THE SERBS AND THEIR LEADERS IN THE TWENTIETH CENTURY

The Serbs and their Leaders in the Twentieth Century

Edited by

PETER RADAN
University of Western Sydney Macarthur
Faculty of Law

ALEKSANDAR PAVKOVIĆ
Macquarie University
School of Modern Languages

Routledge
Taylor & Francis Group
LONDON AND NEW YORK

First published 1997 by Ashgate Publishing

Reissued 2018 by Routledge
2 Park Square, Milton Park, Abingdon, Oxon, OX14 4RN
52 Vanderbilt Avenue, New York, NY 10017

Routledge is an imprint of the Taylor & Francis Group, an informa business

A Library of Congress record exists under LC control number: 97016726

ISBN 13: 978-1-138-36641-1 (hbk)
ISBN 13: 978-1-138-36642-8 (pbk)
ISBN 13: 978-0-429-43031-2 (ebk)

Contents

Preface

The aim of this book is to present a new perspective on the history of the Serbs in the twentieth century. The new perspective is to view this historical period through the lives of its most significant Serb participants. In selecting the lives to be profiled we chose those individuals, who we felt were in positions of real power and influence and significantly shaped the destiny of the Serbs. We do not deny that other Serbs were of importance and influence. We concede that many readers would have chosen a different and/or longer list. Ultimately, any select list of individuals will reflect the views of its compilers, and we readily recognise that the present volume of essays reflects our own personal biases.

The present volume, in no way, pretends to be a comprehensive narrative of Serb history during the twentieth century. Nor, using the biographical perspective, could it be. Nevertheless, even accounting for the limitations of the biographical perspective, there is no biographical chapter covering the period of Yugoslavia's history during the life of Josip Broz Tito. There were two possible candidates for inclusion in this volume from this period - Milovan Djilas and Aleksandar Ranković. Djilas was excluded, in part, on the ground that he did not, in any event, consider himself a Serb. Ranković was ruled out on the basis that very little is known of the degree of influence he possessed during his tenure in office. The ease with which he was removed from office would, however, suggest that it was not of a kind possessed by the other individuals portrayed in this volume.

The contributors of the biographical chapters to this volume represent a diversity of backgrounds. They come from different countries, different academic disciplines, different intellectual traditions, and different generations. Given their varied backgrounds, there was no point in trying to impose upon them a common general framework within which their contributions were to be written. Instead, all the authors were given a free hand as to how they approached the writing of their contribution. As a result, there is no attempt to evaluate the contribution of each author on the basis of a single set of criteria. We recognise such an approach could detract from the value of this volume. However, any such loss, we hope, is more than compensated for by the varied approaches taken by each author.

Each of the individuals profiled in this volume is controversial. To a large extent this is a product of the fact that each of them exercised power and influence at critical times during the twentieth century. Most, if not all, readers will disagree with some, and perhaps all, of the contributions. We would be surprised if it were otherwise. However, one hopes that the present volume will provoke the reader to question his or her own views on its subject matter.

It is hoped that this book will attract the interest of not only the scholarly audience but also of the wider reading public. The specialist readers will recognise that this volume is but a first attempt at providing a different perspective of the historical events covered, and it is hoped that scholars will be inspired to follow with similar efforts. For the general reading public this book aims to provide a sound introduction to the major personalities that helped shape the contours of twentieth century Serb history. In order to provide the necessary background for the biographical essays we have included, as the first chapter, an overview and assessment of the course of the history of the Serbs during the twentieth century.

The Editors
March, 1997

Acknowledgements

The editors wish to thank the contributors to this volume for their efforts. Thanks are also due to the translators, Lana Panić, Melanie Petranović and Ivana Spasić. For technical assistance the editors extend their thanks to Biljana Đurić, Mary Bejte, Andrew Mencinsky and Ilija Vicković.

Particular thanks are due to the Serbian Studies Foundation at Macquarie University in Sydney for its financial assistance in preparing this book for publication. The publication of this book marks the tenth anniversary of the Foundation's activities in support of the programme of Serbian studies at Macquarie University.

List of Contributors

Mile Bjelajac - Research Fellow with the Institute for the Recent History of Serbia, and author of numerous articles and books on the social and military history of Yugoslavia, including *Vojska Kraljevine SHS 1918-1921* (1988) and *Vojska Kraljevine SHS/Jugoslavije 1922-1935* (1994).

Lenard J. Cohen - Professor of Political Science at Simon Fraser University, and author of numerous articles and books on modern Yugoslav politics, including (with Paul Warwick) *Political Cohesion in a Fragile Mosaic, The Yugoslav Experience* (1983), *The Socialist Pyramid, Elites & Power in Yugoslavia* (1989) and *Broken Bonds, Yugoslavia's Disintegration & Balkan Politics in Transition* (1995).

Dimitrije Djordjević - Emeritus Professor of History at the University of California, Santa Barbara, member of the Serbian Academy of Sciences and Arts, and author of numerous articles and books on the modern history of the Balkans, including (with Stephen Fischer-Galati) *The Balkan Revolutionary Tradition* (1981), *Migrations in Balkan History* (1989) and *Ožiljci i opomene I & II* (1994, 1995).

Alex N. Dragnich - Emeritus Professor of Political Science at Vanderbilt University, and author of numerous articles and books on modern Serbian and Yugoslav history and politics, including, *Serbia, Nikola Pašić, & Yugoslavia* (1974), *The First Yugoslavia, Search for a Viable Political System* (1983) and *Serbs & Croats, The Struggle in Yugoslavia* (1992).

Branislav Gligorijević - Senior Research Fellow at the Institute of Contemporary History, and author of numerous articles and books on the history of Yugoslavia, including, *Demokratska stranka i politički odnosi u Kraljevini Srba Hrvata i Slovenaca* (1970), *Parlament i političke stranke u Jugoslaviji 1919-1929* (1979) and *Kralj Aleksandar I Karađorđević* (1996).

David MacKenzie - Professor of History at the University of North Carolina at Greensboro, and author of numerous articles and books on modern Serbian history, including, *Ilija Garašanin: Balkan Bismarck* (1985), *Apis: The Congenial Conspirator, The Life of Colonel Dragutin T. Dimitrijević* (1989) and *The 'Black Hand' on Trial, Salonika, 1917* (1995).

Kosta Nikolić - Research Fellow at the Institute of Contemporary History, and author of a number of articles and books on Yugoslav history, including, *Boljševizacija Komunističke partije Jugoslavije 1919-1929* (1994) and (with Milan Vesović) *Ujedinjene srpske zemlje, Ravnogorski nacionalni program* (1996).

Aleksandar Pavković - Associate Professor within the School of Modern Languages at Macquarie University, and author of numerous articles and books in the fields of Yugoslav philosophy, history and politics, including *Slobodan Jovanović, An Unsentimental Approach to Politics* (1993) and *The Fragmentation of Yugoslavia: Nationalism in a Multinational State* (1996).

Peter Radan - Lecturer in Law at the University of Western Sydney Macarthur, and author of a number of articles on Yugoslav history and international legal aspects of the disintegration of Yugoslavia.

Srdja Trifković - Executive Director of the Lord Byron Foundation for Balkan Studies. He has completed a doctoral dissertation entitled *The Ustaša Movement & European Politics* (1991), and has written a number of articles on Yugoslav history.

1 The Serbs and their History in the Twentieth Century

PETER RADAN

Introduction

War and nationalism have been the dominant themes in the history of the Serbs during the twentieth century. During the nineteenth century era of nationalism which had seen the emergence of the German and Italian nation-states, the idea of a Serb nation-state was a dominant theme in Serb political history. The creation of such a state had its roots in the Serbian uprisings against the Ottoman Empire which ruled most of the territories in which the Serbs lived. However, it was the famous memorandum *Načertanije* (Outline), prepared by Serb statesman Ilija Garašanin in 1844, that provided the blueprint for the unification of all Serb lands into a Serb nation-state.[1] Garašanin has been described as the Balkan Bismarck, but unlike his famous German counterpart, he did not live to see his dream realised. His death in 1874 meant that he did not witness the partial realisation of *Načertanije* in 1878 when the great powers of Europe, at the Congress of Berlin, recognised the independent Serb states of Serbia and Montenegro. At that time the two Serb states, rivals for the leadership role in unifying the Serbs into one state,[2] did not include lands claimed by the Serbs but ruled by the Ottoman and Austro-Hungarian empires.

Pre-World War I Serbia

The year 1903 was a turning point in the modern history of the Serbs. For much of the preceding century internal Serbian politics had been dominated by an intense and often violent dynastic rivalry between the Karađorđević and Obrenović families. The Obrenović family had been in power since 1858. Their dominance came to an end in 1903. In May of that year a conspiracy by military officers led by Dragutin Dimitrijević-

Apis resulted in the assassinations of King Aleksandar Obrenović and his Queen Draga. Aleksandar's personal life, his autocratic tendencies and his pro-Austrian foreign policy had led to considerable opposition within Serbia. His death resulted in the Serbian *Skupština* (Assembly) electing Petar I Karađorđević as King and restoring Serbia's democratic constitution originally promulgated in 1888. Genuine constitutional parliamentary democracy became a notable feature of Serbia's political life.[3] The major political party from then to the outbreak of World War I was the Radical Party led by Nikola Pašić. The Serbian army, under the guidance of General Radomir Putnik, was reformed and modernised.

The dynastic and political restructuring of Serbia in 1903 brought into sharper focus the goal of the unification of all Serb lands into one state. In 1903 a large number of Serbs lived in the neighbouring Ottoman and Austro-Hungarian empires. After the Congress of Berlin, the focus of Serbian expansionism had been towards Kosovo and Macedonia in the south where Ottoman control was in a state of decay. Under the pro-Austrian foreign policy of the Obrenović dynasty, Serbia did not focus its attentions to the region of Vojvodina to its north, nor the province of Bosnia-Hercegovina in the west. The latter region was still formally part of the Ottoman empire but was administered by Austria-Hungary. From 1903 Serbian foreign policy gravitated towards seeking closer ties with Russia. Relations with Austria-Hungary became increasingly tense. This tension was exacerbated by Vienna's formal annexation of Bosnia-Hercegovina in 1908, which signalled an intent on the part of Austria-Hungary that it would countenance no expansion, at the Dual Monarchy's expense, of a Serbian state backed by Russia. Serbia's future continued, as it had during the nineteenth century, to be a by-product of great power rivalry for influence in the Balkans. This rivalry, known as the Eastern Question, had arisen as a result of the decline of the Ottoman Empire and its gradual withdrawal from Europe. The Eastern Question had become the issue that threatened, and ultimately destroyed, the European political order of the nineteenth century, the so-called Concert of Europe, formulated at the Congress of Vienna in 1815.

The penultimate event in the breakdown of the nineteenth century European political order was the Balkan Wars of 1912-1913. In the First Balkan War of 1912, the Balkan states of Serbia, Bulgaria, Montenegro and Greece combined to all but eliminate the Ottoman Empire from Europe. The Second Balkan War of 1913 was between the victors of the

First Balkan War over the territorial spoils. The result of the Second Balkan War was a victory for Serbia, Montenegro and Greece and defeat for Bulgaria. Serbia and Montenegro doubled their size and for the first time shared a common frontier. A further consequence was the emergence of an Albanian state, much to the dissatisfaction of Serbia and Montenegro who both had territorial ambitions over Albanian territory. The Balkan Wars marked the final victory of Serbia's efforts to liberate Serb lands from Ottoman occupation which dated back to the late fourteenth century. Serbia had now recovered most of its historic lands in the southern Balkans, especially Kosovo-Metohija which had been the site of the Battle of Kosovo in 1389, the memory of which became a legendary symbol of the Serb nationalist programme during the nineteenth century.[4]

World War I

Serbia's success in the Balkan Wars aroused considerable concern in Austria-Hungary. Vienna feared that Serbia's next step would be to threaten the empire's recently annexed Bosnia-Hercegovina, where the Serbs were the majority population. Serb unrest in Bosnia-Hercegovina had been steadily mounting and the assassination, on 28 June 1914, of Archduke Franz Ferdinand, the heir to the Austro-Hungarian throne, provided Vienna with the excuse for war against Serbia. Vienna's aims were to eliminate Serbia as a threat and to increase the Dual Monarchy's influence in the Balkans at the expense of Serbia's great power benefactor, Russia. The assassination, carried out by a group of Serb revolutionaries from Bosnia, was seen by Vienna as being masterminded by the Serbian government in Belgrade. Vienna issued an ultimatum to Serbia which Belgrade ultimately did not accept. Acceptance would have been tantamount to Serbia abandoning its sovereignty as a state. On 28 July 1914 Austria-Hungary declared war on Serbia.[5]

After initial success in repelling the invading forces of Austria-Hungary, Serbia was largely overrun by enemy forces and its army forced to retreat south through Albania during the winter of 1915, eventually to gain refuge on the Greek island of Corfu. Austria-Hungary's war against Serbia had by then become World War I. The war's Balkan theatre was less significant than those in western Europe and Russia. However, by 1916 the regrouped Serbian forces in Corfu made a significant contribution to the Allied war effort on the Salonika Front which repelled the enemy forces and liberated the Balkans. The cost to Serbia of the preceding Balkan Wars and World War I was, in human terms, enormous. Over one-third of her adult male population died. This enormous human tragedy played a significant role in moulding Serb political attitudes after World War I.

World War I signalled the end of the nineteenth century European political order. In the Balkans it marked the end of the Austro-Hungarian empire, which, following on so soon after the removal of the Ottoman Empire during the First Balkan War, meant a new political order had to emerge. Serbia was at the centre of this process. The Austro-Hungarian attack on Serbia led to a swift re-ordering of Serbia's foreign policy objectives. After the conclusion of the Balkan Wars, which had considerably taxed Serbia's resources, Serbian foreign policy focused on consolidating its territorial gains and maintaining peace in the Balkans. Whatever her long-term gains were in relation to Serb lands in Austria-Hungary, Serbia was not in a position to pursue them by military means. The radically transformed environment brought about by the outbreak of World War I meant that new policies were required. Serbia's response to the new environment came with the Niš Declaration of 7 December 1914. The Declaration had as its goal the unification of the Serb, Croat and Slovene territories within the Dual Monarchy with Serbia and Montenegro into one South Slav state. Serb national goals had significantly changed as a result of the Niš Declaration. Prior to then Serb national goals, as reflected in Garašanin's *Načertanije*, centred around the creation of a Serb nation-state incorporating all Serb lands in the Balkans. The Niš Declaration replaced this goal with the creation of a state of South Slavs, which included all the Serb lands in the Balkans, but also included lands populated by Croats and Slovenes. The goal of a nation-state had been replaced with that of a multi-national state. However, the multinational character of the future state was downplayed by official statements of Serbian policy that declared that the Serbs, Croats and Slovenes were in fact one nation of Yugoslavs, and that the creation of a nation-state was the goal. In part, such official statements were, especially towards the end of the war, motivated by Serbia's need to present its policy as being within the principle of national self-determination being championed by President Woodrow Wilson of the United States as the basis for the post-war re-ordering of Europe.

Leadership of Serbia during World War I was dominated by its prime minister Nikola Pašić and Prince Regent Aleksandar Karađorđević, who had assumed the royal prerogative from his ailing father Petar I a few weeks before the assassination of Franz Ferdinand. Given the war aims stated in the Niš Declaration, Serbia's contact with the South Slav population of Austria-Hungary became central. The Yugoslav Committee, which had been established in Italy in 1914 by a group of Croat exiles and Serb politicians from Bosnia-Hercegovina, was an important organisation with which Serbia established contacts for this purpose. The aim of the Yugoslav Committee was to represent to Allied governments the views of the South Slavs within Austria-Hungary. The major concern of many members of the Yugoslav Committee was that the collapse of the Dual Monarchy would lead to the annexation of their homelands by Italy. In the initial stages of the war the collapse of Austria-Hungary was not seen as a likely outcome. Indeed the continuity of the empire was assumed by most Croat and Slovene politicians who remained in Austria-Hungary, and their goal was the establishment of a South Slav component within it and thereby, the conversion of the Dual Monarchy to a Triple Monarchy. However, as the war progressed it became increasingly apparent that the Dual Monarchy would not survive. It was at these later stages of the war that Serbia and the South Slavs of Austria-Hungary were pushed towards finding a solution to their common concern about Italian aspirations towards the Adriatic coastline and southern regions of the Austro-Hungarian empire. This common concern led to the Corfu Declaration of 20 July 1917, signed by the government of Serbia and the Yugoslav Committee, which expressed the aim of establishing a constitutional parliamentary democracy under the aegis of the Karađorđević dynasty and encompassing the South Slav lands of the Dual Monarchy, Serbia and Montenegro. The new state was to be called the Kingdom of Serbs, Croats and Slovenes.

Interwar Yugoslavia

The South Slav state envisaged by the Corfu Declaration was proclaimed on 1 December 1918. In the meantime the shifting tides of war had led to the successful Salonika Front which resulted in the liberation of Serbia and the annexation of Bosnia-Hercegovina. In the hectic month of November 1918, with the collapse of Austria-Hungary a fact, Montenegro proclaimed its unification with Serbia on 24 November. The South Slav politicians of the Dual Monarchy, no longer able to realise their plans within the Dual Monarchy, proclaimed their independence as the State of Slovenes, Croats and Serbs on 29 October. On 23 November its government, the National Council, resolved to seek unification with Serbia and a delegation to negotiate unification was sent to Belgrade on 27 November. Prince Regent Aleksandar met with the delegation and the Kingdom of Serbs, Croats and Slovenes was officially proclaimed on 1 December 1918.[6] The major foreign policy objective for the new state was to obtain international recognition. This was achieved at the Paris Peace Conference of 1919, which established a new political order for Europe in the wake of World War I.

The newly created Kingdom was beset with internal political problems from the outset. Although the Corfu Declaration provided for the creation of the new state, it was vague on its internal political structure. This failing of the Corfu Declaration reflected the divisions that existed between the Serbian government and the Yugoslav Committee on this fundamental issue. These matters, according to the Corfu Declaration, were be determined by a constituent assembly elected after the war. The divisions that existed at Corfu, and which continued into the new state, reflected differing conceptions of *jugoslovenstvo* (South-Slavism). For Serb political leaders the new state would ideally be run on a centralised basis with the Serbs, being the largest national group, playing the lead role. This attitude was a reflection of Serbia's historical experience during the nineteenth century struggle for independence. This experience taught the Serbs that a strong centralised government was essential for building a strong state, equally capable of meeting any challenges from neighbouring states and building a viable and modern economy. This view served Serbia well prior to the Balkan Wars when it had a nationally homogenous population. Serbia's political leadership mistakenly believed that this view would function in a nationally heterogeneous state in which the Serbs were only a relative majority and in which other national groups, most notably the Croats, were determined to resist the implementation of a centralised state system.

For the other major national groups, especially the Croats, *jugoslovenstvo* necessarily entailed a federal system in which various national groups would be granted considerable legislative and political autonomy. This had been the essence of the movement for *jugoslovenstvo* championed during the latter part of the nineteenth century by the Croat Bishop Josip Juraj Štrosmajer. Štrosmajer's aim had been to create a third unit in the Dual Monarchy along federal principles, and comprising the South Slav lands of the Austro-Hungarian empire. He did not envisage *jugoslovenstvo* as entailing the unification of the South Slavs of the Dual Monarchy with Serbia and Montenegro. His ideal of *jugoslovenstvo* was the dominant goal of a significant section of Croat political leaders for as long as the Dual Monarchy existed. When its collapse became inevitable this concept of *jugoslovenstvo* was adapted to the reality of the new South Slav Kingdom, and saw the Croats, in particular, demanding a federal internal structure in which Croat lands would be given considerable political and national autonomy. In the new Kingdom the standard-bearer of Croat autonomy was the Croat Peasant Party (CPP) led by Stjepan Radić. In the days of the Dual Monarchy, Radić's party was not a major force within Croat politics. It emerged as the voice of the Croat nation in the 1920s with the political empowerment of the Croat peasantry which resulted from the extension of universal suffrage from pre-war Serbia to the regions of the former Dual Monarchy that now formed part of the new South Slav Kingdom.

Elections in the new Kingdom soon exposed nationalism as being the major threat to the continued viability of the fledgling constitutional democracy. With one major exception all national groups tended to overwhelmingly support the major nationalist party of each nation. The exception was the Serb nation, which split its vote between two parties, the Radicals led by Pašić and the newly formed Democratic Party led by Ljuba Davidović. Both parties, especially the Democrats, sought to establish a following amongst other national groups, but failed and drew their support overwhelmingly from the Serbs. On the other hand both parties did support a centralised state structure. Such a structure was implemented with the passage of the Constitution of 1921, which effectively gave the dominant position in the state government apparatus to the Serbs. This dominance was facilitated by a boycott on political participation in the new state for most of the 1920s by Radić and the CPP. Radić was unrelenting in his drive for Croat autonomy and in the early 1920s supported the secession of Croat lands from Yugoslavia.

A series of elections in the 1920s was unable to resolve the differences between the Serb and Croat parties. Nationalist tensions escalated and ultimately resulted in the curtailment of the Kingdom's experiment with parliamentary democracy. In June 1928 a Serb deputy to the Kingdom's *Skupština* shot and killed a number of Croat deputies during a heated *Skupština* debate. Radić was also shot and wounded. Although he recovered from his wounds he died two months later and was replaced as leader of his party by Vladko Maček. The *Skupština* assassinations led King Aleksandar to appoint the Slovene Anton Korošec as prime minister, in a desperate effort to lead the country out of its crisis. The Korošec administration, the only government to that date not headed by a Serb, proved ineffective, and on 6 January 1929 Aleksandar abrogated the Constitution and assumed personal rule over the country, which on 3 October 1929 was officially renamed the Kingdom of Yugoslavia. A new constitution conferring extensive powers on the monarch was proclaimed in September 1931.[7]

Aleksandar's introduction of the royal dictatorship initially attracted widespread support, including that of Maček. However, this support was short-lived. Aleksandar's attempt at solving the country's crisis was the introduction, from above, of a supra-national identity of Yugoslavism. The country was internally re-organised into nine *banovine* (provinces) that in many cases cut across national boundaries. The *banovine* were given non-national names. In addition all organisations based on national affiliations, including political parties, were banned. Although Aleksandar was a genuine believer in his policy of Yugoslavism, the widespread opposition to his reforms doomed his efforts to failure. Most Croats were against Aleksandar because his policies denied the expression of Croat nationalism. In this sense they saw Aleksandar's personal rule as being worse than the era of parliamentary democracy that preceded it. To them, Aleksandar's personal rule was simply seen as the continuation of Serb dominance in Yugoslavia under the guise of Yugoslavism. A segment of the Croat nationalist opposition went into exile and formed the Ustaša Movement. This extremist group sought the assistance of fascist Italy to overthrow Aleksandar, destroy Yugoslavia and establish an independent Croat state.[8] Serbs also opposed Aleksandar, partly on the grounds that Serb nationalism was suppressed, but also because of the dictatorial nature of his rule. Pre-World War I Serbia had developed a system of liberal democracy following a long struggle with both the Obrenović and Karađorđević dynasties during the nineteenth century. Aleksandar's personal rule attacked the core of the best of Serb political culture. Aleksandar's personal rule came to an end with his assassination in Marseilles on 9 October 1934, an assassination organised by the exiled Ustaša Movement which in turn was financed by Italy.[9]

As Aleksandar's heir, Petar II, was a minor, power in Yugoslavia passed to Aleksandar's cousin Prince Pavle Karađorđević who headed a three-man Regency Council. The system of personal rule continued under Pavle, although Pavle proved to be somewhat less authoritarian than Aleksandar. However, the threat to the European political order posed by the increasingly disruptive foreign policies of Nazi Germany and Fascist Italy added another destabilising factor. Pavle sought to preserve the country's integrity and enhance its security. His priority during the latter half of the 1930s was to find a solution to the Croat question in Yugoslavia. This was designed to bolster the internal security of the country as he sought to shield Yugoslavia from dominance by an increasingly assertive and belligerent Germany. This led to Pavle to negotiate a settlement of the Croat problem by means of the *Sporazum* (Agreement) of 23 August 1939. The *Sporazum* created a Croatian *Banovina* encompassing traditional Croat lands and extensive parts of north-west Bosnia. Significant local autonomy was given to the Croats over territory that was home to a large Serb minority. The *Sporazum* pleased neither Serb nor Croat politicians. Despite its considerable concessions to Croat nationalism the *Sporazum* was seen by the Croat leadership as only a first step towards eventual independence. Serb opposition pointed to the privileged position given by the *Sporazum* to the Croats over other nations within Yugoslavia, and in particular their own. Whereas Serbian opposition to the personal rule of both Aleksandar and Pavle had, to date, been mainly political in orientation, it now became increasingly nationalistic.

Pavle's attempt to keep Yugoslavia out of World War II, which erupted in September 1939, ultimately failed. Abandoned by France and Great Britain, Yugoslavia's allies in World War I and during the interwar period, Pavle was unable to prevent German domination of the Balkans. Germany's desire to secure its southern flank, as a prelude to its planned invasion of the Soviet Union in mid-1941, led to overwhelming pressure on Yugoslavia and ultimately to Yugoslavia's adherence to the Tripartite Pact on 25 March, 1941. This event triggered a putsch which toppled Pavle and saw Petar II installed as monarch even though he was still some months short of majority age. The putsch was led by Serb army officers and enjoyed massive support from Yugoslavia's Serb population.[10] The response of Nazi Germany was swift and decisive. Germany's invasion of Yugoslavia commenced with the bombing of Belgrade on 6 April 1941. Yugoslavia capitulated on 17 April 1941. With its government fleeing the country, Yugoslavia was left to the mercy of Germany and her allies, each eager to share in the spoils of victory. As with the breakdown of the nineteenth century European political order when Serbia found itself entangled in World War I, the breakdown of the interwar European political order saw Yugoslavia entangled in World War II.[11]

World War II

The Axis attack on Yugoslavia led to the partition of Yugoslavia. After the spoils of war were shared between the Axis allies there remained two 'states', both closely controlled by Nazi Germany. Within a week of the German bombing of Belgrade, the population of Zagreb euphorically welcomed the German army as liberators. The Germans created the Independent State of Croatia, a third of whose population was Serb, and installed the extremist Croat Ustaša nationalist Dr Ante Pavelić as head of its government. With German consent, the Ustaša launched a brutal policy of genocide against the Serbs, as well as the Jews and Gypsies, aimed at eliminating Croatia's 'Serb problem'.[12] To the east of the Independent State of Croatia a puppet Serbian state was established with General Milan Nedić, a former army minister in interwar Yugoslavia, soon installed as its president. The aim of the Nedić administration was to keep Serbia subdued and free of the two anti-Axis resistance movements that had commenced operations soon after the collapse of Yugoslavia.

The first resistance movement to arise was that led by Colonel (later General) Dragoljub-Draža Mihailović. Refusing to capitulate to the Germans, Mihailović, together with a small band of officers, launched his resistance movement from central Serbia in May 1941. Mihailović's movement, popularly known as the Četnici, had as its goal the restoration of the pre-war political order in Yugoslavia. Mihailović's military strategy focussed on building up and conserving his forces with the aim of striking at a time when the war turned against the Germans. It also aimed at preventing unnecessary losses to the civilian population, such losses being very high in the light of the brutal reprisal policy adopted by the Germans in late 1941. It was also a strategy that was in line with Allied policy at the time.[13]

The second resistance movement was inspired by the Communist Party of Yugoslavia (CPY) and known as the Partisans. This movement, led by Josip Broz Tito, emerged in the wake of Germany's attack on the Soviet Union in June 1941. Originating in Serbia, the Partisans quickly built upon the CPY's organisation developed in interwar Yugoslavia and established itself in varying degrees of strength in all parts of Yugoslavia. For the Partisans the war represented an opportunity to gain power in a post-war Yugoslavia. The revolutionary tactics of the Bolsheviks in Russia during World War I served as the precedent. The Partisan policy of constantly engaging the enemy and thus provoking German reprisals, was aimed at radicalising the civilian population into joining the Partisan ranks.[14]

Soon after the establishment of the two resistance forces, and after a brief period of cooperation, their diametrically opposed goals and strategies led to conflict. Both Mihailović and Tito realised that the liberation of Yugoslavia from the Germans was not going to be achieved from within Yugoslavia, but rather would be the result of an Allied victory over the Axis forces in Europe and elsewhere. Thus, what began as a war of resistance against foreign occupation became a civil war in which the prize was power in a post-war Yugoslavia.

The brutality of the multi-dimensional civil war that engulfed Yugoslavia during World War II cannot be over-stated. Neither side hesitated at entering into tactical accommodations with its enemies, be they foreign or domestic. At times these accommodations were necessitated by the need to survive. Thus, Četnik accommodations with the Italians in Pavelić's Croatian state, were aimed at saving the non-Croat civilians from the terrors of an Ustaša policy of genocide that was, particularly in the early years of the war, waged with a ferocity that alarmed even the Germans. In Montenegro, the Četnici made accommodations with the Italians in order to survive a brutal Partisan campaign against them. This campaign was launched in the winter of 1941-1942 in the confident expectation that the communist revolution would result in a Partisan victory by mid-1942. At other times tactical accommodations were entered into for purely military reasons. Thus, in early 1942 Partisans in eastern Bosnia cooperated with German forces with the aim of liquidating their Četnik rivals in that region. In Serbia,

Mihailović's Četnici, at various times, were instructed to join the ranks of Nedić government forces for the purposes of attacking Partisan forces. The fact that such arrangements and accommodations took place, does not deny the anti-Axis orientation of either the Četnici or the Partisans. What it does confirm is that the struggle against the Axis occupiers was second in priority to the civil war for power in a post-war Yugoslavia.

In the initial years of the war both resistance forces drew their support overwhelmingly from the Serbs of Yugoslavia.[15] The Četnici, however, were never able to attract widespread support from Yugoslavia's other nations. This became a major disadvantage for them in their struggle with the Partisans. Non-Serbs increasingly saw the Četnici as a Serb nationalist organisation committed to a pre-war political order which in their eyes had been discredited. On the other hand, the Partisans made a conscious effort after mid-1942 to attract non-Serb recruits and support. Their policy of *bratstvo i jedinstvo* (brotherhood and unity), combined with their promise of a federal post-war Yugoslavia based upon the principle of national self-determination, proved successful. As the tides of war turned against Germany, and Allied policy switched to favouring the more militarily active Partisans, the latter were able to ride to power on the back of Allied military victories over Germany.[16] By early 1945 the Partisans had emerged as the future rulers of a communist Yugoslavia.[17]

Communist Yugoslavia

The Yugoslavia that emerged after World War II was a vastly different country from that which entered the war. The CPY, itself dominated by Tito, had replaced the monarchy, and the state was dramatically restructured. The 1946 Constitution guaranteed Yugoslavia's now five constituent nations the right to self-determination including the right of secession. The five constituent nations, Serbs, Croats, Slovenes, Macedonians and Montenegrins, were each based in a republic of their own. A sixth republic, that of Bosnia-Hercegovina was populated by a mixture of Serbs, Slavic Muslims and Croats. (It was only in 1968 that the Muslim nation was officially recognised, with Bosnia-Hercegovina quickly becoming its territorial base.) Two minority groups, the Albanians and Hungarians were given a special status, but one short of a constituent nation. They were given territorial homelands in the form of sub-republican units, known as the autonomous region of Kosovo-Metohija and the autonomous province of Vojvodina respectively. Both these sub-republican units were within the Republic of Serbia. This constitutional structure had the effect of weakening the political influence of the Serbs, as the most numerous nation within Yugoslavia. The watering down of the influence of the Serbs and Serbia was achieved by this structure, given that of all the constituent nations, the Serbs were the ones with the highest proportion of their population living outside their home republic. The anti-Serb thrust of the new constitutional structure was confirmed by the CPY's rejection of a Serb autonomous province within Croatia, where a sizeable minority of Serbs, who had survived the Ustaša genocide, still resided.

In the immediate post-war years Yugoslavia was, of all the Communist bloc states in Eastern Europe, the most loyal to the Soviet Union. However, with Yugoslavia's expulsion from the bloc in 1948,[18] Yugoslavia undertook a skilfully executed policy of exploiting both East and West in the Cold War era that lasted until the 1980s. However, a new socialist ideology had to be crafted to justify the CPY's hold on power. The Yugoslav ideology that emerged was built upon three bases, namely, the war of national liberation, as the civil war during World War II came to be known, the system of workers' self-management, and Yugoslavia's leading role in the Non-Aligned Movement. The CPY was re-named as the League of Communists of Yugoslavia (LCY) and, through Tito, it managed to wield absolute power.

On the issue of the national question there was a genuine belief, immediately after 1945, that nationalism would, in accordance with marxist ideology, pass. However, following the split with the Soviet Union, Yugoslavia had to create a state national identity as a means of bolstering its internal stability and external security.[19] Just as external factors impacted on Prince Pavle's attempts to solve the national question in the 1930s, so too did the external threat from the Soviet Union in the late 1940s and early 1950s impact on Yugoslavia's treatment of the national question. This prompted the LCY, following the footsteps of King Aleksandar in the early 1930s, to introduce a policy of Yugoslavism from above. This Yugoslavism stressed that the future of national relations lay in social relations developing a Yugoslav consciousness. There was no explicit renunciation of separate national self-determination, but Yugoslavism relegated national identification to questions of language and culture only.

The high point of this form of Yugoslavism was the Seventh Party Congress of the LCY in 1958. However, it was soon to meet the same opposition that Aleksandar's Yugoslavism had met in the 1930s. To Croats and Slovenes Yugoslavism was seen as a mask for Serb hegemony. During the 1960s it was evident that nationalism, especially Croat nationalism, had not been suppressed, and the regime quietly abandoned Yugoslavism in favour of seeking some accommodation with the forces of nationalism. The nationalist debate was not conducted in the language of nationalism. Overt nationalism was taboo and suppressed, as was illustrated by the suppression of the so-called Croatian Spring of the late 1960s and early 1970s. Instead, the nationalist debate was conducted in the coded language of economic reform. The debate within the LCY over economic reform was over centralisation versus decentralisation of the economy. During the 1960s the debate swung in favour of the decentralisers beginning with the Economic Reform of 1965 and culminating in victory for them with the 1974 Constitution.[20]

The 1974 Constitution devolved economic and political power to the six republics and two autonomous provinces of the federation, except in a very few matters. Any of the republics and autonomous provinces was able to veto major policy initiatives at the federal level. Political careers with real power were brokered at the republican level, not at the federal level. The seeds had been sown for the later partition of the country. All that was required was a climate that facilitated such an event. What kept Yugoslavia together during this period, and through to the end of the 1970s, was a product of three factors. First, there was the enormous authority of Tito who was able to anoint the various republican elites that remained loyal to him and to the preservation of Yugoslavia. Second, an enormous inflow of foreign capital masked underlying economic problems, and created the illusion of economic prosperity, thereby minimising the prospects of mass grass-roots discontent emerging as a threat to the country. Third, the international political order created by the Cold War and Yugoslavia's position in that order as a maverick socialist state, meant that Yugoslavia's integrity was fostered by both East and West. The Soviet Union tolerated Yugoslavia's relative independence from the Eastern bloc given that, except on issues of direct concern, Yugoslavia generally supported the Soviet Union in international matters. For the West, Yugoslavia, as a maverick communist state, served as a useful propaganda tool, with the West keen to preserve Yugoslavia's integrity at any cost. The facade of unity and prosperity masked the reality of a state whose society was increasingly alienated by the chronic corruption of its political establishment, and whose economy began to stagnate because of incompetence and mis-management.[21]

The Final Partition of Yugoslavia

The threads that had held Yugoslavia together began to unravel in 1980.[22] In May of that year Tito died, and the Yugoslav polity became increasingly fractured and fragmented once his cohesive force was gone. Yugoslavia's post-1974 political and economic structure of eight regional political and economic establishments, each firmly based in one of the republics or autonomous provinces, meant that a new Tito, capable of appealing to all parts of the country, could not emerge.[23] It was no coincidence that, within a year of Tito's death, Yugoslavia faced its first major challenge to its internal security and territorial integrity, with the riots by Albanians in Kosovo demanding republic status for their autonomous province. These demands, and the exodus of Serbs and Montenegrins that they provoked, struck at the core of Serb sensitivities. For the Serbs, Kosovo was sacred Serbian soil, it being the site of the legendary Battle of Kosovo in 1389.[24] Serbian nationalism was aroused and came to the fore. Nationalism increasingly, and openly, became the language of political debate.[25]

The second challenge to Yugoslavia's integrity was rooted in economics. In the 1980s the time had come for Yugoslavia to account for its economic sins of the past.[26] Foreign credit dried up, and the large foreign debt was being called in by an increasingly demanding and unsympathetic international financial community. The economic pain this caused to the country was reflected in increasing antagonism between the republics over the causes and cures of the country's economic ills. The economic restructuring which the international financial community forced upon Yugoslavia exacerbated conflict between Yugoslavia's republics. It also created increasing popular unrest, given that the masses bore the brunt of the price Yugoslavia was paying for the economic mis-management of previous decades. The increasingly volatile populace was ripe for political mobilisation, and given that the political elites were based in the republics, nationalism became the convenient means for such mobilisation.[27]

The final challenge to Yugoslavia's integrity was posed by the decline of the Soviet Union as the leader of the East in the Cold War. The Soviet Union's decline, reflected in President Gorbachev's policies of *glasnost* and *perestroika*, led to her losing her grip on Eastern Europe and eventually abandoning those countries to their own fates. With the end of the Cold War Yugoslavia ceased to be of strategic and political importance to both East and West. Its fate was increasingly in its own hands.

In this volatile political climate the problems of Yugoslavia in some respects resembled the problems of Yugoslavia in its first few years after World War I. The constitutional structure of the state was at stake. Serbs politicians again argued for an increasingly centralised state. To non-Serb politicians, this was again not the preferred option. However, the world of the 1920s was not the world of the 1980s. In the 1920s the Croats and Slovenes had no alternative to joining and remaining in Yugoslavia. By the late 1980s, leaving Yugoslavia was not an unrealistic option for the Croats and Slovenes. By the end of the 1980s the critical question for Yugoslavia was no longer its future structure but whether it had any future at all. The national question was at the heart of the debate, but in one sense it had been transformed. Whereas the national question had been mainly concerned, in the past, with the 'Croat Problem', it was now concerned with the 'Serb Problem'. In the past it had been the Croat politicians who had sought change to Yugoslavia's constitutional order. Now it was their Serb counterparts who sought change.

Serbian dissatisfaction with the constitutional structure of 1974 coincided with the demands of the international financial community for more stringent and centralised control of Yugoslavia's economy in order that the country's foreign debt be reduced and repaid. This presented an opportunity to press for a change to the constitutional structure that would enable Serbia to play a more dominant role in Yugoslavia's affairs. The wealthier northern republics of Slovenia and Croatia, intent on preserving their relative economic prosperity as compared to the rest of Yugoslavia, resisted any centralisation of the economy, and in Serbia's anxiety over Kosovo saw only the threat of Serb hegemony over Yugoslavia.[28] The LCY elites in the various republics, no longer under the control of a dominant unifying figure such as Tito, and beholden to nobody except their own republican constituencies, became increasingly detached from one another as they attempted to deal with an increasingly severe economic climate and the rise of overt nationalism. This breakdown in the cohesiveness of the LCY was most dramatically manifested by Slovenia's decision, in 1989, to amend its republican constitution. These amendments effectively declared the supremacy of the Slovenian constitution over the Yugoslav constitution, and asserted the right of Slovenia to unilaterally secede from the federation. A precursor to Slovenia's eventual secession occurred in January 1990 when the Slovenian delegation walked out of a Special Congress of the LCY. Slovenia had assumed the leadership role in resistance to Serbia's push for centralisation of Yugoslavia.

Yugoslavia's troubles were being played out against a background of a dramatically changed Eastern Europe. The end of the Cold War, symbolised by the fall of the Berlin Wall in 1989, unleashed dramatic change in Eastern Europe. The winds of change ushered in by this momentous event blew over into Yugoslavia. The pressure for political change was overwhelming. The change was most clearly seen with the holding of multi-party elections in all of Yugoslavia's republics in 1990. These elections brought to the fore new leaders in many of the republics. All these new leaders were representatives of nationalist, anti-communist parties.[29]

However, the 1990 elections did not result in new leaders coming to power in all of Yugoslavia's republics. In Serbia the LCY (by then re-named the Socialist Party of Serbia), won a comfortable victory. Serbia's political elite had been transformed in 1987 with the emergence of Slobodan Milošević as president of Serbia. Milošević's political aspiration was to fill the vacuum left by Tito's death. Milošević exploited dissatisfaction in Serbia over Kosovo to engineer a party coup and install himself as leader of Serbia. He mobilised popular support by openly appealing to Serb nationalism. His drive for power in Yugoslavia resulted in new and loyal party elites being installed in Montenegro and both of Serbia's autonomous provinces. By 1989 he was able to curtail the power of the communist elites in these provinces by amendments to Serbia's republican constitution. However, Milošević's political tactics also meant that he would never achieve his ultimate ambition of becoming a new Tito. His manipulation of Serb nationalism raised alarm bells in the other republics, especially in Slovenia. The 1990 elections in both Slovenia and Croatia swept nationalist parties into power determined to resist Milošević. Both republics declared their intention of seceding from Yugoslavia. During the first half of 1991 a series of meetings of the country's six republican presidents, all elected or re-elected in 1990, failed to resolve their political differences. In late June 1991, Slovenia and Croatia both declared their independence from Yugoslavia.

Secession and War

The Slovenian and Croatian secessions ignited a brutal war in Yugoslavia. The war was over the borders of the future states that would emerge in its wake. The seceding republics claimed that Yugoslavia's internal republican boundaries should be the new international borders. In this attitude they were joined by Macedonia and Bosnia-Hercegovina, who effectively seceded by seeking international recognition in late 1991, after it became apparent that Yugoslavia would not survive. Serbia and Montenegro disagreed with this view claiming that Serb majority areas in Croatia and Bosnia-Hercegovina should be permitted to stay in what remained of Yugoslavia. This view necessitated a redrawing of borders along national lines. By the end of 1991 the international community adopted the position of the seceding republics. During 1992, Slovenia, Croatia and Bosnia-Hercegovina were internationally recognised, to be followed in 1993 by the recognition of Macedonia.

Slovenia's independence was quickly accepted by Serbia's government, as the population there was overwhelmingly Slovene. However, in Croatia and Bosnia-Hercegovina, Serbia supported Serb forces that rebelled from the two new states and sought unification with Serbia and Montenegro. Serbia's support of the Serbs in Croatia and Bosnia-Hercegovina was condemned by the international community. In mid-1992 stringent economic sanctions on Serbia, Montenegro and the Serb-controlled regions of Croatia and Bosnia-Hercegovina were imposed by the Security Council of the United Nations (UN). In Croatia a UN-brokered peace was implemented in early 1992 and relative calm returned to Croatia.[30] However, Croatia was effectively split, with the Croatian government losing control of one-third of its territory to its rebellious Serbs who organised themselves as the Republic of Serbian Krajina. This relative peace lasted until mid-1995.

In Bosnia-Hercegovina war raged uninterrupted from April 1992 until late in 1995. International efforts to quell the fighting all proved unsuccessful. Various peace plans were proposed but none were acceptable to all three combatant groups, the Muslims, Serbs and Croats.

The international community's response to the war in Bosnia-Hercegovina was marked by differences of opinion between the United States and the Europeans, and an unwillingness to get involved beyond providing humanitarian assistance to the victims of war.[31] Up until mid-1995, neither side in the war, namely, the Serbs, who had declared the independence of their state of Republika Srpska, nor the fragile Muslim-Croat coalition, was able to obtain any decisive military victory over each other.[32]

By mid-1995 circumstances had changed dramatically. The effects of sanctions against Serbia and Montenegro led Serbia's president Milošević to end his support of the Serbs in Bosnia-Hercegovina and Croatia. Croatia and the recognised government of Bosnia-Hercegovina greatly improved their military strength as compared to the Serbs, despite an international arms embargo against all of former Yugoslavia being in place since late 1991. Finally, the divisions within the international community were caste aside at the insistence of the United States, which asserted its authority over the Europeans. The international community now openly supported the governments of Croatia and Bosnia-Hercegovina. This support came in the form of military assistance and more importantly a NATO-led bombing campaign against the Serb-held regions of Bosnia-Hercegovina in August-September 1995. Denied the support of Serbia and faced with an increasingly better equipped and trained enemy supported by NATO, the Serbs of Croatia and Bosnia-Hercegovina were unable to sustain their efforts on the battlefield.

By August 1995, following two brief and successful military campaigns, Croatia had recovered most its territory held by the Serbs.[33] By September 1995 the Muslim-Croat coalition, backed by NATO air power, had retaken Serb-held territory in northern and western Bosnia and threatened to take territories held by the Serbs in eastern Bosnia.[34] It was at this time that the United States' government forced the combatants and all other relevant parties to the negotiating table at Dayton in the United States. The major provisions of the Dayton Agreements provided for the eventual re-integration of Serb-controlled Eastern Slavonia into Croatia and the creation of a loose confederal structure for Bosnia-Hercegovina. The latter was to consist of two entities, Republika Srpska and the Muslim-Croat Federation. Significant powers were to devolve to the two entities with only few powers for the central government. NATO forces were charged with the responsibility of facilitating the implementation of the Dayton Agreements. By late 1996 the implementation of the Dayton

Agreements was by no means assured. Elections in Bosnia-Hercegovina in September 1996 saw the electorate voting almost exclusively for the same nationalist parties that they had voted for in 1990, and, to all intents and purposes, supported in the 1992 referendum on independence. The possibility of further armed conflict remained, especially after the withdrawal of NATO forces, due to take place by the end of 1996.

In human terms, the suffering and dislocation of the populations of Croatia and Bosnia-Hercegovina was enormous. Tens of thousands died, and hundreds of thousands were forcibly displaced from their homes. No accurate statistics of the losses suffered by Serbs, Croats and Muslims are yet available. For the Serbs the war resulted in the biggest dislocation of people in their history. Virtually the entire Serb population of Croatia and northern and western Bosnia, numbering approximately 400,000, was expelled. In those parts of Bosnia which formed the entity of Republika Srpska, most Muslims and Croats were expelled. An International War Crimes Tribunal for the Former Yugoslavia, established by the UN Security Council in May 1993, has been given the responsibility of bringing to justice all those guilty of war crimes in the former Yugoslavia.[35]

Conclusions

As stated at the beginning of this chapter war and nationalism have been the dominant themes in the history of the Serbs in the twentieth century. Wars and the threats of war were significant in moulding the course of that history. The Balkan Wars were significant events in the expansion of the Serbian state which had first been internationally recognised in 1878. World War I led to a fundamental transformation of Serbia's goal of an expanded nation-state to that of an expanded multinational state. The threat of war in the 1930s gave birth to the *Sporazum* as a means of bolstering the security of Yugoslavia as it attempted to stay out of World War II. World War II brought about the communist revolution which transformed Yugoslavia into a state in which the power and influence of the Serbs was significantly reduced. The possibility of real war during the Cold War era in many respects acted as a brake on the independence aspirations of non-Serbs in Yugoslavia. The victory of the West in the Cold War contributed to bringing about the wars over the partition of Yugoslavia in the 1990s. Some see the wars of the 1990s as being facilitated, or at least exacerbated, by the conflicting interests of Europe and the United States over the spoils of the Cold War.[36] That war and the threats of war have been significant in shaping Serb history is not surprising given the geo-political significance of the Balkans to the great powers.

Nationalism has been the second dominant theme of Serb history in the twentieth century. At the dawn of the twentieth century a small Serbian nation-state was bent on creating a larger Serbian nation-state. By the end of World War I Serbia's aim had been transformed into creating a multinational South Slav state as a homeland for the Serbs of the Balkans. However, the new South Slav state was one in which the Serbs were only a relative majority of the population. Although Yugoslavia appeared to represent an acceptable solution to the goals of Serb nationalism, it was nevertheless a fundamentally different state to the ideal of a Serb nation-state that found its expression in Garašanin's *Načertanije* and which had been the dominant theme in Serbia's politics of the nineteenth century.

However, the state of Yugoslavia could only survive if its nations were able to find a formula for co-existence within one state. As long ago as 1920 the eminent Serb scholar Slobodan Jovanović observed that pre-World War I Serbia was not the Prussia of the Balkans.[37] It had neither the military might nor the disciplined political tradition to enable it to dominate Yugoslavia as Prussia dominated the unified German state after 1871. Given this reality and the fact that the Croats and Slovenes only entered into Yugoslavia out of necessity, Yugoslavia's viability was always going to be tenuous. In its early history the fragility of Yugoslavia was exposed by the persistent demands of the Croats for autonomy. The Serbs were unable to placate the Croats in the 1920s and King Aleksandar's attempts to suppress Croat nationalism in the early 1930s similarly failed. Croat aspirations were partly realised with the *Sporazum* of 1939, but this arrangement, too, was one born out of necessity. Croat aspirations to statehood, but not full political independence, were realised in 1941 with the proclamation of the Independent State of Croatia. But being a creation of Nazi Germany it was only going to survive if Hitler emerged victorious in World War II. Hitler's loss, and the horrors of the Ustaša genocide which alienated many Croats, meant that a new Yugoslavia, dominated by Yugoslavia's communists, emerged in the wake of World War II.

The Yugoslavia fashioned by Tito and the CPY was in some respects similar to the interwar kingdom. The Serbs appeared content as they all lived in one state and were still the largest national group in the state. The Croats, as after World War I, accepted Yugoslavia for the reason that they had no alternative. Tito's attempts to create a Yugoslav identity met with the same fate as Aleksandar's attempt of the 1930s. However, communist Yugoslavia differed in one major respect from its monarchical predecessor. Whereas the Serb political elites did, to a large extent, control the levers of power in interwar Yugoslavia, that was not the case in the Tito era. Beginning with the constitutional arrangements of 1946, Serb power and influence over Yugoslavia gradually decreased in comparison to the days of the monarchy. The culmination of this process was the 1974 Constitution. Significant and widespread Serb discontent with the 1974 arrangements was slow to emerge, but it did so in the turbulent 1980s. Many Serb intellectual dissidents saw the solution to Yugoslavia lying in Serbia asserting real control over the federation.[38] The continuation of a Yugoslav state was not the problem, rather it was the decline of Serb control and influence over it. However, this option was never going to succeed. If, as Jovanović opined, Serbia was not a Prussia in 1920, then Slobodan Milošević was certainly not the Bismarck of the 1980s.

The political environment of the 1980s, both domestically and internationally, had conspired against Yugoslavia. The preservation of Yugoslavia was not in the interests of its non-Serb nations, and the changed international environment of the late 1990s meant that the international community had no great stake in saving it. The Croats, Slovenes, Bosnian Muslims and Macedonians, were now in a position to do what the Croats had been unable to do at any other time in Yugoslavia's short history. Independent statehood was available for the taking if they wanted it. When the Serb political and intellectual elites realised that the survival of Yugoslavia was in question, the divisions within the Serb elites over their future interests, revealed that the Serbs were not in a position to defend Yugoslavia. Some Serbs favoured the aim of preserving Yugoslavia. Others saw the opportunity to create their own nation-state. As the problem of Yugoslavia increasingly became the resolution of the 'Serb problem', the Serb response was unable to display the cohesion of the type displayed by the Croats in the interwar era. The contradiction in Serbia's response to the secessionist aspirations of

Slovenia and Croatia was exemplified in the politics of Milošević. Milošević, who was not a nationalist, sought to control Yugoslavia, but his politics was bathed in the rhetoric of Serb nationalism. The result of this policy was that he alienated the non-Serb nations and stiffened their resolve to leave Yugoslavia, whilst at the same time alienating many Serbs. The Serb nationalists were finally alienated by his abandonment of the Serbs of Croatia and Bosnia-Hercegovina. The political left was alienated by his increasingly authoritarian tendencies. Serbia's political programme by early 1997 consisted of little more than the retention of power by the Milošević elite.

As the twentieth century approaches its end, the Serb nation is increasingly confronted with the realisation that its history is at a major cross-road. Serb political and intellectual elites are divided over the issue of their optimal national goals in the wake of Yugoslavia's disintegration.[39] The dream of a nation-state that was so prevalent at the beginning of the century no longer informs Serb politics. The idea of a multinational Yugoslavia has been shattered. With the partition of Yugoslavia not yet settled and completely finalised, the Serb nation is in a state of considerable anxiety and uncertainty as it awaits the dawn of the twenty-first century.

Notes

1 For a detailed profile of Garašanin see MacKenzie (1985).

2 Aspects of the Serbian and Montenegrin rivalry are covered in Treadway (1983).

3 On the dynastic and constitutional struggles in Serbia in the nineteenth century see Petrovich (1976), Dragnich (1978), and Stokes (1990).

4 On the Battle of Kosovo and its significance as a political symbol see Emmert (1990).

5 On the events leading to the Sarajevo assassination see Dedijer (1967). For an account of Serbia's response to the Austro-Hungarian

ultimatum see Cornwall (1995). For a summary of the literature on the causes of World War I see Langdon (1991).

6 On the creation of Yugoslavia see Djordjevic (1980).

7 For an account of Yugoslavia's political turmoil to 1929 see Dragnich (1983), pp. 14-73, Critchley (1975), and Fogelquist (1990).

8 On Italian support for the Ustaša and Croat separatism and relations between the Ustaša and Maček see Sadkovich (1987).

9 For an account of Aleksandar's personal rule see Dragnich (1983), pp. 74-98, and Bigelow (1974), pp. 160-163.

10 On the putsch see Ristić (1966) and Petranović & Žutić (1990).

11 For an account of Yugoslavia's political situation during Pavle's rule see Dragnich (1983), pp. 99-134, Bigelow (1974), pp. 163-172, and Hoptner (1962).

12 Shelah (1990).

13 On the Četnici see Karchmar (1987), Tomasevich (1975), and Milazzo (1975).

14 On the Partisan movement see Shoup (1971), and Irvine (1993).

15 That the Partisans, in the first 18 months of the war, got their support predominantly from the Serbs of Yugoslavia, despite post-war claims to the contrary, was confirmed by Tito himself in an article he wrote in December 1942. The article, 'The National Question in Yugoslavia in the Light of the National Liberation Struggle', is reprinted in Rusinow (1995), pp. 309-316.

16 On Allied policy towards Yugoslavia see Roberts (1973), Wheeler (1980), Deroc (1988), and Ford (1992).

17 For a brief account of World War II in Yugoslavia see Pavlowitch (1971), pp. 107-172.

18 On the Yugoslav-Soviet split see Banac (1988).

19 On the transformation of Yugoslav ideology see Johnson (1972).

20 For an account of the national question to 1966 see Shoup (1968).

21 For an account of the national question from 1966 to the end of the 1970s see Burg (1983).

22 On the political developments in Yugoslavia in the 1980s see Pavković (1996), pp. 75-84, Cohen (1995), pp. 45-195, and Woodward (1995), pp. 47-113.

23 On the process and consequences and consequences of political and economic regionalism see Pleština (1992).

24 Serb feelings on Kosovo were amply demonstrated in 1989 with the celebrations marking the 600th anniversary of the Battle of Kosovo. Over 2 million Serbs attended the official celebrations in Kosovo in June. Massive media, scholarly and literary attention was given to Kosovo, its history and its significance to the Serbs. The then president of the Writers' Association of Serbia and distinguished Serb poet, Matija Bećković, captured the mood of the time when he wrote: 'On this Earth six centuries ago nothing of greater significance occurred than the battle at Kosovo Polje. And today, after six hundred Vidovdans, nothing is more critical for the Serb people than the present struggle in Kosovo and for Kosovo...Kosovo is the dearest of Serb words. It has been paid for with the blood of the whole nation. Because of that price it is entrenched at the throne of the Serb language. Without blood it could not be bought, without blood it cannot be sold.' See Bećković (1989), pp. 7, 8.

25 On the emergence of nationalism in Yugoslavia in the 1980s see Pavković (1996), pp. 85-98.

26 See Lydall, (1989).

27 Woodward (1995), pp. 39-40, 69-70, 74-81.

28 Woodward (1985), pp. 58-63.

29 On the elections in 1990 and the emergence of new political elites see Pavković (1996), pp. 99-121.

30 For an account of the 1991 war in Croatia see Glenny (1993), pp. 98-137.

31 A detailed account of the international community's response is provided by Lord Owen, one of the major participants, in Owen (1995).

32 For an account of the war in Bosnia-Hercegovina see O'Ballance (1995).

33 Klemenčić & Schofield (1996), pp. 38-40.

34 On the deployment of NATO air forces see Nicholls (1996).

35 For details of the wars in Yugoslavia from 1991 see Pavković (1996), pp. 122-185, Cohen (1995), pp. 227-237, and Woodward (1995), pp. 223-332.

36 Petras & Vieux (1996), p. 12.

37 Jovanović (1920), p. 368.

38 This was the solution proposed by the 'Memorandum' prepared by a committee of the Serbian Academy of Arts and Sciences that surfaced in 1986. For the text of the 'Memorandum' and a discussion of the controversy it sparked see Mihailović & Krestić (1995).

39 See Pavković (1995).

References

Banac, Ivo (1988), *With Stalin Against Tito, Cominformist Splits in Yugoslav Communism*, Cornell University Press, Ithaca & London

Bećković, Matija (1989), *Kosovo - Najskuplja Srpska reč,* Biblioteka 'Glas Crkve', Valjevo.

Bigelow, Bruce (1974), 'Centralization Versus Decentralization in Interwar Yugoslavia', *Southeastern Europe*, Vol 1, No 2, pp. 157-172.

Burg, Steven L. (1983), *Conflict and Cohesion in Socialist Yugoslavia, Political Decision Making Since 1966*, Princeton University Press, Princeton.

Cohen, Lenard J. (1995), *Broken Bonds, Yugoslavia's Disintegration and Balkan Politics in Transition*, 2nd ed., Westview Press, Boulder, San Francisco & Oxford.

Cornwall, Mark (1995), 'Serbia' in Keith Wilson (ed), *Decisions for War, 1914*, UCL Press, London, pp. 55-96.

Critchley, Winnifred H. (1975), *Political Restrictions on Leadership Response to Political Instability: Yugoslavia, 1921-1929*, Unpublished Doctoral Dissertation, Columbia University, New York.

Dedijer, Vladimir (1967), *The Road to Sarajevo*, MacGibbon & Kee, London.

Deroc, M (1988), *British Special Operations Explored, Yugoslavia in Turmoil 1941-1943 and the British Response*, East European Monographs, Boulder.

Djordjevic, Dimitrije (ed) (1980), *The Creation of Yugoslavia 1914-1918*, ABC-Clio Press, Santa Barbara & Oxford.

Dragnich, Alex D. (1978), *The Development of Parliamentary Government in Serbia*, East European Quarterly, New York.

Dragnich, Alex D. (1983), *The First Yugoslavia, Search for a Viable Political System*, Hoover Institution Press, Stanford.

Emmert, Thomas A. (1990), *Serbian Golgotha, Kosovo, 1389*, East European Monographs, New York.

Fogelquist, Alan F. (1990), *Politics & Economic Policy in Yugoslavia 1918-1929*, Unpublished Doctoral Dissertation, University of California, Los Angeles.

Ford Jr, Kirk (1992), *OSS and the Yugoslav Resistance, 1943-1945*, Texas A & M University Press, College Station.

Glenny, Misha (1993), *The Fall of Yugoslavia, The Third Balkan War*, Revised Edition, Penguin Books, London.

Hoptner, Jacob B. (1962), *Yugoslavia in Crisis, 1934-1941*, Columbia University Press, New York.

Irvine, Jill A. (1993), *The Croat Question, Partisan Politics in the Formation of the Yugoslav Socialist State*, Westview Press, Boulder, San Francisco & Oxford.

Johnson, A. Ross (1972), *The Transformation of Communist Ideology, The Yugoslav Case, 1945-1953*, MIT Press, Cambridge & London.

Jovanović, Slobodan (1920), 'Je li federalizam kod nas mogućan' in Radovan Samardžić & Živorad Stojković, *Sabrana dela Slobodana Jovanovića*, Vol. 1, Bigz, Belgrade, pp. 363-368.

Karchmar, Lucien (1987), *Draža Mihailović and the Rise of the Četnik Movement, 1941-1942*, Garland Publishing, New York & London.

Klemenčić, Mladen & Schofield, Clive (1996), 'Calm After the Storm? Croatia's Strategic Outlook', *RUSI Journal*, Vol. 141, No. 1, pp. 37-44.

Langdon, John W. (1991), *July 1914, The Long Debate, 1918-1990*, Berg, New York & Oxford.

Lydall, Harold (1989), *Yugoslavia in Crisis*, Clarendon Press, Oxford.

MacKenzie, David (1985), *Ilija Garašanin: Balkan Bismarck*, East European Monographs, Boulder.

Mihailović, Kosta & Krestić, Vasilije (1995), *'Memorandum SANU', Odgovori na kritike*, Srpska akademija nauke i umetnosti, Belgrade.

Milazzo, Matteo J (1975), *The Chetnik Movement and the Yugoslav Resistance*, Johns Hopkins University Press, Baltimore & London.

Nicholls, D. V. (1996), 'Bosnia: UN and NATO', *RUSI Journal*, Vol. 141, No. 1, pp. 31-36.

O'Ballance, Edgar (1995), *Civil War in Bosnia, 1992-94*, St Martin's Press, New York.

Owen, David (1995), *Balkan Odyssey*, Victor Gollancz, London.

Pavković, Aleksandar (1995), 'Intellectual Dissidence and the Serb National Question' in Aleksandar Pavković, Halyna Koscharsky & Adam Czarnota (eds), *Nationalism and Postcommunism, A Collection of Essays*, Dartmouth Publishing Company, Aldershot.

Pavković, Aleksandar (1997), *The Fragmentation of Yugoslavia: Nationalism in a Multinational State*, Macmillan, London.

Pavlowitch, Stevan K (1971), *Yugoslavia*, Ernest Benn Ltd, London.

Petranović, Branko & Žutić, Nikola (1990), *27. mart 1941. Tematska zbirka dokumenata*, Nicom, Belgrade.

Petrovich, Michael Boro (1976), *A History of Modern Serbia 1804-1918*, Harcourt Brace Jovanovich, New York & London.

Petras, James & Vieux, Steve (1996), 'Bosnia and the Revival of US Hegemony', *New Left Review*, No. 218, pp. 3-25.

Pleština, Dijana (1992), *Regional Development in Communist Yugoslavia, Success, Failure & Consequences*, Westview Press, Boulder, San Francisco & Oxford.

Ristić, Dragiša N. (1966), *Yugoslavia's Revolution of 1941*, Pennsylvania State University Press, University Park & London.

Roberts, Walter R. (1973), *Tito, Mihailović and the Allies, 1941-1945*, Rutgers University Press, New Brunswick.

Rusinow, Dennison (1995), 'The Yugoslav Peoples' in Peter F. Sugar (ed), *Eastern European Nationalism in the Twentieth Century*, American University Press, Washington.

Sadkovich, James J. (1987), *Italian Support for Croatian Separatism, 1927-1937*, Garland Publishing, New York & London.

Shelah, Menachem (1990), 'Genocide in Satellite Croatia During the Second World War' in Berenbaum, Michael (ed), *A Mosaic of Victims, Non-Jews Persecuted and Murdered by the Nazis*, New York University Press, New York & London, pp. 74-79.

Shoup, Paul (1968), *Communism and the Yugoslav National Question*, Columbia University Press, New York & London.

Shoup, Paul (1971), 'The Yugoslav Revolution: The First of a New Type', *Studies on the Soviet Union (New Series)*, Vol. XI, No. 4, pp. 215-243.

Stokes, Gale (1990), *Politics as Development, The Emergence of Political Parties in Nineteenth-Century Serbia*, Duke University Press, Durham & London.

Tomasevich, Jozo (1975), *War and Revolution in Yugoslavia, 1941-1945: The Chetniks*, Stanford University Press, Stanford.

Treadway, John D. (1983), *The Falcon & the Eagle, Montenegro and Austria-Hungary, 1908-1914*, Purdue University Press, West Lafayette.

Wheeler, Mark C. (1980), *Britain and the War for Yugoslavia, 1940-1943*, East European Monographs, Boulder.

Woodward, Susan L. (1995), *Balkan Tragedy, Chaos and Dissolution After the Cold War*, The Brookings Institution, Washington.

2 Nikola Pašić

ALEX N. DRAGNICH

Introduction

Nikola Pašić was born in Eastern Serbia in 1845, at a time when Serbia was beginning to achieve *de facto* independence after nearly 500 years of subjugation by the Ottoman Empire. By the time that he had completed his education and was emerging as a young political leader, Serbia had been recognised *de jure*, in 1878, as a fully sovereign state. As events unfolded Pašić was to be on the political stage for fifty years, from 1875 until his death in 1926, longer than any other Serbian or Yugoslav political leader. Most of his political career was pursued in his native Serbia, but the last eight years were spent in the service of the new Yugoslav state, which he helped to bring into being in 1918 and of which Serbia was the largest component.

Pašić lived and acted in times that were turbulent and fateful not only for his nation but also for Europe and the world beyond. He played a key role in guiding the destinies of his native Serbia and in shaping the future of the Balkans during the years the Ottoman empire was in decline. His task was how to go about rebuilding the nation while also working toward the liberation of other Serbian lands and at the same time not becoming a victim of the great-power rivalry - Russian, Ottoman, and Austro-Hungarian.

Approximately one half of his career was devoted to the struggle for the establishment of a democratic parliamentary system. The other half was spent in building and improving that system, in combating the efforts of the Austro-Hungarian monarchy to strangle Serbia, and in seeking to redeem Serbian lands under foreign rule and ultimately to bring about a union of all South Slavs in one national state.

The Struggle for Democracy

Pašić's political ideas were in large part shaped during his days as a student at the Federal Polytechnic Institute in Zurich, Switzerland, one of the best institutions of its kind at the time. His early schooling was in his native Zaječar, supplemented by intermediate work in Negotin, Kragujevac, and Belgrade. Subsequently, he studied technology at the *Velika Škola* (forerunner of Belgrade University) and then was given a government stipend to continue his studies in Zurich.

At Zurich, in addition to his technological studies, Pašić immersed himself in the study of politics, including the democratic institutions of the Swiss political system. Moreover, he became acquainted with Russian emigre revolutionists, including the anarchist Bakunin, and established a close friendship with fellow Serb Svetozar Marković, who became the first socialist theoretician in Serbia. Pašić quickly rejected Bakunin's anarchist ideas because he could not get a satisfactory answer to his question about what was to be done after the destruction of the existing political system. And he early recognised that Marković's socialist ideas were not applicable to Serbia. He could see that political success required the adaptation of abstract political ideas to the needs and aspirations of the Serbian peasant masses. Hence his practical bent in searching for political solutions.

Upon his return to Belgrade in 1873 he was appointed professor of geodetics, but this was vetoed for political reasons, whereupon he began a career as an engineer. Two events resulted in that career being cut short - the rebellion of the Serbs in Bosnia-Hercegovina against the Turks in 1875 and the death in the same year of Svetozar Marković. At that point Pašić concluded that he could best serve his country by going into politics, and for the next fifty years he was a major actor on its political stage. He became the central figure of the political group that began to take shape at the Zurich Polytechnic. His initial effort to gain political office was frustrated by government decree, leading him to go to Bosnia-Hercegovina, and to join the army. After the conclusion of the war with the Treaty of San Stefano in 1878, and Russia's creating thereby of a Great Bulgaria, earning the enmity of Serbia, Pašić returned to political battles. In October 1878 he was elected a deputy to the *Skupština* (Assembly) at age thirty-three, the first of his circle to be elected to the national parliament.

In launching the fight for democracy, Pašić built on the works of his predecessors. The struggle for constitutional monarchy and parliamentary supremacy had its inception in the ideas of the young liberals, most of whom had been students in Western Europe and were the nucleus of the first Serbian political party, the Liberals. Their leader, Jovan Ristić, was first regent in the years (1868-1872) when Serbian Prince Milan Obrenović was a minor. He drafted the Constitution of 1869, patterned on that of Belgium, which was a long step toward recognising constitutional monarchy. Under that constitution the principle of ministerial responsibility was first proclaimed and shortly thereafter, as prime minister under Milan, Ristić formulated its classic defence.[1]

With Pašić in the forefront, a new political party was in the making - the Serbian National Radical Party. It was the first political party in Serbia to organise systematically. In 1880 Pašić brought together parliamentary deputies of similar views. A party caucus was formed, party statutes were formulated, and a detailed programme worked out and in January 1881 published in the newly founded party organ, *Samouprava* (self-government). Pašić was chosen the party leader without opposition, a position that he was to hold, except for a brief interval at the turn of the century, until his death in 1926.

The party programme dealt almost exclusively with needed domestic reforms - legislative, administrative, judicial, financial, educational, and military. Heading the list of needed reforms was one to amend the constitution so that the *Skupština* would be directly and freely elected, that it meet annually on a set date, and that it have full legislative powers. The programme also called for strengthening local self-government, the enactment of a progressive income tax, and for educational opportunities irrespective of means. The programme was signed by Nikola Pašić and thirty-seven other deputies and subscribed to by another thirty-nine unnamed deputies. This was a majority of the elected deputies, although not a majority of the total.

Before the constitution could be amended to achieve such reforms, the party programme called for enactment of legislation that would guarantee: (1) full freedom of the press, (2) freedom of speech, (3) freedom of association, (4) communal self-government, (5) security of person and property. Pašić continued to emphasise the relationship between basic freedoms and a constitutional state.

In foreign affairs, the programme called for closer relations with Montenegro and Bulgaria and building a league of Balkan peoples. In addition, it stressed the need for educational and cultural work among 'our people' in regions where they were under foreign rule.

The programme demonstrated to the people that the Radical party was not, as some had depicted it, a collection of wild-eyed idealists, and they flocked to its colours. The monarchy and its supporters, however, saw in the party a threat, and proceeded to nullify its electoral victories.

From 1880 to 1882 elections were held three times, and the result each time was a defeat for the non-Radical parties. In elections held in September 1883, the Radical party won a clear majority of seats in the *Skupština*, but Prince Milan wanted nothing to do with the new parliament. In October he opened it with one decree and adjourned it with another, all in a matter of ten minutes.

Soon thereafter, a rebellion broke out in the Timok region, the extreme northeastern part of Serbia. The immediate cause was the cabinet's attempt to collect state arms of the national militia. The idea was to disarm one area at a time, and the authorities began in the region where the Radical party was the strongest. The regime struck hard at Radical leaders of the rebellion in the region, mainly teachers and priests, sentencing ninety-four to death and imprisoning over six hundred. It also suppressed the rebellion that had spread to adjoining regions. Blaming the top Radical leadership, the regime arrested all of those who were in the capital, except Pašić, who had fled by way of Austria-Hungary with the intention of joining the rebellion in eastern Serbia. Before he could get there, however, he learned that the rebellion had been put down. Consequently, he went to Bulgaria, where he spent most of his six years of exile. During that exile he was concerned with the question of how to change things in Serbia. To that end he sought to get arms from Russia, but with little success. He also devoted a good deal of thought to how Serbia could liberate Serbian lands that were under foreign rule, particularly 'Old' or 'South' Serbia, which at one time had been part of Serbia's medieval kingdom.

The basic cause of the Timok Rebellion, of course, was the smouldering dispute between the Radicals, who saw their electoral victories denied them, and Prince Milan, who completely distrusted them. He was convinced that they were revolutionary and anti-dynastic elements.

During Pašić's exile the Radical party was without an acknowledged leader in Serbia. Prince Milan's actions against the party faithful left the party further disorganised and in considerable disarray. Milan sought to govern through politicians willing to do his bidding, mainly the conservatives who had formed the Progressive party, but his moves were generally unpopular. In 1882, in the hope of improving his status, Milan proclaimed himself king. And in 1885 he embarked on a war against Bulgaria, which Serbia lost.

These ill-fated moves and his difficulties with his estranged wife Natalija, whom he had not yet divorced, led Milan to conclude that he should abdicate. Before doing so, however, he sought to secure two objectives: (1) he wanted to protect Aleksandar, the young heir to the throne, from Natalija's influence, and (2) he wanted the Serbian treasury to guarantee his future financial security.

He believed that he could best achieve these objectives if he brought the Radicals to power. He would grant them a liberal constitution, provided that he could appoint the Royal Regency to rule while Aleksandar was a minor. To that end he granted pardons to the important Radical leaders, except Pašić who, as noted above, was in exile. And he pressured the Metropolitan of the Serbian Orthodox Church to grant him a divorce decree from Natalija. Two days after the decree was published, he called for elections to a parliament that would change the constitution. Milan insisted that this be the common work of all political parties, and appointed the leading personalities to a constitutional committee. He guided the work throughout personally. The constituent assembly ratified the document, which was certainly one of the most democratic in Europe.[2]

Milan was motivated by a number of considerations. At different times he gave varied reasons (marital troubles, fear of insanity, disloyalty of Serbian politicians, distaste for ruling by force). There is a fair amount of evidence that he believed that Serbia was not ready for democracy, and as a consequence, the chaos that would result from the new system would lead the European powers, within a couple of years, to beg him to come back to restore order. In this expectation he was sadly disappointed.

The Radicals formed the first cabinet under the regency. Four days after his abdication, Milan as a 'friend' of the regency recommended an amnesty for Pašić, and the next day the regency obliged. Pašić returned in triumph in March 1889. Following the September elections, he was made president of the *Skupština*, and in February 1891, he became prime minister for the first time.

The Radicals proved that they could rule in a democratic, progressive and competent manner. Yet during much of their four-year governance (1889-1893), they were beset with spending much time in dealing with the Milan-Natalija problem. Despite Milan's abdication he continued to interfere in Serbian politics. He broke the agreements he had made, and sought additional money from the government. Pašić even engineered a million dinar loan from Russia - in fact a gift - to Milan. But Milan always wanted more, partly to cover gambling losses and costs of high living in European cities. He even sought the help of the regency to oust the Radicals from power, but without success, even though he had appointed its members. Natalija also tried to counter his moves.

In large part, because he was forced to concern himself with the conflict between the parents of Aleksandar, Pašić's first cabinet seemed colourless and without coherent political direction. He appeared to permit his cabinet colleagues to go their own way. He waited and wavered. Many of his Radical colleagues could not understand why it was necessary to bribe the ex-king, but Pašić early in his political career accepted the principle that in dealing with an opponent it was better to use money than force. Nevertheless, many thought that his star was fading. But it was just the beginning of a new decade of struggle for parliamentary democracy.

The Struggle for Democracy Continues

As a last resort, Milan engineered a coup against the regency in April 1893. Aleksandar dismissed the regency and proclaimed himself king, even though he was not quite seventeen years of age. In effect, Serbia became a duarchy of son and father, to say nothing of mother Natalija's role. The fact that Pašić had obtained from Milan, in writing, a renunciation of his rights as a member of the royal household, as well as Serbian citizenship, did not phase him. Milan's action seemed to have been precipitated by the death of one of the regents. Because the constitution provided that filling of a vacancy in the regency was the prerogative of parliament, and because the Radicals were in a majority, Milan was sure it would choose Pašić'. And that was the last thing that he wanted.

The decade of Aleksandar's rule (1893-1903) began with a coup and ended with a coup. In 1893 he seized power, and in 1903 a conspiracy ended his life and that of the Obrenović dynasty. During those turbulent years, Aleksandar sought to reign *and* to govern. He suspended and abolished constitutions as if they were toys. Elections did not mean much to him. In that decade he had twelve cabinets; all ministries were made and unmade in the palace. He sought to end party government and even to take the lives of some Radical leaders, including Pašić. He entered into an extremely unpopular marriage, which culminated in both he and his queen being shot in 1903.[3]

In those years, Milan and Natalija came and went, and in their separate ways sought to influence Aleksandar's politics. The mother advised him to work with the Radicals and in no case against them, while the father advised him to work with anyone but the Radicals. In the first phase of his reign he seemed to have taken his mother's advice; several cabinets had Radical Party members, but not Pašić, who however agreed to Radical participation. During the second phase he was primarily influenced by his father. After his intention to marry the widow Draga Mašin became known, however, Milan told his son that if he should go through with such an impulsive act, he would be the first to greet the cabinet that would overthrow him. In January 1901, Milan died in Vienna, a grieving and dejected 'old man' of forty-seven.

Aleksandar's troubles did not end with the death of his father. He had difficulty putting together a cabinet that would sanction his marriage. Subsequently, when it turned out that the announced pregnancy of the queen was false, he became even more disliked. The strained relationship between Aleksandar and the Radical leaders continued, but he managed to bring some of them into cabinets, with the blessing of Pašić. Whenever there was a cabinet crisis, Aleksandar returned to personal rule. Although the Radicals were his principal opponents, they were not involved in the army coup that ended the lives of the royal couple in May 1903. Pašić had been approached, but refused, and on the fatal day he and his family were on their way to the Adriatic coast, then under Austrian rule.

The turbulent decade of Aleksandar's rule was an exceedingly trying one for Nikola Pašić and the Radical party. Although the party won a majority whenever there was a free election, it was not given power. On the contrary, it was subject to persistent persecution. In 1898 Pašić went to prison for nine months because of an alleged press slander against the dynasty. Pašić had no sooner returned from prison in the summer of 1899 when he and other leading Radicals were arrested in connection with an attempt on Milan's life. While Milan was convinced that the Russians were behind the plot, he was determined that the Radicals must bear the full responsibility. The public, influenced in part by the reopening of the Dreyfus case in France, was not convinced of the Radicals' guilt, especially before any evidence had been presented. Milan, however, held fast that at least Pašić and Kosta Taušanović must be sentenced to death.

The intervention of Russia and Austria-Hungary, for quite different reasons, saved the lives of the two Radical leaders. But Pašić did not know this. Milan sent Đorđe Genčić, minister of interior and Pašić's former collaborator, to talk to Pašić behind prison walls. Genčić asked Pašić to provide the king with a way out from a difficult situation - to admit to Radical activities that could have destroyed the dynasty, and to promise that he would no longer tolerate Radicals who were known to be working against the dynasty. In that event the crown would spare the lives of all except that of the assassin. Failing this, the king would view the Radicals as incapable of reform and in that case would order up to twenty heads to fall.

Pašić was in terrible turmoil. He was reluctant to admit anything, yet he knew that some elements in the party had engaged in anti-dynastic activities. He weighed the consequences for the Radicals and for Serbia of making or not making such a 'confession'. He was disturbed about the reaction of the public and the Radical followers, especially when they could not be told of Genčić's visit as an intermediary between Pašić and the king.

Pašić's difficulties were compounded by the attitude of the court. He was on trial for treason and yet he was told that he could not have witnesses unless their names and the questions that would be put to them were submitted in advance. When he complied, the judge told him that witnesses could not be called to testify against government witnesses. This meant, in effect, that he was sentenced in advance.

Nevertheless, he concluded, especially since a number of lives hung in the balance, that it was better to accept responsibility for the acts of others and thereby save their lives and the party. In so doing, he recognised that he was also sacrificing his political future. In court he denied any implication of guilt, but he did recognise political errors. He admitted the existence of anti-dynastic elements in the party and that he had not taken sufficiently energetic measures against them. The court sentenced Pašić and several others to prison terms, but Pašić was almost immediately pardoned.

The reaction of the public was predictable. His behaviour in court was condemned as cowardly. He was abused from all sides as a man who did not have a speck of moral worth. The noted Serbian historian,

Slobodan Jovanović, observed: 'He became the most unpopular man in the whole country; he experienced the greatest amount of disdain a politician can experience.'[4] Although believing that he had not betrayed the party, Pašić saw no point in seeking to defend himself if the public could not recognise his merits.

Pašić's behaviour in court served to widen an already existing rift in the party. That schism resulted more from differences over tactics than from disagreement over basic principles. Pašić and the other older Radicals were viewed by the younger members as too conciliatory toward the autocracy of the Obrenovićes and their followers. The split chrystalised over the Constitution of 1901 and the Progressive-Radical agreement that brought it about. The younger Radicals, condemning what they considered opportunism, began calling themselves 'Independent Radicals' or just 'Independents.' They soon founded a separate political party, the Independent Radical Party. Pašić, for his part, began publishing a paper, *Zakonitost* (legality), the only Radical paper published at that time, which he hoped would be a rallying point for dispersed party elements. That activity served as the beginning of his political rehabilitation.

Pašić and Radical Party Rule, 1903-1918

The perpetrators who ended the Obrenović dynasty turned power over to an all-party coalition, which legitimised the return of parliamentary rule by calling into session the existing parliament. It merely ratified previously agreed-upon acts - mainly the choice of Petar Karađorđević as king and the return of the democratic Constitution of 1888, now to be known as the Constitution of 1903. Serbia again became a constitutional parliamentary monarchy.

It was obvious that the first order of business was legislation to implement the new constitution, ie. judicial and administrative reforms. New elections were needed and they were held, but the party complexion of parliament was far from clear. In November 1904, Pašić formed a Radical cabinet even though lacking a solid majority. In 1906, however, the Radicals won a solid majority, and except for a brief period when for tactical reasons he found it prudent to have another Radical at the helm, Pašić was prime minister until the formation of the Yugoslav state in 1918.

Even though the Pašić cabinet was to face several difficult domestic and foreign policy problems, important political and administrative reforms were made. Economic growth was facilitated, educational and cultural opportunities were improved, and the nation's defenses strengthened. Yet all of this was done while maintaining sound and responsible fiscal policies. State budgets were balanced and Serbian currency was on par with those of the major European countries.

Pašić's approach to the new epoch in Serbia's history came about as a result of much thought about domestic and foreign affairs. In domestic politics he was guided by the knowledge of and faith in the democratic political system. In foreign affairs he was influenced by his knowledge of history, especially recent history, and by a serious assessment of the intentions and capabilities of Serbia's enemies as well as her friends.

Along with the ambitious domestic reforms, Pašić and his colleagues were forced to deal with several critical domestic questions, some of which were related to foreign affairs questions. The first one concerned the question of the army conspirators who overthrew the Obrenovićes. That act horrified much of Europe, and Great Britain even broke diplomatic relations. There were demands for punishment, but in Serbia this could not even be mentioned. Hence the only way out was to pension them. Some, including King Petar, thought this drastic, but Pašić was unwavering, cool, and logical. Through long and patient talks, he got the older conspirators to retire by giving them full pay, and King Petar approved. This was not strictly legal, but it resolved a delicate question without quarrels or scandal. The younger conspirators, who at that time were not involved in politics, were allowed to remain in active service, with the understanding that they would not get involved in politics. The fact that they failed to abide by this agreement was to continue as a source of latent conflict between the civil and the military authority.

Another critical question involved getting a loan to build up Serbia's army. Austria-Hungary, on whom Serbia had long been dependent economically, was confident that Pašić had no alternative but to get loans and to buy arms from Vienna, for the simple reason that most of Serbia's foreign trade was with the Dual Monarchy. Pašić knew that he was risking an economic war, and he got it - the so-called 'pig war'. His answer was to get a loan from France and to buy cannons for the Serbian army from French firms. The tariff war continued for several years, and caused Serbia serious economic difficulties, but the decisiveness of Pašić's cabinet promoted Serbia's political and economic independence.

A different but delicate problem involved getting Prince Đorđe, the heir to the throne to abdicate. This question came about as a result of several factors. The immediate cause was the death of his orderly, whom Đorđe had kicked in the stomach. More important were some of his anti-parliamentary statements, and especially his animosity toward Pašić. Prince Đorđe knew what he was doing. His father had told him that a king does not dare go against the will of his ministers, 'for they represent the people and the people's will is law.' But such admonitions had little impact on Đorđe, who sought to communicate directly with the *Skupština*. In the years after World War II, he authored a book in which he said that he told his father that he would never collaborate with Pašić. A number of antics in Đorđe's personal life also led Pašić to conclude that Đorđe was not fit to be king. In 1909, Prince Đorđe abdicated, and thereby his younger brother, Prince Aleksandar, became heir to the throne.

As suggested above, the nagging problem of civil-military relations continued to confront Pašić and the Radicals. For a time it was dormant, but after the Balkan Wars it surfaced when Pašić ordered the newly-liberated territories placed under civilian rule. The military commander in Skoplje, General Damjan Popović, refused to abide by the order and was promptly dismissed. The moving force in the Serbian patriotic society, Union or Death, Colonel Dragutin Dimitrijević-Apis, even suggested that it would be a good thing if some of the civil administrators were forced to leave for home with their baggage. Pašić was firm and after a time King Petar reluctantly agreed, but at the same time (1914) transferred the royal powers to Aleksandar, who became Prince Regent. The question was finally resolved in blood when conviction by a military court in Salonika, Greece near the end of World War I led to the execution of Apis and two of his colleagues. The charge was attempting to assassinate Prince Aleksandar. Whatever one may think of the evidence presented, the appropriateness of the penalties, or the motives of the principals on both sides, it is clear that Pašić and Aleksandar - who had no love for each other - were in agreement that some settling of accounts could not long be delayed. And whatever one may think of their judgment, there seems little doubt that Apis and his collaborators exceeded the proper role of the military in a democratic political system.[5]

Many knowledgeable observers believe that Pašić's greatest achievements were in the realm of foreign policy. In that sphere he faced great obstacles. As we have seen, he was prime minister during the tariff war with Austria-Hungary. He led Serbia in the Balkan Wars and in World War I. And he engineered the creation of the Kingdom of the Serbs, Croats, and Slovenes, later known as Yugoslavia. In all of these actions, it can be said that he contributed to the fall of two empires, the Ottoman and the Austro-Hungarian. Pašić had precious little help from the outside. It is sometimes said that he relied on Russia's support. At times he had it, but it is worth noting that in 1878 the Russians favoured Bulgaria over Serbia and agreed to Vienna's occupation of Bosnia-Hercegovina, and at a later date (1908) agreed that ultimately occupation could be changed to annexation.

Although Pašić had by the spring of 1907 concluded trade agreements with England, France, Italy, Switzerland, and Sweden, and in 1908 a Radical cabinet not headed by Pašić concluded a trade agreement with Austria-Hungary, the latter refused to ratify the agreement until 1911, which finally ended the tariff war.

It was in 1908 that Vienna announced the annexation of Bosnia-Hercegovina. The Serbian populace was outraged, the *Skupština* passed a resolution protesting the annexation and announcing that it was ready for any and all sacrifices, and that it would approve all measures which the cabinet might undertake. The cabinet knew that Serbia was in no position to go to war. Early in the crisis Pašić had gone to St Petersburg in the hope of preventing Russia's recognition of the annexation, but it was not to be. Russia was afraid that if it failed to extend recognition, Vienna might seek to destroy Serbia. The Russians knew that a month before the crisis, Vienna's foreign minister told his German counterpart that Serbia should be divided between Austria-Hungary and Bulgaria. Moreover, Russia was in no position to help because she had just met defeat at the hands of Japan in 1904.

England, France, and Russia declared that the annexation was a violation of the agreement at the Congress of Berlin of 1878. Yet not only was the annexation recognised, but, in addition, Russia was compelled to exert pressure on Serbia to have the Belgrade government declare, in writing, that Serbia's rights were not impaired by the annexation and that she would give up her protests. Vienna took other steps designed to weaken Serbia, such as the projected railway across

Novipazar, which never materialised. Moreover, Vienna engineered treason trials in Cetinje and Zagreb in the hope of discrediting Serbia, but the documents presented at the trials were patent forgeries.

In the meantime, Serbia and the other Balkan nations were plotting to oust the Ottomans from Europe. A successful alliance was concluded in 1912, first between Serbia and Bulgaria, and subsequently extended to include Greece and Montenegro. One of Pašić's Radical colleagues was prime minister when the alliance was negotiated; understandably he was consulted. He was prime minister when the war against Turkey was launched in October. In November the Turks sued for peace, asking the great powers to intervene. The latter were surprised by Turkey's quick defeat. In Austro-Hungarian circles it was believed that Turkey would defeat the upstart Balkan nations.

Before the great powers could act, Serbian troops drove to the Adriatic at Durazzo (Drach) and established a common frontier with Montenegro. Simultaneously, the Montenegrins captured Skadar (Scutari). The great powers, including Russia, decided to create an Albanian state and thereby denied to the Serbs and Montenegrins their gains on the Adriatic. Pašić was under immense domestic pressure not to give in, but he knew that he could not buck the great powers when they were united. Pašić stated his case, but indicated Serbia's desire for peace and her trust in the judgment of the great powers. The result: both Serbia and Montenegro were denied significant victories, and in that sense it could be said that Austro-Hungarian anti-Serb policies won out. But her triumphs were leading her on the road to destruction.

For Pašić and Serbia that was not the end of the war. The problem of dividing up the lands liberated from Turkey was complex and difficult, particularly in drawing the boundary between Serbia and Bulgaria. Their agreement had specified where part of the boundary should be, with the proviso that the Russian tsar would arbitrate in case of unresolved differences. After the defeat of Turkey, the Serbs proposed a revision of the agreement because the Bulgarians had not lived up to their part of it. Moreover, Serbian forces had to rescue Bulgarian units. The Serbs also believed that the Bulgarians should take into account the fact that Serbia's victories in the drive to the sea were taken away by the great powers.

Since Bulgaria was in no mood to seek a peaceful resolution, Pašić was in a difficult position. Given past Russian actions that favoured

Bulgaria, could he trust them to be fair in this situation? Typically, not wanting to cast the first stone, Pašić must nevertheless have had doubts as to the wisdom of a wait-and-see attitude. The members of the *Skupština* were adamant, passing a resolution that the cabinet must not, under any circumstance, sacrifice Serbia's vital interests in Macedonia. Despite all of his fears, Pašić finally told the *Skupština* that the cabinet had agreed to arbitration by the Russian tsar.

While he was still in the *Skupština*, he received word that Bulgarian forces had attacked on all fronts, and that they had also attacked Greece. Fortunately for Serbia, the Bulgarians had alienated the Romanians and they also came into the fray. In a month the Bulgarians were defeated and suing for peace. Pašić's gamble paid off, and in addition, Serbia's international prestige was boosted.

In surveying what Serbia had gone through in the past few years, Pašić concluded that the Austro-Hungarian leaders in Vienna must have viewed the outcomes as defeats. He could also see that those leaders were increasingly annoyed because Serbia was more and more becoming an attraction for the South Slavs of the Dual Monarchy, who viewed democratic Serbia as the Piedmont of a Yugoslav state. Pašić was convinced that Vienna would not desist from other aggressive acts, even war against Serbia.

In the early spring of 1914, he conveyed his fears personally to the tsar in St Petersburg and asked for Russian help and protection in the event of an Austro-Hungarian attack. He explained his thinking in detail. The tsar listened but was still incredulous. In the end, he promised Russian protection in case of an unprovoked attack. Following this assurance, Pašić decided on new elections in the summer, mainly because his parliamentary majority was a narrow one.

Pašić's fears, that Austria-Hungary was determined to cow Serbia and if need be to crush her, turned out to be justified. The leaders in Vienna were successful in convincing their allies in Germany that a preventive war against Serbia was an absolute necessity for the salvation of the Dual Monarchy. Berlin gave its consent. All of this was before the assassination of the heir to the Austrian throne in Sarajevo on Serbia's most important holiday, *Vidovdan* (28 June). The assassination was the work of the Dual Monarchy's Serbian subjects, but Vienna nevertheless used it as a pretext for war against Serbia.

Austria charged that agents from Serbia, with the knowledge of the Serbian cabinet, were behind the plot. While there is no proof of this allegation, Serbian intelligence agents were no doubt travelling to and from the area. Even if some of them were involved, there is no proof that Pašić's cabinet knew. Pašić must have been uneasy about the announced visit of the Austrian archduke to Sarajevo, because he had asked his minister in Vienna to caution the Austrians about his making a trip to Bosnia to inspect Austrian troops on the Serbian holiday.

In any case, it can be said unequivocally that Pašić did not desire war with anyone in 1914, and this was true of all Serbian political leaders. Serbia had been badly depleted by the Balkan Wars. Serbia's military preparedness was poor. Moreover, Pašić knew that in case of war with Austria, Serbia would have another enemy, Bulgaria. He was in the midst of the civil-military controversy, discussed above, and he had much work to do in organising the newly-liberated areas of South Serbia. Finally, he had dissolved the *Skupština* and was in the midst of an electoral campaign. He and most other leaders were on the campaign trail when the Austrian ultimatum was presented to the acting prime minister on 23 July 1914.

The ultimatum, with a forty-eight hour time limit, was unbelievably humiliating, and seemingly drafted so that Serbia could not accept it. Even so, Pašić and his colleagues decided on a serious and conciliatory answer. Among other things, they agreed (1) to amend the press law so as to prevent attacks on Austria-Hungary, (2) to dissolve the patriotic organisation *Narodna odbrana* (National Defence), and (3) to oust teachers, civil servants, and military officers who carried on anti-Austrian activities. But the Pašić cabinet could not accept the demand that Austro-Hungarian agents participate in various investigations on Serbian soil.

The rulers in Vienna, however, were not even interested in considering the Serbian answer. After a hasty reading of the note that Pašić had personally handed to him, Baron Giesl, the Austro-Hungarian minister, declared that diplomatic relations between the two countries were being broken. His bags and those of his staff were already packed, and all of them were ready to leave on the evening train within two hours after Pašić had handed him the Serbian answer.

Neither the Austrians nor the Germans had been able to find any evidence of Serbia's complicity in the assassination. The most that Austria could do was to demonstrate that the Serbian cabinet had tolerated anti-

Austrian organisations in Serbia. In the light of these facts, Germany was satisfied with the Serbian answer to the ultimatum. Austria-Hungary, however, was not and declared war on Serbia on 28 July 1914.

World War I and the Creation of Yugoslavia

Austro-Hungarian forces attacked. The Serbian forces withdrew, regrouped, and waited. Pašić and the cabinet had withdrawn to the city of Niš, because Belgrade was on the frontier and the object of enemy shelling. When the Austrian units moved toward the Serbian interior, they were badly beaten in several battles, with Serbian forces in hot pursuit into Austrian territory. By the end of the first year of the war, the Serbs were back in Belgrade, with no enemy soldiers on Serbian soil.

Serbia's victory, however, was short-lived. In the summer of 1915, a concerted German-Austrian campaign was launched, coordinated with an attack by Bulgaria. Fighting on two fronts, out-gunned by superior German artillery, and with no significant Allied assistance, the Serbian forces fell back. With two courses open to them - either fight and die, or retreat across the Albanian mountains in winter - Pašić and his cabinet chose the latter course, which resulted in painful material and human losses.

Tragic as the Albanian retreat had been, it earned for Serbia enormous respect in Paris and London. Even today a visitor to the main entrance of the British foreign office will see a huge fresco on the wall in which Britain is depicted as a large lady embracing two children, one wrapped in the Belgium flag and the other in the Serbian flag. There were at that time no more popular small states than Belgium and Serbia. And Serbia's exodus in winter only served to enhance its prestige.

There was also a negative side. In 1905, Vienna had viewed Pašić as an able and dangerous political leader. In the winter of 1915-1916; however, he seemed a pathetic figure, driven from his country, with huge losses incurred by the nation's proud military forces. Even many of Pašić's own military commanders, to say nothing of his political opponents, were blaming him for the debacle. But he was not defeated. In the not exactly friendly atmosphere of the Greek island of Corfu (where the Serb army and cabinet were settled), he husbanded his resources, secured Allied help to re-equip an army of 115,000 men, which in April

1916 went to the Salonika front. From there the army proceeded to take part in the eventual liberation of their homeland.

In the course of the war, Pašić and his countrymen played a crucial role in the formation of the Yugoslav state. The idea of a South Slav state was not the monopoly of one man or group of men. Serbs, Croats, and Slovenes contributed in a variety of contexts. One of the leading personalities advancing that idea was Croat Bishop Juraj Štrosmajer. Practical steps in this direction were not, however, undertaken until the First World War. Pašić did report in a memorandum of his conversation with the Russian tsar in early 1914 (when he hoped to find a Russian princess for the heir to the Serbian throne) that he told the tsar that if circumstances permitted she might become princess of the 'Serbo-Croat Yugoslav people.'

In less than two months after the outbreak of the war, Pašić assembled a variety of experts who recommended the goal of a common South Slav state. Shortly thereafter he sent instructions to his ministers in the Allied capitals, setting forth in fairly precise form the projected boundaries of the new state after the defeat of Austria-Hungary. These boundaries would have given Yugoslavia even more territory than it got after World War II. However these aspirations may be depicted, they are not the aspirations for a Great Serbia.

On 7 December 1914, the *Skupština* approved a declaration of the Pašić cabinet which put forth as Serbia's principal war aim the unifications of all Serbs, Croats, and Slovenes. This is known as the Niš Declaration because the Serbian government was at that time in the city of Niš. Pašić was earlier made aware of South Slavs in Austro-Hungary who shared these aspirations. In October he had suggested the creation from among the emigres from the Dual Monarchy a committee that would collaborate with the Serbian government in seeking that goal. Pašić's emissary met in Rome with a group of these emigres in November, who approved in principle, but the man who was to become president of that committee, Ante Trumbić (a Croat from Dalmatia), wanted to postpone action for a time. In May 1915, the Yugoslav Committee was organised, with headquarters in London.

The timing was in large part influenced by another action in London the previous month, the conclusion of a secret agreement, the Treaty of London, whereby Serbia's main allies - Britain, France, Russia - agreed to give Italy large areas of Austro-Hungarian territory, mainly along the northern Adriatic, in return for Italy's leaving the Triple Alliance and joining the Allied side. The regions promised to Italy contained large areas populated by Croats and Slovenes, which was in conflict with Serbia's declared war aim of liberating all Serbs, Croats, and Slovenes. In an effort to win over the Serbs, the framers of the Treaty of London promised to Serbia all of Bosnia-Hercegovina, large parts of what is now Croatia, and most of the southern part of the Dalmatian coast. The other Serbian ally, Montenegro, was promised a small part of Southern Dalmatia, including the city of Dubrovnik.

The framers of the Treaty were, in effect, offering to Pašić and his cabinet a Great Serbia on the proverbial silver platter. This arrangement also fitted in with their reluctance to consider dissolving the Dual Monarchy, while plans for the creation of a Yugoslav state would really mean the end of Austria-Hungary. The Yugoslav Committee, especially its Slovene and Croat members, was fearful that the terms offered to Serbia would be difficult for them to turn down. But the Serbs failed to accept the offer, and proceeded to work toward the creation of a Yugoslav state. With the benefit of hindsight, it must be clear to all Serbs that it was a great tragedy for the Serb nation that Pašić and his colleagues did not accept the offer. Defenders of Pašić insist, however, that he was carrying out the strong desire of Prince Regent Aleksandar.

The Yugoslav Committee was ecstatic with the Serbian decision, and pushed for an early agreement with the Serbs on the organisation of the new state. The Yugoslav Committee was greatly disturbed by the declaration in May 1917 by South Slav deputies in the Vienna parliament that urged the union of the provinces of the Dual Monarchy where Slovenes, Croats, and Serbs lived into one unit under the sceptre of the Habsburg dynasty. The Pašić government, for its part, felt weakened by the Russian Revolution of March 1917, which meant the loss of a key ally. Hence, both stood to gain by an agreement that would seek the end of the Austro-Hungarian state.

Consequently, the two parties met on the island of Corfu and worked out an agreement, which was signed on 20 July 1917, by Pašić on behalf of the Serbian government and by Trumbić on behalf of the Yugoslav Committee. The agreement came to be known as the Corfu Declaration. It was full of sentiments of unity, brotherhood, and indications of common interests which in the past had been thwarted by

Austria-Hungary. Understandably, the Declaration got immediate international attention.

There were fourteen specific points about the organisation of the future state. The first point stated that a state of Serbs, Croats, and Slovenes would be a 'constitutional, democratic, and parliamentary monarchy with the Karađorđević dynasty at the head.' Point thirteen made reference to local autonomy based on 'natural, social, and economic' conditions. The last point provided that a constituent assembly should adopt a constitution 'by a numerically qualified majority.' These three provisions became points of contention in the following months and years.

While Trumbić expressed high praise for Serbia's leadership in the common effort, he increasingly sought some kind of power-sharing with Pašić, which the latter pointed out would be in violation of the Serbian constitution. Thereupon, he and some of his friends began spreading rumours that Pašić was betraying the Corfu Declaration and that Serbia wanted to impose its will on the other South Slavs. In this campaign they got the support of the noted English publicists R. W. Seton-Watson and Wickham Steed. These persistent efforts to set up a dual authority - the Yugoslav Committee and the Pašić cabinet - were overtaken by events. As Austro-Hungarian authority was disintegrating in October 1918, an independent power came into being in the Croat centre, Zagreb. Prominent Serbs, Croats, and Slovenes there proclaimed an independent state of Slovenes, Croats, and Serbs, and established a governing body, the National Council.

The Yugoslav Committee could no longer really pose as a representative of the South Slavs in the Dual Monarchy. At the same time the National Council delayed talks with the Serbian government. That delay led an assembly in Vojvodina to declare for union with Serbia. At the same time, forty-two out of fifty-two districts in Bosnia-Hercegovina voted for union with Serbia. In Montenegro, the Large National *Skupština* proclaimed union with Serbia. And the council for Dalmatia gave the National Council in Zagreb five days in which to decide on union with Serbia.

These developments, together with the movement of Italian military forces into Slovene and Croat areas to claim what was promised Italy in the Treaty of London, caused Croats and Slovenes to beg for Serbian troops to protect them. These same considerations led the National Council to send a delegation to Belgrade without delay. It asked the delegates to take certain conditions with them. Among these were: the constituent assembly should decide by a two-thirds vote whether the new state should be a monarchy or a republic; only certain specified government functions would be entrusted to the central government; and that Prince Regent Aleksandar should exercise power until the constituent assembly made its decisions.

When the delegation arrived on 28 November 1918, most of the Serbian government was back in Belgrade, but Pašić was out of the country. The delegation met with Aleksandar, and made the following points:

1. That sovereign authority be exercised by the Prince Regent,
2. That through agreement a responsible cabinet and a temporary parliament be established and that the parliament remain in session until the meeting of the constituent assembly'
3. That during the transitional stage existing administrative authorities remain, but under control of the cabinet, and
4. That the constituent assembly be chosen on the basis of universal, equal, direct, and proportional right to vote.

No other conditions were presented. Aleksandar accepted the statement and on 1 December 1918 proclaimed the coming into existence of the Kingdom of the Serbs, Croats, and Slovenes.

After the establishment of the provisional government, the National Council in Zagreb and the Serbian *Skupština* in Belgrade declared their respective missions concluded and, thereafter, ceased to exist. The first great power to recognise the new state was the United States in February 1919.

Pašić's Role in the New State

Most observers thought that in the flush of victory and the achievement of unification it would be difficult to deny Pašić the honour of being the first prime minister of the new state. All parliamentary parties and groups were unanimous in agreeing that he should head the first cabinet. Even a list of ministers was selected. But Aleksandar, who had had some differences with Pašić during the war, refused. Instead he appointed a cabinet that was virtually the same as the one proposed, but minus Pašić.

The new prime minister, Stojan Protić, was one of Pašić's long-time collaborators. Aleksandar explained his action by saying that he needed Pašić to head the country's delegation to the Versailles peace conference.

In less than two full years, Aleksandar had six cabinets, none of which could do much with the provisional parliament, where all sorts of problems confronting the new state were discussed but without concrete results. It did provide in late 1920 for the election of the constituent assembly, which met in January 1921.[6]

Aleksandar concluded that if the country was to have a constitution, he had to call upon Pašić, whose work at Versailles was completed. At the peace conference the basic decisions were made by the great powers. The Yugoslav state failed to gain certain areas on the Adriatic to which it thought it was entitled. Because of the disintegration of Yugoslavia in the 1990s, it seems desirable at this point to take brief note of two treaties as a part of the Versailles settlement - Trianon and St. Germain. They treated the new kingdom as the successor state of Serbia. All international agreements to which Serbia was a party were transferred to the Yugoslav state. These international acts, as in the case of the Treaty of London, were conveniently overlooked by those who, in the Yugoslav tragedy of the 1990s, seemed to think that Serbia had no rights beyond the narrow borders which Communist leader Tito had contrived.

Pašić's first Yugoslav cabinet was installed in January 1921, which proceeded with constitution-making, completing the task in June.[7] Pašić faced great odds at the outset. Sixteen parties succeeded in electing 419 delegates. The newly-formed Democratic Party had 92; Pašić's Radicals 91; the Croat Peasant Party 50; the Communists 58; Agrarians 39; Slovene and Croat Populists 27; Yugoslav Muslim Organisation 24. The remaining seats went to several minority parties.

The Croat Peasant Party, headed by Stjepan Radić, refused to participate, and the Communists proclaimed that the real constitution would be written with blood in the streets. In guiding the assembly, therefore, Pašić relied on the cooperation of the Democrats, the Muslims, and the Agrarians. One bone of contention was the needed majority to adopt the constitution. The Corfu Declaration had said 'a numerically qualified majority,' not otherwise defined. The constituent assembly, in adopting rules of procedure, decided that an absolute majority of the total number of the elected delegates, ie. 210, would meet that proviso. In the final vote on 28 June 1921, 223 voted for, and 35 against, with 161 not voting. Because it was adopted on Serbia's leading holiday, *Vidovdan*, it came to be called the *Vidovdan* Constitution. As foreseen by the Corfu Declaration, the constitution provided for a constitutional, parliamentary and hereditary monarchy. The new state was organised on a unitary basis, the constituent assembly having rejected federalism. The Radicals and the Democrats both argued that old historic regions were not natural, and that they could become nests of separatism dangerous to the new state. Hence the state was divided into 33 administrative units, similar to the French prefects.

There are a number of misconceptions about the *Vidovdan* Constitution. One of the most prevalent is that it gave the Serbs and Serbia a privileged and preeminent position, which just was not so. Neither Serbs nor Serbia had any privileges or rights not enjoyed by other citizens. And there were no provisions comparable to the those in the constitution of the German Empire, which guaranteed a privileged position for Prussia.

Many observers, with the benefit of hindsight, have argued that a federal arrangement would have been preferable, but that was not a realistic alternative at the time. Pašić was not against federalism in principle, but in reflecting on Corfu he said, 'when we began to draw boundaries on the map, we saw that it was impossible.' Moreover, at Versailles he had told a colleague that in terms of the country's and the people's future, it was important that domestic state authority be strong and based on the national unity of Serbs, Croats, and Slovenes and not on the basis of their particularities.

Be that as it may, the Croat parties that had participated in the provisional parliament were defeated in the elections for the constituent assembly by Stjepan Radić's Croat Republican Peasant Party. Radić wanted an independent Croatian state. More than that, the Croats were uncomfortable being only half as numerous as the Serbs, and this fact continued to remain a psychological barrier in the search for a viable political system. Moreover, unlike the Serbs who enjoyed politics and who had confidence in governmental authority, the Croats were uncomfortable with politics and distrustful of government. For centuries they had fought and connived against governmental authority. Their sudden liberation in 1918 did not immediately rid them of lifelong suspicions. They found it difficult to believe that the opportunities for determining their own destiny were real. The Serbs, for their part, contributed to the distrust. For example, the adoption of the constitution on the most famous of Serbian holidays lacked sensitivity.

The failure of the Croats to participate in constitution-making was a great disappointment to Pašić. And their failure to take part in governing once the constitution was adopted even more puzzling. He had hoped that once they saw the value of working together in a democratic setting, understanding and cordiality would grow. And indeed, when in 1925 he succeeded in getting Radić and his Peasant Party to accept the monarchy and the constitution, and to join the cabinet, Pašić was convinced that he had been right. In less than a year, however, Radić, in April 1926 precipitated a cabinet crisis, which signalled the end of Pašić's governmental career.

In the period 1921-1926, except for an interlude of four months in 1924, Nikola Pašić was prime minister of the Kingdom of the Serbs, Croats, and Slovenes. He headed ten cabinets with an average life per cabinet of six months, very close to the average life of French cabinets in the Third and Fourth republics. The instability suggested by the brevity of the life of Yugoslav cabinets is countered by the fact that many of the ministers held posts in several cabinets. Overriding this, however, is the fact that at no time during that period did any political party have a majority in the *Skupština* or even close to one. Pašić's cabinets had to depend on support outside the Radical party, either by way of coalitions, abstentions, or benevolent tolerance. Political bargains had to be struck at every turn; agreements on coherent programmes were next to impossible.

Pašić's cabinets in the first two years dealt with the production of the constitution and implementing it. This was a time when a number of emergency problems needed attention, especially in some Croat areas where government authorities were ignored or their work sabotaged. Stjepan Radić travelled abroad and openly worked against the state. On his return he was convicted of anti-state activities and sent to jail. In Serbia and Montenegro the ravages of the war were everywhere evident. Outside the kingdom, revisionist forces were at work, but the Little Entente (Yugoslavia-Romania-Czechoslovakia), a French-sponsored agreement, was concluded to guard against external threats.

Pašić's first cabinets were largely Radical-Democratic coalitions (Pašić and Svetozar Pribičević). After a brief interval in 1924, when the nominal head of the Democratic Party, Ljuba Davidović, attempted to forge an alliance with the Croats and failed, Pašić was brought back. This time he again teamed up with Pribičević, who had split with Davidović and formed the Independent Democratic Party. The cabinet was short-lived, mainly because of successful negotiations between Pašić's Radicals and Stjepan Radić's Croat Republican Peasant party. As indicated above, Radić recognised the monarchy and accepted the *Vidovdan* Constitution. In addition, he dropped the word Republican from the party's name, and in 1925 joined the cabinet. Within a few months, however, he was criticising the very cabinet of which he was a part. That activity created a cabinet crisis leading to Pašić's resignation in April 1926, ending his career as a governmental leader.[8]

In December Pašić died at age 81. It is interesting to note that in the years 1921-1926, he was the only prime minister of World War I vintage still holding the reins of power.

Pašić in Historical Perspective

Over one hundred years have gone by since Nikola Pašić entered politics, at a time when Serbia had barely regained independence after more than 400 years of Turkish rule. He was born and reared in an otherwise primitive and unstable political system. An assessment of his political leadership and performance must focus on his two broad aims: (1) domestically, a democratic political system; (2) in foreign affairs, a unification with Serbia of his fellow-countrymen still under alien rule. In the pursuit of both of these aims he had considerable success, although at times it was not unqualified and in some respects it did not come up to his high aspirations or those of the people.

Except for a brief interval, Pašić was the leader of the Radical party from its beginning until his death nearly fifty years later. He and the party deserve great credit for waging a successful struggle for the establishment of democracy in Serbia. Perhaps Pašić merits the most credit for the consolidation of parliamentary rule in the years before World War I. In those years, the parliamentary system functioned as well in Serbia as in most of the parliamentary states of Western Europe. And it should not be forgotten that parliamentarism had not yet won its way in such states as Austria-Hungary and Germany, to say nothing of Russia. He had an abiding faith in the people as judges of public policy. In some ways, elections were for him the high points of the political process, when the direction of politics was determined by popular participation. And he was always willing to abide by the verdict.

Pašić had difficulties with the *Skupština*, both in Serbia and Yugoslavia. Given the fact that his majorities in Serbia were for the most part exceedingly narrow and in Yugoslavia nonexistent, he managed remarkably well. His difficulties were considerably greater in Yugoslavia, with its plethora of political parties. Yet through bargaining with various *Skupština* groups in the years 1921-1926, he managed to stay in power. For Pašić, parliament was a means to an end. He was a pragmatist who preferred reaching an agreement on a matter rather than leave a controversy unresolved. And although he believed in give and take and would readily make concessions, he held firm in matters of principle. His pragmatism led him to conclude that in politics there are no absolute solutions.

Pašić's position toward the crown was precise and consistent. He was a monarchist if for no other reason than that the political culture demanded it. While seeking to establish parliamentary democracy, Pašić saw the need of retaining the monarchy as the cement that would bind the political system into a significant whole. He realised that for the people the crown was the source of authority and therefore political legitimacy.

At the same time, he was firm in his conviction that in a democracy, the monarch should be above partisan political battles. Political decisions, he said, should be made by the elected representatives. Cabinets should be selected by the party or coalition of parties that could command a majority in parliament. And they should be responsible to parliament.

In the course of his political career, Pašić dealt with four kings: Milan and Aleksandar Obrenović prior to 1903, and Petar and Aleksandar Karađorđević after 1903. He was in almost constant trouble with the Obrenovićes. As noted above, he was twice at death's door. Whereas he always seemed hostile to Milan, he tended to be conciliatory toward his son Aleksandar, in the hope that the young lad of thirteen would grow up to be a constitutional monarch, which did not come about.

Petar I Karađorđević, brought to the throne in 1903, was a constitutional monarch in the best sense of that word. He accepted the decisions of ministers who had the confidence of the *Skupština* majority. It was during the reign of Petar I that Pašić reached the height of his power. After Petar transferred the royal powers to Aleksandar in 1914, however, harmony between the cabinet and the crown began to erode. Unlike his father, Aleksandar was not satisfied to be a king who reigns but does not govern. While World War I continued, differences between Aleksandar and his prime minister were not a problem. During his years in power in the Yugoslav state, Pašić knew that the young king barely tolerated him. But Pašić always avoided open conflict for fear of the consequences to the nation.

Pašić often compared the proper relationship between the prime minister and the king to a man and the fire in the fireplace. 'If you are too close it is no good; you will get scorched. If you are too far it is also no good; you will be left out in the cold.'

In dealing with political opponents, Pašić exhibited measured tolerance. In the course of five decades of public life, he made many political enemies. He could be tough in political combat, and was usually brief and factual. He respected the press and followed it closely, but he did not let himself be provoked into replies. For him, opposition was the price of democracy. He did not respond to personal attacks. But, as one of his scholarly opponents observed: 'He could hate, but he did not allow hate to blind him. He economised on hate, and for that reason, despite a large number of political opponents, he had few personal enemies.'

In the new Yugoslav state, in addition to political opposition, Pašić was forced to deal with nationality antagonisms, mainly that of the Croats. He was able to get one or more representatives of major Slovene parties to join his cabinets, as well the leader of the Yugoslav Muslim Organisation. But despite his awareness of the difficulties and complexities of national feelings, Pašić's handling of the Croats was something short of successful.

True, he got them to recognise the constitution and the established order, and he brought them into the cabinet. But the Croats, especially their leader Radić, were not satisfied. With the Serbs being twice as numerous as the Croats, the latter were afraid that they would always be outvoted. In defence of Pašić, it should be said that those who came before him and those who came after him were no more successful. Perhaps there were too many factors beyond Pašić's or anyone else's control. The union came unexpectedly and too rapidly for too many people. Given the composition of the new country, involving national and religious groupings, as well as the proportional representation system, it is difficult to imagine how any party, or any leader, or any programme, could have produced coherent and satisfactory solutions.

In foreign affairs Pašić had great achievements. He had an almost prophetic vision of coming events. He did not provoke any war, but he concluded that the political aims and methods of Austria and Russia in the Balkans would lead to war, and he realised that the Ottoman empire could not long hang together. In those circumstances, he believed that Serbia's aspirations could best be served by relying on Russia, although there were times when he resisted or rejected Russian advice.

Pašić's work is sometimes compared to that of Cavour in the unification of Italy and that of Bismarck in the unification of Germany. Neither of the two, however, had to overcome the obstacles, make the sacrifices, or endure the tribulations that were Pašić's lot. Neither of the two had to flee his homeland in the difficult circumstances that faced Pašić in World War I, when he reached the height of his wisdom, determination, and moral strength. The disintegration of the Yugoslav state under leaderships that came much later does not diminish Pašić's successes.

Pašić's great strength lay in his realistic knowledge of politics, and in his refusal to bow before reverses. He was unsparingly self-sacrificing. Almost never did he know moments of peace, yet he possessed a certain Olympian peacefulness. Engaged for much of his lifetime in demolishing absolutism at home and in seeking to tear down two empires, he was patient and self-confident, and he was confident of history's judgment. As an objective fellow countryman of his, not a friend of Pašić's or the Radicals' once observed: 'he left tracks not only in our but also in the world's history.'

Notes

1 Dragnich (1978), pp. 55-56.
2 For more detail see Dragnich (1974), pp. 32-35.
3 For phases of Aleksandar's rule and Pašić's actions, see Dragnich (1974), 38-58.
4 Jovanović (1934-1936), Volume II, p. 452.

5 Dragnich (1974), pp. 70ff.
6 On the political goings on in the provisional government, see Dragnich (1974), pp. 139-154.
7 Dragnich (1974), pp. 154-188.
8 For a discussion of Pašić's ministries, 1921-1926, see Dragnich (1974), pp. 163-188.

References

Adams, John C. (1942), *Flight in Winter*, Princeton University Press, Princeton.

Dedijer, Vladimir (1966), *The Road to Sarajevo*, Simon & Shuster, New York.

Dragnich, Alex N. (1974), *Serbia, Nikola Pašić, and Yugoslavia*, Rutgers University Press, New Brunswick.

Dragnich, Alex N. (1978), *The Development of Parliamentary Government in Serbia*, East European Monographs, Boulder.

Dragnich, Alex N. (1984), *The First Yugoslavia: Search for a Viable Political System*, Hoover Institution Press, Stanford.

Jovanović, Slobodan (1962), *Moji savremenici: Nikola Pašić*, Windsor.

Jovanović, Slobodan (1934-1936), *Vlada Aleksandra Obrenovića*, Geca Kon, Belgrade.

Lederer, Ivo J. (1963), *Yugoslavia at the Peace Conference: A Study in Frontiermaking*, Yale University Press, New Haven.

Mamatey, Victor S. (1957), *The United States and East Central Europe, 1914-1918*, Princeton University Press, Princeton.

Marcovitch, L. (1920), *Serbia and Europe*, 1914-1920, London.

McClellan, Woodford D. (1967), *Svetozar Marković and the Origins of Balkan Socialism*, Princeton University Press, Princeton.

Seton-Watson, R.W. (1911), *The Southern Slav Question*, London.

Sforza, Carlo (1940), *Fifty Years of War and Diplomacy in the Balkans: Pashich and the Union of the Yugoslavs*, Columbia University Press, New York.

Thaden, Edward C. (1965), *Russia and the Balkan Alliance of 1912*, University of Pennsylvania Press, University Park.

Vucinich, Wayne (1954), *Serbia Between East and West: The Events of 1903-1908*, Stanford University Press, Stanford.

3 Dragutin Dimitrijević-Apis

DAVID MacKENZIE

'Please tell my friends that I do not regret that I die from Serbian Guns because it is for Great Serbia, which I wish to see realised soon.' Apis to Colonel Dabić, 13/26 June 1917.[1]

Introduction

In a ravine outside of Salonika, Greek Colonel Dragutin Dimitrijević, nicknamed Apis, awaited execution at the hands of the exiled Serbian government for deeds he had neither committed nor even envisioned. Bidding farewell to the goalers who had accompanied him to the execution site and holding a half smoked cigarette, Apis leaped straight into his open grave. Then, blindfolded as the firing squad prepared to shoot, Apis shouted from the grave: 'Long live Greater Serbia and Yugoslavia!' To Captain Milan Stojković, commander of Salonika Officers' Prison, where the Colonel had been imprisoned since mid-December 1916, Apis at that moment looked young, resolute and powerful. After two salvoes Apis was stretched out neatly in his grave. None of the bullets had struck his massive head - the soldiers had heeded his plea not to shoot him there. Shrieking vultures circled over the ravine where Apis, Major Ljubomir Vulović, and Rade Malobabić had died at sunrise on 13/26 June 1917. 'We have brought them down,' commented one officer calmly. 'Should we one day fall into their hands, then let the friends of Apis do the same to us.'[2]

Apis' heroic death near Salonika marked the end of a dramatic and turbulent life. It made him a martyr for nationalistic Serbs and triggered efforts of partisans of 'Unification or Death!', popularly known as the 'Black Hand', to arrange a retrial of the Salonika defendants. Before the caravan of automobiles had left Salonika Prison for the execution site, Apis had written his beloved nephew, Milan Živanović: 'I die innocent...They found us guilty and deserving death for reasons purely of internal policy...I am convinced...that my death...It is necessary for the good of Serbia.'[3]

Early Years

Dragutin T. Dimitrijević was born in Belgrade on 5 August 1876, just three days after Prince Aleksandar Obrenović, whose murder he would organise twenty-seven years later. He descended from peasant Cincars, an enterprising people from Macedonia. While his father and two brothers worked as tinsmiths, Dragutin grew up with two older sisters. Losing his father at age nine and surrounded with female love and attention, young Dragutin felt a profound need to prove his manhood, deciding early on a military career. When his elder sister Jelena married Živan Živanović, a politician and historian, the whole family moved from Niš back to Belgrade. During his last year at the classical secondary school there, the sixteen year old Dragutin decided rather abruptly in 1892 to enter the Belgrade Military Academy as a cadet. His fellow students soon called him Apis (The Bull) because of his powerful physique and dynamic energy. An excellent and conscientious student, Dragutin completed the Academy's lower school in 1896, sixth in his class. Two years later he enrolled in the higher school there to prepare himself to become a General Staff officer. As a dedicated officer who soon became deeply interested in politics, Apis apparently never seriously considered marriage or having his own family, although he was fond of women. During his whole life his sister's family remained the centre of his personal world; their home on Sveti Sava Street in Belgrade was his emotional headquarters. Dragutin invariably displayed deep affection for all family members, notably for his sister's children, with whom he had grown up, and later for his nephew Milan Živanović.[4]

The May Coup of 1903

Apis' first major political action was his organisation and leadership of an officer conspiracy against the last rulers of the Serbian Obrenović dynasty: King Aleksandar and Queen Draga Mašin. In April 1893, soon after Apis entered the Military Academy, seventeen year old Aleksandar Obrenović, prompted by his father, ex-king Milan, suddenly removed a regency, assumed full royal power, and dismissed the assembly whose chairman was Apis' brother-in-law, Živan Živanović. The self-willed, cruel, and obstinate young monarch soon became the most disliked and unpopular of all the Obrenović rulers. Ruling arbitrarily and despising the people and their political leaders, King Aleksandar in ten years of personal rule implemented three palace coups, abolished two constitutions and suspended a third, creating a virtual political vacuum in Serbia.

To the dismay of his father and army leaders, Aleksandar decided in the summer of 1900 to marry his mistress, Draga Mašin, widow of a Czech engineer and lady-in-waiting to his mother, Queen Natalia. Visiting his mother in Biarritz, France in 1897, Aleksandar had fallen hopelessly in love with the seductive Draga who was much older than he. On 18 July 1900, despite widespread rumours that Draga had slept with many prominent men in Belgrade, the official Serbian press announced their formal engagement; they were married soon thereafter. However, the King found it difficult to find political leaders willing to support his marriage to an obscure, disreputable women commoner. Finally, a 'wedding cabinet' of second rate politicians was installed. An ambitious lieutenant colonel, Miloš Vasić, named war minister, advised the king to summon his Belgrade officers and demand they support his marriage. Complying, Aleksandar warned the officers not to interfere in his personal affairs. A few senior officers shouted loyally: 'Long live the King!', but the rest departed silent and dejected.

Leaving the hall in dismay, junior officers vented their indignation against their senior colleagues for preventing them from speaking out openly, then against the King for dishonouring them. Lieutenant Dimitrijević-Apis expressed their anger most dramatically. Shrieking with rage and towering over the others, Apis shouted: 'Cowards! Scum! All this must be refuted and reversed!' His outburst galvanised the others to protest loudly the King's decision to marry Draga Mašin.[5]

Their unpopular marriage of July 1900 sparked an army conspiracy organised chiefly by Apis, a junior captain from December 1902. Queen Draga's arrogant behaviour soon endangered the Obrenović dynasty. To secure its future the infatuated king longed for a son. That December Draga told Aleksandar she believed she was pregnant; a Russian specialist, examining her and predicted an heir. However, as months passed all signs of Draga's pregnancy vanished causing a public scandal that undermined the dynasty's credibility. Rumours spread that

Draga's disreputable brother, Nikodije Lunjevica, would soon be named heir to the Serbian throne.

By that time Apis and Lieutenant Antonije Antić were urging their fellow junior officers to remove the Obrenovićs or at least expel Queen Draga from Serbia. By the summer of 1901 an officer conspiracy began to take shape to remove the Obrenovićs with Apis as its chief leader. Such political activity was prohibited to all army personnel.

Lieutenant Pavle Panković, serving with the General staff, often dined at the Belgrade Officers' Club with other junior officers, including sometimes Apis and Antic. Walking one evening with Apis, Panković castigated Draga's false pregnancy and rumours that the Queen's brother might become heir. Apis queried: 'Would you like to join a society which would work to remove Aleksandar and Draga from the throne?' When Panković nodded, Apis invited him to join the discussions of his junior officer group. Initially they favoured just expelling the Obrenovićs, but by fall 1901 they had resolved to kill them and thus end the lengthy quarrel between Serbia's two royal dynasties: Obrenović and Karađorđević. Some officers favoured replacing the Obrenović with an English, German or Montenegrin prince; a few even advocated a republic. The rest, headed by Apis, argued that Serbia had its own alternative ruler. Why not enthrone Pretender Petar Karađorđević, a professed constitutional monarchist, then living in Swiss exile? After much debate the officers agreed that Petar should become king. Credit for this outcome, affirmed Panković, belonged entirely to Apis; without him neither Petar nor his heirs would have mounted the Serbian throne.[6]

In August 1901 the officer conspiracy's seven founders convened at Lieutenant Antić's home where Apis drew up a plan to murder the King and Queen during a scheduled celebration of her birthday at Belgrade's 'Kolarac' restaurant. When the King failed to attend this party, Apis' plan died. A plan to kill the King during fall military manoeuvres at Ub near Belgrade also failed.[7] With officer salaries months in arrears and discipline sagging, the army became increasingly dissatisfied with King Aleksandar. By 1903 it was no longer reliable and except for the infantry was woefully unprepared. Young officers, resenting Obrenović neglect of national goals, kept entering the conspiracy. The Serbian national idea of becoming the South Slav *Piedmont*, noted Apis later, had been wholly abandoned. 'The unfortunate secret convention with Austria, and blind surrender into Austria's embrace was a most shameful betrayal of Serbian traditions.' Only a change of regime and dynasty could rescue the country from humiliation. 'I realised that Serbia must once more in full measure undertake her role as *Piedmont*.'[8]

Dominating the youthful conspirators by force of personality, Apis met with them often at his family's home on Sveti Sava Street. In 1902 Apis composed there a written oath to bind the conspirators, blaming King Aleksandar and Queen Draga for the plight of Serbia:

> 'We swear and obligate ourselves with our signatures that we will kill them. To the throne of Serbia,...we shall bring Petar Karađorđević,...son of the legitimate prince, the late Aleksandar Karađorđević.'[9]

Only when a new member had revealed his attitude toward the Obrenovićs and had signed the oath did the founders describe their true purpose, thus maintaining secrecy among over 120 members recruited in Belgrade and the interior. Warning against broadening the conspiracy excessively, Apis told Panković: 'Great ideas have always been the work of a few people.' Next to Belgrade the Niš garrison contained the largest group of conspirators with 36 officers by the end of 1902. Travelling through eastern Serbia in the summer of 1902, Apis personally enlisted a number of officers. Also recruited were some senior officers including Colonel Aleksandar Mašin, brother of Queen Draga's deceased first husband, and Lieutenant Petar Mišić, commanding a battalion of Belgrade's Sixth Regiment, who would later preside over the Salonika Trial. Some prominent political leaders such as Đorđe Genčić joined the plot, but Captain Apis' original group still directed the conspiracy, apparently the only successful coup in modern European history organised and led by junior officers.

Speeding the coup was a great demonstration of 23 March 1903 involving almost half of Belgrade's population that protested King Aleksandar's decision to set up a personal dictatorship. When the crowd defied the impatient King's order to clear the streets, palace police and troops opened fire killing many students and apprentices. This slaughter mobilised all Belgrade against the Obrenovićs and accelerated recruitment into the conspiracy.

The plotters' decision to attack the royal palace the night of 28-29 May 1903, Apis revealed later, was reached when they realised their people that night would control the key posts. Apis then made detailed plans for the actual assault. Directing and controlling an extensive secret movement, Captain Apis, then only in his late twenties, revealed personal magnetism, boldness and cool resolve.

Apis knew the coup could only succeed if the King and Queen were killed quickly, the government seized, and a new multiparty regime proclaimed. The King was guarded by his adjutant, General Lazar Petrović and a palace guard of three officers, forty-five cavalry men, and a police detachment. Although the pending assault appeared highly risky, King Aleksandar's despotic rule had roused general opposition. Serbia's finances lay in ruins, and its standing abroad had been wrecked. Unless the Obrenović were removed then, Apis and his friends believed, Serbia faced destruction and collapse. According to Apis' battle plan, office conspirators from five cafes near the palace would gather at the Officers' Club about 1am. Once Colonel Mišić's battalion had arrived there, twenty-eight officer conspirators would advance to the palace whose main gate was to be opened by Lieutenant Petar Živković. In overall command of the supporting military forces would be Colonel Mašin.

Initially, the coup followed Apis' plan closely. At first it was strictly an officers' revolt; the troops could be involved only after the royal murders. All twenty-eight conspirators, mostly junior General Staff officers, reached the Officers' Club, some reportedly having imbibed liberally at the nearby cafes. When Mišić's troops failed to arrive, realising he must adhere to his 2am departure time, Captain Apis ordered resolutely: 'Gentlemen officers, double time forward!' Without Apis' coolness and determination, concluded fellow conspirator Vladimir Tucović, Colonel Mišić's tardiness might have doomed the plot.[10]

The officers approached the palace some 550 yards from the Officers' Club where they were joined belatedly by Mišić's battalion. Captain Apis led the advance to the main gate where Živković arrived tardily fumbling confusedly with the heavy bunch of keys. Finally, he managed to open the gate, then hurled to the ground by it, he arose and fled humiliated into the night. Once inside the officers seized General Petrović, the King's adjutant, but he managed to momentarily distract the guards and cut off the electricity plunging the entire palace into darkness.

Seeing someone fleeing in the right-hand corridor, Apis rushed down the steps in pursuit with his revolver. In the lower corridor he exchanged fire with two guards wounding one but was struck with three bullets. Overcoming the guards, his comrades rushed onward leaving Apis gravely wounded supported against the wall, revolver still in hand. Asked later by his brother-in-law, Živan Živanović, why he had not sought cover, Apis replied: 'It would be disgraceful for an officer, even in that difficult situation, to seek cover!'[11]

Apis' wounds removed him from the struggle, but once candles had been brought his comrades implemented his plan. Apis was carried into the guard room and bandaged but insisted on remaining until the coup succeeded. Not until 3-50am, when his adjutant was induced to call him, was the King finally discovered. As he appeared in the doorway, Captain Mihailo Ristić fired at him. A total of thirty rounds were fired at the King and eighteen at the Queen. Then the two corpses were stripped and sabred. Captain Ristić ordered their nude bodies hurled into the garden below to show the assembled troops, as he proclaimed: 'Tyranny is no more!' Questioned later by Živanović why he had ordered this brutal act, Ristić declared: 'So that it would be clear to all that the King and Queen were no more.' This momentous and terrible outcome, concluded Živanović, 'was accepted by the entire people,...by the majority with joy.'[12]

For ten days Captain Apis remained in a critical condition in a hospital while his comrades immediately handed over political power to a provisional government representing all major Serbian political parties. It promptly restored the Constitution of 1901 and the parliament. Then the Assembly almost unanimously elected Petar Karađorđević King of Serbia. The Karađorđević dynasty owed an enormous debt to Apis and his friends for its restoration, ending a century long dynastic feud. A close colleague of Apis, Vladimir Tucović, linked Apis with Serbia's resurrection:

> 'Driven by the vision of national genius which recognises no obstacles, Apis lit the revolutionary flame in the Serbian officer corps. From the flame sprang the May tragedy and the wars to liberate the nation.'[13]

Conspirator in Politics, 1903-1909

Believing firmly that the post-Coup regime would pursue Serbia's national goals, Apis declared while in the hospital: 'And now that we have carried out what we sought to achieve, I don't mind if I should die'.[14] Senior conspirators occupied all key Belgrade army commands, leading cabinet posts, and court positions. Fearing them, King Petar remained subservient to their wishes helping to provoke a 'Diplomatic Strike' in January 1904 as most foreign envoys boycotted court functions and left Belgrade. King Petar then promoted and removed leading conspirators from court, but they continued to dominate the War Ministry. Finally, in May 1906 the new Radical cabinet of Nikola Pašić, seeking to restore normal relations with Britain, had senior conspirators retired and pledged they would not be re-employed.

After passing written examinations for service with the General Staff, Captain Apis spent 1905-1906 in Berlin on a leave of absence studying the organisation and training of the German army, Europe's best. Attending the great German army manoeuvres of 1906, Apis submitted to the Serbian War Ministry a lengthy report praised in Belgrade for its clarity and perceptive analysis. Back in Serbia, he was assigned to the General Staff section of the War Ministry.

Forced resignations of the senior conspirators provided Apis with an opportunity to exert growing leadership in army affairs. Surrounding himself with energetic younger officers and winning the friendship of senior commanders such as General Radomir Putnik, Apis even as a captain exerted remarkable influence. Applying what he had learned in Germany, he and his friends worked assiduously to improve the Serbian Army's training and weaponry, applying pressure on the government and Assembly to provide more funding and obtain modern weapons. Though his political ideas remained ill-defined, Apis, with his influence with the court and the General Staff, caused Radical leaders such as Pašić to consider him a dangerous power competitor, suspecting him of praetorian aims. Around Apis gathered national revolutionaries advocating a ruthless struggle against Austria-Hungary to liberate and unite its Serbs with Serbia. Opposing him were officers jealous of his growing power, including some May conspirators such as Petar Živković and older ones content with the *status quo*. From this rivalry would later develop the 'Black Hand' and 'White Hand' officer factions.

Captain Apis headed a group of able junior officers mostly of peasant origin who often disregarded legal forms and militant hierarchy. After 1906 many regarded Apis as *de facto* war minister, and from 1909 as the grey eminence of Serbian politics. His persistent rise provoked bitter feuds with senior conspirators such as Colonel Mišić and Major

Josif Kostić who later gained their revenge at the Salonika Trial. Apis campaigned to remove old drones, blocking needed reforms, from the army. Partly through his influence younger, more innovative officers were elevated into command positions and assisted him to democratise the army. In the General Staff commission Apis regularly persuaded more senior officers to adopt new policies without their realising these were his suggestions. He won over his superiors by appearing to defer to them and by massaging their self-esteem.[15]

How did Apis obtain such a remarkable hold over higher ranking officers? 'For me,' explained one, 'he (Apis) is something more than an ordinary person, but a secret force at whose disposal I am compelled to place myself, although my reason gives me no cause to do so'. He continued:

> 'He was the only one among us who solely by his presence was able to turn my thoughts into his stream and with a few words spoken in the most ordinary manner could make out of me an obedient executor of his will.'[16]

Every 29 May the officer conspirators assembled at Belgrade's 'Kolarac' restaurant with Apis acting as genial and convivial host. Sharing beer and comradeship, they considered these reunions as virtually a holy communion. All those who attended considered it imperative to seek out Apis, often in preference to more senior colleagues. To him came the written excuses of those unable to attend. As the May conspirators dwindled in number Apis recruited new celebrants.

Apis exerted an irresistible power over his friends and colleagues. Casting a virtual hypnotic spell, he embodied for them with his dynamic energy the Serb national ideal and the unceasing struggle to achieve its goals. Always smiling, charming and approachable, Apis treated the gravest matters in such a relaxed, lighthearted manner that others did not realise their gravity. His ideas, thrown out casually without command or overt pressure, were generally accepted as orders to be obeyed. The sympathetic Apis would listen patiently to his comrades, then face them with clear decisions. Exuding a self-confident ease, he dominated the thought of others.

Apis' antechamber attracted young officers waiting to explain their missions and to receive instructions. He was an idol for the impatient, anxious to do something for the nation. Apis supplied them with moral nourishment, always promising something and stimulating them to act. Whether fellow May conspirators or new recruits, all were attracted to him like moths to a flame as he constantly sought opportunities to work for the national cause or exert influence in its behalf.

Apis and other May conspirators fostered Serbian interests persistently in a Macedonia disputed among Serbs, Bulgars and Greeks. In 1904 he joined a secret committee that coordinated guerrilla activities there against the Bulgars, hailing this as an essential part of Serbia's role as the South Slav *Piedmont*. Among the Serbian officers leading guerrilla bands into Macedonia was Lieutenant Vojislav Tankosić, soon a renowned guerrilla leader and later Apis' colleague in 'Unification or Death!' The substantial successes scored after 1903 in this Macedonian guerrilla warfare convinced Apis that Serbian unification could best be achieved by revolutionary and militant action.[17]

Thus, in the years following the May Coup, Apis rose swiftly to military and political prominence. Remaining on excellent terms with King Petar and his sons, he also won the trust of Serbia's top military man, General Putnik. From 1906 he was the May conspirators' virtually undisputed chief. His growing influence within the officer corps, however, provoked jealousy from those who had been sidetracked or removed.

Apis and the 'Black Hand', 1909-1912

Austria-Hungary's sudden annexation of the Turkish provinces of Bosnia and Hercegovina in October 1908 provoked an angry outburst of patriotic sentiment in Serbia and other lands inhabited by Serbs. Soon a public national organisation was formed centred in Belgrade, entitled *Narodna Odbrana* (National Defence) to mobilise Serbs morally and even militarily against Austrian rule. Its efforts to recruit volunteers from the Serbian youth to cross into Bosnia was supported by the Belgrade regime. However, Serbia, lacking Russian military support, in the spring of 1909, had to yield to an Austro-German ultimatum. Henceforth, *Narodna Odbrana* had to limit its activities to peaceful agitation and the cultural realm. Militant Serbian nationalists such as Major Apis were dismayed. 'In our view,' he declared later, '*Narodna Odbrana* did not do much or what we considered necessary to do'.[18] During the ensuing lull in national activity, as Belgrade halted guerrilla activities in Macedonia, the Bulgars erased earlier Serbian gains there. Ardent nationalists and revolutionaries sought a secret, militant organisation to continue the Serb struggle for liberation and unity.

Convinced that only revolutionary struggle against the Bulgars and Young Turks could save Serbs in Macedonia and Old Serbia, late in 1910 Bogdan Radenković, a leading civilian activist of the Serb movement, travelled to Belgrade to win official support for a new guerrilla campaign in the south. Unable to interest the Serbian Radical government, Radenković resolved to form a secret, nationalist organisation, 'Unification or Death!', to direct national revolutionary activities outside Serbia proper. In Belgrade Radenković shared his ideas with three Serb militants, meeting frequently with them to discuss forming such an organisation. One of them, Captain Velimir Vemić, Apis recalled early in 1911, first informed him about 'Unification or Death!' enjoying secrecy. When Apis displayed interest, Vemić introduced him to its initiators: Bogdan Radenković and Ljuba Jovanović-Čupa, an idealistic pro-Yugoslav nationalist. Apis recalled first meeting with them and Vemić in his office at the Cavalry Division where he served as Chief-of-Staff. He agreed to join their secret organisation warning that he was overburdened with staff work. However Major Božin Simić, who joined the organisation subsequently, asserted it had been Apis who had conceived 'Unification or Death!' in order to provide direction for Serb national revolutionaries.

At the Salonika Trial Apis ascribed the Constitution and Rules of 'Unification or Death!' chiefly to Radenković and Jovanović-Čupa. Only after those basic documents were drafted had Apis joined the original seven man Central Executive Committee (CEC) of the organisation, remaining an ordinary member of that board. Lacking time to recruit additional members, Apis promised in his spare time to aid his colleagues and to place his numerous connections with top government and army leaders at their disposal. 'They all seemed satisfied with this, did not elect me president, and spared me also from other duties in the Central Executive Committee.' Queried by court chairman, Colonel Mišić, why he had entered a secret organisation forbidden to all military personnel, Apis replied that the Austrian annexation of Bosnia and Hercegovina and Turkish pressure in Macedonia had created 'a desperate time for the Serbs'. To solve the Macedonian question in their favour, argued Radenković, Serbs required such a militant organisation. 'Earlier,' noted Apis, 'I had been involved personally in similar secret committees (in

Macedonia), so I was not worried about its secrecy. I entered the organisation especially because of Bogdan.'[19] Major Apis thus had voluntarily subordinated his obligations as an officer to his convictions as a Serb nationalist.

'Unification or Death!', or 'Black Hand' as it soon became known popularly, had engaged in revolutionary struggle solely outside of Serbia's borders, Apis affirmed. Inside Serbia it had never undertaken illegal actions. Furthermore, it had disclosed its foreign activities promptly to the Serbian government and court. Responding to the request of Jovanović-Čupa, Apis agreed to act as intermediary between the organisation and the Serbian foreign ministry. 'I informed (Foreign Minister) Dr Milovan Milovanović about the organisation, often going to see him at his home or to his office in Belgrade.' Much impressed, after listening to Major Apis, Milovanović had declared: 'Place, young friend, your 'Black Hand' at my disposal, then you will soon see what Milovanović will do for Serbia.' Apis pledged that his group would do nothing harmful to the national interest. 'We passed directly to discussing negotiations with Bulgaria for an alliance.' During that winter of 1911-1912, at Apis' urging, 'Black Hand' became virtually an instrument of the Serbian Foreign Ministry in preparing the way for that alliance and the subsequent Serbo-Turkish War. The Foreign Minister declared: 'I had never met such a brilliant officer.'[20]

Asked by Colonel Mišić at the Salonika Trial why they had adopted as 'Black Hand's' insignia a skull and crossbones, knife, bomb, and poison, Apis reaffirmed its intimate connection with the desperate Serbian struggle in Macedonia. On the secret committee where in 1904 he had begun his national work, a famous Belgrade University professor had insisted on the need to employ all means 'to save Serbdom with bombs, knives and rifles.' In secret foreign national work, poison was utilised: 'All guerrillas carried it both as a means of attack and to save someone if he fell into enemy hands. That is why such emblems entered the organisation's seal and it was a sign that these people were prepared to die.'[21]

The 'Black Hand' was most active and dynamic during its first year until the Serbo-Turkish War. In Belgrade, new members were constantly being recruited, especially younger officers who were told it was a patriotic group aiming to unite all Serbs. During a visit to Belgrade by Serb and Croat students from Zagreb in April 1912, a banquet was held for them at the Moskva Hotel. Apis presided at a long table with some twenty of the students. One, Oskar Tartaglia, later a Croat journalist, was deeply impressed by this imposing man who could win people over at a glance. Cultured and well-read, with the exquisite manners of a cosmopolitan:

> 'He (Apis) was the spirit, leader and organiser of the national-revolutionary movement who always kept in mind not just Serbia but all other regions where our people lived and were under foreign tyranny...He was a soldier and a politician, simultaneously the Garibaldi and Mazzini of the Yugoslav war for liberation.'[22]

A few days later Tartaglia became the first Catholic Croat to join the overwhelmingly Serb 'Black Hand'.

Apis soon became the true leader of 'Black Hand', its chief dynamic force, and its main link with the May conspirators. His devoted friends in the CEC informed him of the 'Black Hand's' various activities: in *Narodna Odbrana* by Major Milan Vasić, among Serbian guerrillas by Major Tankosić, and with intellectuals and youth by Jovanović-Čupa. Major Apis' close ties with Foreign Minister Milovanović and General Putnik provided key connections with the Serbian government and high command. Still warmly regarded by King Petar, Apis had persuaded Prince Aleksandar, already heir to the Serbian throne, to contribute 20,000 dinars to *Piedmont*, the organisation's newspaper. By 1912 Apis had attained the peak of his power and influence. Even his enemies admitted his uncanny ability to win over his superiors and persuade them to follow his policies. Formidable in appearance, with seemingly inexhaustible energy and dedicated to the national cause, to young officers Major Apis embodied Serbia's martial values and highest ideals.

While Serbia's preparations as leader of the Balkan League for war against Turkey neared completion in August 1912, Major Apis and several 'Black Hand' colleagues carried out for the General Staff dangerous reconnaissances in Turkish-ruled Albania and Macedonia. Apis' group, including the civilian, Bogdan Radenković, was to ascertain the attitude of the key Albanian chieftain, Isa Boljetinac, who talked with them both. Apis pressed Boljetinac to commit himself to Serbia: 'We helped you Albanians during your struggle against the Turks, so now we expect you to assist us when the Turks are threatening us.' Boljetinac finally pledged neutrality as Apis and his colleagues fulfilled General Putnik's assignment.[23]

As Serbia faced a showdown with Ottoman Turkey, Apis addressed the CEC of 'Unification or Death!':

> 'With us are the Bulgars, Greeks and Montenegrins. In Belgrade and Sofia are to be made these days the final decision on war. Unfortunately, neither our nor Bulgarian ruling circles are bold enough.'

Apis remained in constant touch with General Putnik, encouraging him and urging cautious politicians to resolve on war:

> 'As far as I can, I am encouraging them either personally or through others, but you must do so too. Get in touch, I beg of you, with every influential person you know, then give them as big an injection of courage as possible.'

If the Serbs could defeat the Turks in initial battles, Apis affirmed, they would drive right to the Aegean Sea. 'That we young officers will always be in the forefront of the soldiers in battle no one should doubt.'[24] Vindicating Apis' prediction, the Serbian army, reformed partly through his efforts, amazed Europe with its victories over the Turks.

However, Apis could not contribute personally to that triumph as he had wished. At Cavalry Division staff he fell ill of blood poisoning and Maltese fever contracted during his Albanian reconnaissance. After writing out detailed marching orders for his division and over his heated protests, Apis was sent to the Belgrade Military Hospital. For more than three weeks he remained unconscious, hovering between life and death. Responding to urgent pleas by his friends, Dr Cinn, a bacteriology professor from Berlin, came and saved his life. He was not discharged from the hospital until 30 March 1913. He then went to Berlin on convalescent leave to continue treatments with Dr Cinn.

Chief of Serbian Military Intelligence, 1913-1914

Promoted to lieutenant-colonel in January 1913 while still in hospital, Apis returned home from Germany after Serbia had defeated Bulgaria in the Second Balkan War. That August he was named chief of the General Staff's intelligence division. In his new post Colonel Apis controlled agents inside Austria-Hungary responsible for determining its military strength and intentions towards Serbia. With this work Apis was aided by the two men executed with him at Salonika four years later: Major Ljubomir Vulović and Rade Malobabić. As intelligence chief Apis worked in General Staff headquarters on the Kalemegdan, the old Turkish fortress overlooking Belgrade where the Danube and the Sava rivers joined. In his office there he received Slobodan Jovanović, chief of the War Press Bureau and later Serbia's leading historian. Apis expressed himself indefinitely, often not finishing his sentences 'as if he had suddenly remembered that it would be best for him not to disclose everything he knew'. Not yet fully recovered from his illness, seated behind a table with his huge body, double chin and almost completely bald, Apis at age thirty-six resembled a powerful Mongol:

> 'Towards us 'civilians' he adopted a very different behaviour than towards most officers. He spoke mostly in that half-joking, half-serious tone of voice in which cafe conversations are often conducted.'[25]

Searching for a reliable top agent to coordinate intelligence gathering in Austria-Hungary, Apis consulted 'frontier officer' Colonel Dimitrije Pavlović who recommended enthusiastically Rade Malobabić, a Serb born in a Croat village, as a highly intelligent, courageous, dedicated Serb patriot. Receiving Malobabić warmly, Colonel Apis quickly accepted him as the General Staff's chief agent for the Dual Monarchy, assigning him the vital task of creating a network of Serb agents inside Austria-Hungary. Dispatched on repeated missions by Apis, Malobabić invariably returned with valuable information. For his achievements and dedication Apis came to love Malobabić like a brother; he became the Colonel's chief assistant in intelligence operations. Malobabić brought back key information about the strength, disposition and readiness of Austrian commands and units. Detained several times by the Austrian authorities, Malobabić always escaped, once swimming across the frigid Drina River. For his historic exploits, concluded Colonel Pavlović, Malobabić deserved Serbia's highest award.[26] Instead, he would be executed by the Serbian regime.

Early in 1914 Malobabić was the first to report to Colonel Apis the planned visit to Sarajevo of Archduke Franz Ferdinand, heir to the Austrian throne, and upcoming Austrian military manoeuvres there. He assured Apis this marked Austria-Hungary's final preparations for a preemptive war against Serbia.

'Frontier officer' Colonel Čedo Popović, a 'Black Hand' member, described the dispatch of weapons, supplies, and Serb spies across the Drina River into Bosnia based on explicit written orders from Colonel Apis or Supreme Command. 'Each such dispatch had a confidential number, a seal and a signature...of someone I knew and trusted.' Most often Apis had signed, but he concealed this by adding: 'On orders of the chief of the General Staff.' All such activity, insisted Popović, had been 'for the holy future of our country', and concluded: 'Dragutin, Vulović, and all these young Bosnians were for me the embodiment of patriotism and heroism.'[27]

In his only published report as intelligence chief,[28] Colonel Apis praised highly Malobabić's work for the General Staff, denying heatedly accusations that Malobabić had operated as an Austrian spy or double agent. National leaders in Zagreb had assured Apis that Malobabić was a patriotic Serb and wholly trustworthy. However, even Apis' best efforts and strong defence could not prevent Malobabić from falling victim to the bitter civil-military rivalry in Serbia on the eve of World War I.

The May Crisis of 1914

While Colonel Apis served as intelligence chief a major internal crisis erupted in Serbia between the officer corps and political opposition on the one hand and the Radical cabinet and Crown Prince Aleksandar on the other; elderly King Petar was caught in between. As chief spokesman for the officer corps, Apis played an important if somewhat mysterious role. Early in 1914 the issue arose whether army officers or civilians should enjoy 'priority' at public ceremonies in recently conquered Serbian Macedonia. The Serbian army then, after smashing victories over Turks and Bulgarians, was self-assertive and popular. Military leaders quarrelled with the Radical Interior Minister, Stojan Protić, who soon after the Balkan Wars told General Putnik, Serbia's venerable architect of victory: 'You are just a government clerk!'[29]

As 1914 began General Miloš Božanović, a leading May conspirator, resigned as war minister after failing to get cabinet support for an adequate military budget. With much difficulty the Pašić cabinet lured into that post a junior colonel, Dušan Stefanović, with promises of an increased budget. Stefanović was hostile to Apis and 'Black Hand' leaders. Amidst rumours the cabinet might name a civilian as war minister, Apis and other 'Black Hand' leaders met at the Danube Division's staff room on 15 January to plot strategy. Rumours were spreading that the government would retire Apis, Vemić, and other top 'Black Handers'.

That crisis blew over, but a graver one soon erupted. In April 1914 Interior Minister Protić issued a Priority Decree prescribing that civilian officials, many of them corrupt and junior in length of service, would enjoy pride of place over senior officers at official functions in Macedonia. The Pašić cabinet, screamed *Piedmont*, 'Black Hand's' newspaper, was 'a band of state anarchists' undermining the national interest and army morale. By humiliating the officer elite in Macedonia, the Priority Decree created a gulf between the police and army there. General Damjan Popović, military commander of Skoplje, denouncing the Decree, and asserted precedence over the civil prefect at an army review. Protić promptly retired him from military service, but Popović was then elected president of the Belgrade Officers' Club. Without foundation Protić then asserted the club was a 'Black Hand' tool and ordered it investigated. By early May the issues of the Officers' Club, 'Black Hand', and the Priority Decree were linked in a civil-military power struggle. Apis and Putnik, the most influential army leaders, became embroiled with the Crown and Radical Party.

By then 'Black Hand', having lost many leaders in the Balkan wars, was virtually defunct. By 1914 its CEC met rarely and then only as the friends of Colonel Apis. Many considered it had achieved its national goals in the Balkan Wars. At first Apis played no role in officer protests, chiefly from Macedonia, against the Priority Decree. Only in mid-May did he become an intermediary between officers in Serbia proper and those in Macedonia. Reacting angrily to the Decree like other officers, he soon united most Serbian officers under his leadership. Asked at the Salonika Trial why he and other relatively junior officers had led agitation against the Decree, Apis replied: 'We never had any right to do this, nor were we called upon, but from the general resistance to this insult, we took it upon ourselves to obtain satisfaction.' He had acted similarly - preempting the role of senior officers - in preparing the May Coup. Inquired Colonel Mišić: 'By what magical means did you, as a lieutenant-colonel without relying upon the 'Black Hand' induce junior and senior officers to follow you?' Colonel Apis responded:

> 'I succeeded in making the disturbances in the officer corps that great through agitation. Naturally, I turned first to my closest friends which I had among higher and lower officers and utilised them all. The organisation was dead at that moment, and I did not think of utilising it anyway...We were aided by Opposition leaders (against the Pašić cabinet). Since the number of my friends was very great, the agitation succeeded quickly.'[30]

'Black Hand' officers headed the movement against the Priority Decree only because of the key posts they held; the organisation itself took no action. Soon after General Popović was removed from his Skoplje command, Colonel Apis acted, although without his earlier abundant energy. Weakened by illness and the loss of many close comrades, he was no longer so decisive. Nonetheless, the Pašić cabinet and Crown Prince Aleksandar considered him their chief opponent. Heading the so-called 'White Hand' officer faction at court, Major Petar Živković, now a bitter foe of Apis, played on Aleksandar's uncontrollable fear of the formidable colonel, in order to dominate the Crown Prince. However, Apis' personal magnetism still proved effective. Around his famous table at Belgrade's 'Kolarac' restaurant gathered friends and associates. As the ever congenial host, with his eternal cigarette between his teeth, Apis smiled enigmatically and with lighthearted jokes disarmed his admiring audience. Meanwhile his supporters awaited decisive action impatiently.

About mid-May Apis went to see the chief-of-staff, General Putnik, arguing that the officer corps, angry over the Decree, should receive satisfaction. Putnik agreed to employ his strong influence with King Petar and backed Apis' efforts to win support from the political Opposition. Apis talked also with General Petar Bojović, Macedonian troop commander. Colonel Milutin Lazarević, his chief of staff, assured Bojović that the officer corps solidly opposed the Decree.

Apis urged his friends in southern garrisons to reinforce General Putnik's efforts in Belgrade by telegraphing King Petar directly against the

Decree. In a major political move Apis conferred with leaders of the Opposition to the Pašić cabinet. To Liberal leader, Vojislav Veljković, and the Independent Radical chieftain, Milorad Drašković, he emphasised that it was high time for the united Opposition to achieve power. Apis found them favourable to the officer's cause. Remaining in constant touch with Opposition leaders and with General Putnik, Apis carried their messages back and forth. Independent Radical leaders, notably Drašković, apparently even agreed that a military coup might be the solution to the crisis.[31] By this open intervention in Serbian politics Apis was clearly violating military regulations.

Colonel Apis' controversial subsequent instructions to his friends in Skoplje, Macedonia followed these discussions with political leaders. Opposition leaders, Apis claimed later, would have welcomed 'a little scandal' in order to oust the Pašić cabinet. Apis had sought no authorisation from the 'Black Hand' CEC to negotiate with the Opposition: 'I did this as an ordinary member of 'Black Hand' which was not directly involved in those talks with the politicians.'[32] Apis employed his great powers of persuasion to unite the Opposition knowing that could produce an Assembly majority in the upcoming parliamentary elections.

On 21 May General Bojović wrote War Minister Stefanović from Skoplje about his officer's dissatisfaction with the Decree. Prince Aleksandar reacted angrily to the publication of their protests in *Piedmont* while the Pašić cabinet and Aleksandar ignored officer requests to withdraw the Priority Decree. Apis then apparently sought to trigger the Pašić government's collapse by a local 'putsch' in Serbian Macedonia by replacing some civil officials there with military officers. By then Apis may have feared retribution from Pašić for his role in unifying the Opposition. Colonel Lazarević believed that Apis urged his friends to make a dramatic gesture in order to force new elections but not to orchestrate a full-scale military coup.

At the Salonika Trial Apis stated that on 26 or 27 May he had written his comrades in Skoplje 'to persuade county and district chiefs to assume police power temporarily' without planning any similar action in Serbia proper. However, his friends refused to act while keeping the matter quiet. Apis' relative, Lieutenant Colonel Dušan Glišić, to whom Apis' letter had been addressed replied:

> 'Here there is not a single person who would agree with your proposal...With it would be caused irreparable damage bringing into question the most vital interests of the country; the officer corps would be split as never before.'[33]

Thus accusations at Salonika that Apis had plotted a full-scale military coup in Macedonia and Serbia remain unproven. Indeed, Apis stated under oath, and he was no liar: 'Never either then or later did it enter my head that the army should take power into its hands...I worked for and wished strongly that the officers be given satisfaction (over the Decree).'[34] Apis' intense patriotism suggests he would never have taken action likely to provoke civil war because that would have invited armed Austrian intervention. However, his actions during the May Crisis were improper for an officer in a parliamentary country.

With everything hanging in suspense at the end of May 1914, Apis the politician and conspirator seemed to lose his formidable aura. War Minister Stefanović, backed by the cabinet, drafted stringent measures against the Apis group that would have retired him and other 'Black Hand' officers, transferred others to the interior, and appointed their opponents to key Belgrade posts. This plan was blocked by the War Ministry's operations chief, Colonel Krsta Smiljanić, because of the danger of and an Austrian invasion. Avoiding a direct confrontation with the cabinet, Apis sought compromise sending fellow 'Black Hand' leader, Colonel M G Milovanović, to Prince Aleksandar. With Russia strongly supporting its protégé, Pašić, the cabinet remained but the Priority Decree was withdrawn. Apis receded into the background and King Petar handed over his royal powers to Crown Prince Aleksandar. The latter, viewing the May conspirators and Apis as obstacles to his control over the army, resolved to destroy them at the first opportunity. The May Crisis therefore undermined Apis' political influence and prestige. Only the outbreak of World War I soon after saved him and his friends from removal or reassignment.

Role in the Sarajevo Assassination of June 28, 1914

In the spring of 1914 Serbian political and military leaders agreed that the country required years of peace to integrate conquered Macedonia, recover from the two Balkan Wars, and equip the army. Colonel Apis as head of military intelligence believed the chief external threat to Serbia was the Austro-Hungarian 'war party' headed, he believed, by the heir Archduke Franz Ferdinand. Apis viewed the Archduke as a dynamic and able leader who alone could regenerate the Habsburg monarchy and who was planning to destroy Serbia. The planned visit of Franz Ferdinand to Sarajevo and Austrian manoeuvres in eastern Bosnia Apis viewed as preparatory to an invasion of Serbia. Milan Živanović, Apis' nephew, argued that the trialist program adopted by the Archduke, if implemented, would have forced Serbia under indirect Austrian rule: 'Austria intended to achieve unification of the South Slavs within the framework of the Danubian monarchy.' However, an Austrian scholar insisted that Franz Ferdinand's purpose was defensive and that he strongly opposed annexing any Serbian territory. Nevertheless, had his trialist scheme been achieved, a Great Serbia would have been impossible.[35]

How great was Colonel Apis' role in the Sarajevo assassination? Milan Živanović ascribed it chiefly to him, declaring he decided upon the murder and implemented it in practice. Gavrilo Princip, the chief assassin, had met with Apis in Belgrade to receive instructions and the final stimulus to commit the assassination. After gathering voluminous data about his uncle's career, Živanović concluded: 'His (Apis') role in carrying out the Sarajevo assassination was predominant.' His close associate, Major Vojislav Tankosić, the guerrilla leader, had instructed the assassins in the use of firearms and bombs. Securing their passage from Serbia into Bosnia, Apis had supplied them with revolvers and bombs: 'Apis directed their preparedness to its true goals.' While Bosnian students had planned to kill high Austrian officials, their hatred had focused chiefly on the governor of Bosnia, general Potiorek. Apis then had convinced them that 'one must strike the snake in the head,' by killing the irreplaceable Archduke Franz Ferdinand.

Serbia's national revolutionary movement, claimed Živanović, centred then in the General Staff where Colonel Apis, supported fully by chief-of-staff, General Putnik, held everything in his hands. The 'Black Hand' and its CEC no longer really operated, neither planning nor implementing the assassination:

> 'In Serbia in all this the main and decisive role was played by Colonel Apis with a few of his closest colleagues, all of whom

> were members of 'Unification or Death!' and with the collaboration of Rade Malobabić.'[36]

Deciding to implement the Archduke's murder in Sarajevo after receiving assurances that Russia would back Serbia in case of war, Apis entrusted to his closest colleagues, Major Vulović and Malobabić, the task of transporting the assassins across into Bosnia and sending their weapons. Asserted Živanović:

> 'Malobabić was the first to propose to Apis to kill Franz Ferdinand as the leader of the imperialistic Balkan policy of Austria-Hungary and thus avert the chief danger threatening Serbia.'[37]

Colonel Apis' written hand statement to the Salonika court in 1917 seems to confirm his nephew's assertions:

> 'After Rade (Malobabić) had begun work, believing Austria was preparing for war with us, I thought that with the removal of...Ferdinand, that the military party...would lose its strength and that thus the danger of war would be removed or at least delayed somewhat. For that purpose I hired Malobabić to organise an assassination of Ferdinand upon his arrival in Sarajevo. I decided on this definitively only after (Russian Military attaché) Artamonov had assured me that Russia would not leave us undefended if Austria should attack us.'

Then followed the most controversial portion of Apis' secret report:

> 'Malobabić carried out my instructions, organised and carried through the assassination. Its chief participants were all in my service and received small honoraria which I sent them through Malobabić.'[38]

That document, emphasised Serbian Radical leaders, had prevented Prince Aleksandar from commuting the Salonika Court's death sentences imposed on Apis, Vulović and Malobabić. Other Apis colleagues reinforced these assertions. Thus, Aleksandar Blagojević affirmed much later in a newspaper article:

> 'Those three great dead patriots (Apis, Vulović and Malobabić) are the only ones who prepared and executed that affair, and all other suppositions are baseless.'[39]

And responding to inquiries by Sarajevo's chief archivist, Colonel Vojislav Gojković, another close officer colleague of Apis, declared:

> 'I affirm also that in that affair (Sarajevo assassination) were involved only Apis, Vulović and Tankosić. Only those three knew who was to carry out the affair. Both of the others were reliable and devoted to Apis.'[40]

However, *Young Bosnia and the Sarajevo Assassination*, a well-researched book by the Bosnian scholar, Dragoslav Ljubibratić, presents a very different view of who initiated and implemented the Sarajevo murder:

> 'The Sarajevo assassination was not the work of Apis but of Princip, not merely because Princip carried it out, but because of all the participants he alone remained insistent from beginning to end in executing the decisions reached.'[41]

Princip and his fellow anarchist, Čabrinović, affirmed Ljubibratić, were inspired to commit the murder by previous attempts on the lives of Austrian leaders. Apis' statement to the Salonika court had sought to quash the treason charges against him and his colleagues by depicting them as heroic patriots. Bosnian revolutionary youths were convinced the initiative for the Sarajevo murder had come exclusively from their ranks, notably from Vladimir Gaćinović, who believed that such a murder would rouse the Slav element in Austria-Hungary to revolution and bring freedom to Bosnia. Gaćinović, claimed Ljubibratić, had selected Princip to kill Franz Ferdinand after concluding he was determined and reliable. The Bosnian youths had sought weapons from Major Tankosić who had secured Apis' agreement for the conspirators to leave for Sarajevo.

Ljubibratic's account minimised the role of Colonel Apis and 'Black Hand' in the whole affair.

In 1915 Apis told 'frontier officer' Colonel Čedomir Popović that initially he had concurred with Major Tankosić's proposal to dispatch the young Bosnian assassins across into Bosnia:

> 'But when I, after some time, thought a little more about this, I decided to try to return the youths who had left and in every way to prevent the assassination. This attempt was made through the guerrilla, Đuro Šarac.'

Explained Apis: 'At that moment I did not believe such an attempt could succeed and that perhaps they would not even undertake it.' Dubious about the immature Bosnian youths, Apis wished to employ Tankosić's guerrillas for the murder. He entrusted the organisation of this plot to Malobabić, summoned him to Belgrade, and put him in touch with Major Vulović. Then Apis persuaded Šarac to recall Princip and his friends. However, Princip and Grabež refused to abandon their assassination attempt. Apis informed Čedomir Popović: 'they did not wish to hear of this'.[42] Of the young Bosnians only Princip remained determined to kill the Archduke, achieving his goal, when the others failed, by cool resolve on behalf of revolutionary Yugoslav youth, and with considerable luck.

R W Seton-Watson, a leading British scholar, gave the affair a still different twist. Noting that Colonel Apis was the central figure in 'Black Hand' and a dedicated Serb patriot, he concluded that Apis was 'entirely lacking in balance or common sense, ruthless in ambition'. Concluding from secret intelligence information that Austria-Hungary was about to attack Serbia, Apis decided to forestall this by a sensational terrorist act to disorganise the Austrian leadership. Receiving confirmation on 2/15 June of Russia's promised support in event of war, Apis convened the CEC of 'Black Hand' that very day. When he told his colleagues he had sent Tankosić's two Bosnian pupils to kill the Archduke, their opposition to such a move was so strong that Apis promised to abandon his plan. Then he either attempted to recall the assassins without success, or he neglected to try to halt the murder. Short of holding the youths forcibly in Belgrade, even Apis probably could not have prevented their action. Seton-Watson also concluded that the initiative for the Sarajevo murder had come from inside Bosnia. As a survivor of 'Young Bosnia', Borivoje Jevtić later affirmed: Sarajevo was 'not the work of an isolated individual in national exaltation, but of the entire youth of Bosnia'.[43]

Both Apis and 'Young Bosnia' aimed to eliminate the Archduke for different reasons. Idealistic young Bosnian revolutionaries viewed the murder as beginning a struggle to destroy Austria-Hungary and free their homeland; Apis sought to prevent or defer an Austrian attack on Serbia by removing the 'war party's' alleged leader. Apis' assertions to the Salonika court appear to have been a deliberate exaggeration of his role and that of his colleagues in initiating and implementing the murder. Milan Živanović's assertions that Apis deserved virtually sole 'credit' for the assassination comprise part of his effort to portray him and his colleagues as martyrs in the cause of Serbian national unification.

Role in World War I, 1914-1916

After the Austrian ultimatum of 23 July 1914, Colonel Apis, realising war was likely, worked intensively at the General Staff on Serbian mobilisation. On 25 July, while other General Staff officers left for a new headquarters in interior Kragujevac, Apis remained in Belgrade to confer with his chief agent, Rade Malobabić. After talking with Apis once, Malobabić was arrested by the Belgrade police on suspicion of being an Austrian agent. Without him Apis' intelligence network inside Austria-Hungary collapsed. Malobabić fell victim to Apis' conflict with the Radical regime. Unable to locate his agent, Apis proceeded to Kragujevac still as chief of intelligence and of the information bureau. There his relations with Prince Aleksandar as Supreme Commander deteriorated before their open breach early in 1915.

On Marshal Putnik's instructions, Colonels Apis and Čedomir Popović created a guerilla volunteer corps designed to conduct partisan warfare in the event the enemy reached Serbia's interior. Its four detachments were all commanded by experienced guerilla fighters closely associated with Colonel Apis and 'Black Hand'. In November 1914 Serbia defeated a second powerful Austrian invasion of the country.

Serving with the press bureau in Kragujevac, the historian, Slobodan Jovanović recalled:

> 'The Apis I knew at Supreme Command did not resemble the picture created about him by the public. He was neither hot-tempered nor arrogant; he was more what one would call a 'good comrade.''[44]

Jovanović soon began to appreciate some of Apis' finer qualities. Much concerned with his comrades' advancement, he never blew his own horn. His devoted comradeship and efforts on behalf of his friends amazed others. Apis did not shield his friends from dangerous enterprises, but that danger merely enhanced his attractiveness and prestige.

What provoked the fateful breach early in 1915 between Apis and Prince Aleksandar? Later, on Corfu Aleksandar enumerated Apis' shortcomings, citing numerous denunciations by informants from his entourage dominated by the 'White Hand'. In the army Apis was being called 'the second heir to the throne.' The Prince was dismayed that for some Apis enjoyed more prestige than he did, threatening Aleksandar's position as commander-in-chief and future king. The Prince's homosexual intimate, Colonel Živković, exploited such reports to turn the Prince against Apis. As old comrades fell on the battlefield, Colonel Apis' influenced waned.

In March 1915 at Prince Aleksandar's insistence Apis was removed from Supreme Command and named chief-of-staff of the minuscule Užice Army. There he formed a Bosnian volunteer battalion to assist in a planned Serbian offensive towards Sarajevo. Dušan Marinković, a Serbian intellectual, later recalled that Apis' young officers had been enthusiastic about liberating Bosnia; he viewed them as dedicated patriots:

> 'I did not dream that official (Radical) circles regarded them differently. I saw in Apis and his friends people with wholly sincere intentions and discerned nothing of which they were later accused. I knew there was nothing suspicious about their ties with Bosnia.'[45]

In the fall of 1915 a massive Austro-German offensive from the north, supplemented by a Bulgarian assault from the east, brought Serbia to the verge of total defeat. When the offensive began Colonel Apis was in Zaječar in eastern Serbia at Timok Army (formerly Užice) headquarters. During the ensuing Serbian retreat, Apis' closest friend,

Major Vulović, secured the release of the unfortunate Malobabić from prison. He and Apis transported the severely ill former agent with them to Corfu. Resisting desperately, the Serbian army retreated through the frigid mountains of Montenegro and Albania to the Adriatic. There its emaciated remnants were rescued by Allied ships and taken to the Greek island of Corfu. Apis' unit, defending the approaches to the Albanian port of Durazzo (Durres), was the last to evacuate the mainland. His foes later accused Apis and his 'Black Hand' colleagues, without real evidence, of plotting in Durazzo to overthrow Serbia's dynasty and regime.

During early spring 1916 Colonel Apis wound up the remaining affairs of the dissolved Timok Army, while surviving Serbian forces were reorganised and reequipped, then were inserted on the Allied Salonika Front. At Corfu's cafes, flocking to see the congenial Apis, were numerous officer friends, supplicants, and spies employed by Prince Aleksandar and the Radical regime. As Apis' influence declined, association with him became dangerous. Pointing to him, one colleague commented:

> 'That man is indifferent to everything! His friends and comrades have died, but no matter, he seeks new people...He will continue his work with new people and will not rest until he finds someone ready to struggle and intrigue.'[46]

On Corfu Slobodan Jovanović discussed with Apis his perilous situation. He and his remaining 'Black Hand' colleagues were at odds with Prince Aleksandar and the Pašić regime. The historian urged Apis to repair his relations with one or the other. Affirming that neither the Prince nor Pašić would act against him, the Colonel assured Jovanović that he intended no political action or intrigue. Informed by the new chief-of-staff, General Petar Bojović, of rumours that 'Black Hand' was plotting a military coup, Apis assured him: 'These were false reports by spies. "Black Hand" is a defunct patriotic organisation.' Colonel Apis mistakenly declined to meet personally with Prince Aleksandar, instructing Colonel Milutin Lazarević to assure the Prince he would adhere strictly to his military duties. 'From that moment', declared Apis later, 'I acted in no way to violate the Supreme Commander's desires.'[47]

As Third Army's assistant chief-of-staff, Colonel Apis in May 1916 proceeded to Salonika, then north to the Macedonian front. For seven months he served there with the refurbished Serbian army, busy day and night with military duties. Apis helped plan a Serbian advance late that summer that penetrated into Serbia. However, by late November a curious lull had settled over the Salonika Front. Serbian forces suffered from exhaustion, heavy losses and falling morale.

Did Colonel Apis serve Serbia effectively and loyally on the Salonika Front? In March 1917, evaluating Apis' work as Third Army assistant chief-of-staff, when Apis already faced trial, Colonel Mihailo Jovanović, the new chief-of-staff, jeopardising his own career, provided this positive assessment:

> '(Apis) carried out the tasks entrusted to him quickly and with complete dedication. He grasps orders given extremely quickly, and in every situation is in full command.'[48]

All indications are that Colonel Apis was an extremely valuable member of the Third Army. Nor is there evidence that he engaged there in any anti-regime activities, as alleged at the Salonika Trial.

At the Salonika Trial of 1917

The arrest of Colonel Apis on 15 December 1916 followed months of work by 'The Committee of Ten for the Liquidation of Colonel Apis', directed by Colonel Petar Živković, Prince Aleksandar's vindictive crony. Charged with preparing to destroy the Apis group was the corrupt, repressive 'Salonika regime' directed by Serbian Interior Minister Ljubomir Jovanović-Patak. It employed many spies and informers to gather derogatory and false information about Apis and his colleagues. General Miloš Vasić, an Apis foe, named Third Army commander that summer, in negative and false reports accused the Colonel of insubordination and neglecting his duties. Paving the way for the Apis group's arrest was the interior Minister's lengthy 'Prezidijal' (memorandum) of 12 December accusing it of illegal political agitation and of plotting to overturn the regime: 'From the beginning leading this subversive circle stood Colonel Dragutin Dimitrijević.' The Interior Minister urged War Minister Božidar Terzić to order the entire Apis group arrested. Already on 14 December Colonel Dimitrije Pavlović, leading Supreme Command's legal division, concluded in his report:

> 'Colonel Dimitrijević intentionally and with definite plan recruited individuals and worked to carry out the assassination of the Heir, to overthrow the present regime and legal order and the Karađorđević dynasty and to introduce the supreme power of ten to fifteen men. It would depend on this military organisation and eliminate all those standing in the way, especially Premier Pašić.'[49]

About noon on 15 December Colonel Milan Dunjić, Salonika's military commandant, designated as chief investigator, arrived in Ostrovo with warrants to seize Apis' personal effects and arrest him if anything incriminating were found. Arrest was no great surprise to Apis who had been warned by friends repeatedly. 'They told me', declared Apis in prison. 'I knew I was going to be arrested.'[50] Colonel Dunjić, an old enemy of Apis, could not restrain his joy at discovering in Apis' trunk copies of 'Black Hands'' Constitution, Rules, and a list of its original Central Executive Committee with authentic signatures. Apis had preserved these as of merely historical significance. For Dunjić and his superiors, however, that find was a goldmine enabling them to imprison and try Apis. The first 'Black Hand' leader arrested, Apis was taken under guard to Salonika Officers' Prison. Soon his closest colleagues and friends were likewise arrested and sent to the Salonika prison. For the next three months all remained there in solitary confinement, carefully supervised by prison commandant, Captain Milan Stojković, who described their conversations and behaviour to the sinister Colonel Živković. In prison they were interrogated separately, chiefly by Colonel Dunjić. As the investigation neared competition, the 'Salonika regime' purged the military courts that were to try the 'Black Hand' leaders and review the verdict. The new judges were mostly bitter personal enemies of Apis and thirsting for revenge. Meanwhile the Pašić regime on Corfu sought a scapegoat in case Serbia had to conclude a separate peace with Austria-Hungary. Apis clearly filled the bill.

The Salonika Trial of Colonel Apis and his chief associates from 20 March to 23 May 1917 comprised eighty-two semi-public sessions. All ten defendants and over 100 witnesses, all called by the prosecution, some released from prison for that purpose, testified. The outcome was preordained with only the severity of the sentence in doubt. The accused were brought daily under guard to the courtroom. Recalled the eyewitness author of 'Salonika Affair':

> 'Once I saw Apis being brought to the court building. He went quickly up the stairs with his eternal cigarette in his teeth, in an easygoing manner as if wishing to reduce the impression of the gravity of the moment. His face was slightly darkened; one could detect tiredness. But clearly he was in full control of himself and had lost none of his moral strength.'[51]

Arrayed against him, Apis knew, were the 'Salonika regime' and the most despicable elements in Salonika avoiding their service at the front. In the courtroom a tragi-comedy was played out, staged by the Crown Prince, Živković, the Radicals, and their appointee, Colonel Petar Mišić. Some of Apis' chief colleagues turned against him during the trial, denounced him, and blamed him for their imprisonment and trial. When the junior prisoner officer Lieutenant Josif Protić commented; 'Yes, Colonel Apis is always in such a good mood, always smiling, but I believe nonetheless he knows...what his fate will be,' Colonel Čedomir Popović, Apis' fellow defendant, responded:

> 'Apis smiles because that's the way he is, because he is a giant, a hero, a lion. Apis smiles because he knows they will shoot him!...He smiled that evening (May 29, 1903) in the Officer's Club as if he was going to a wedding...You don't know such people: when they smile, they are most dangerous.'[52]

Early in the trial it grew evident the defendants had done nothing subversive; the charge of fomenting mutiny in the Serbian army was dropped for lack of evidence. Then on 27 March the prosecutor read a supplementary indictment accusing Rade Malobabić of shooting at Prince Aleksandar on 29 August/11 September 1916 at Apis' instruction as the Heir returned from the front by automobile. All the accused were considered Malobabić's accomplices. The only alleged eyewitness, Temeljko Veljanović, had been released from prison after telling investigators about an assassination attempt several months afterwards.

Colonel Apis reacted sceptically: 'What could one gain, I ask you, by killing the heir to the throne while the King is still alive? Would I act in such a way? As an old conspirator would I arrange things so stupidly?' To Captain Stojković he added: 'This (attempt) is either a personal act of vengeance against the Heir or arranged by those who wanted to bring us here.'[53] Shortly thereafter Apis submitted his report to the Salonika court assuming responsibility for the Sarajevo murder; it apparently doomed him, Vulović, and Malobabić. Apis also wrote a long, emotional letter to Prince Aleksandar seeking reconciliation. denying any role in the alleged attempt on the Prince's life, Apis wrote: 'I would have to be, Your Highness,...a monster if I even thought of doing any harm to your person.' Why not end the Salonika Trial and absolve him and his friends of unfair accusations of treason and murder?

> 'Your Highness, I implore you to halt this affair. You must not allow a Serbian military court for officers to complete the verdict of the Austrian court in Sarajevo...and place the brand of treason on the brows of officers who dreamed of liberating the entire Serb people for the glory of your name.'[54]

Both in the courtroom and in his secret report to the Salonika court Colonel Apis accepted maximum responsibility for 'Black Hand' activities, revealing himself as a generous friend anxious to spare his comrades. On his way to execution he told his goaler, Captain Stojković: 'If I had a hundred lives, I would not regret losing them as much as I regret that because of me perished so many true friends and comrades.'[55]

Responding in court to Chairman Mišić's questions, Apis denied that anyone in 'Black Hand' had even considered conducting revolutionary activity inside Serbia. During 'Black Hand's' brief existence: 'We merely aided the government's work, and that was our sole activity.' After the Balkan Wars they concluded their mission had been achieved. Thus, CEC meetings in 1914 had only been gatherings of close friends. Showing amazing trust in Chairman Mišić's fairness, Colonel Apis replied fully and frankly to all questions about 'Black Hand' and his relations with Malobabić and the Bosnian volunteers. Apparently, he believed that telling the whole truth would exonerate him and his comrades. Instead, the Lower Military Court issued nine death sentences, including the three involved in the Sarajevo murder. The High Military Court, reviewing that draconian verdict, also consisted chiefly of Apis' foes, and confirmed seven death sentences. With the final power of pardon Prince Aleksandar commuted the sentences of four defendants to prison terms. Despite numerous protests from Allied countries, the Prince, however, insisted on the execution of Apis, Vulović, and Malobabić.

Assessing Apis' Role

Colonel Apis remains a highly controversial historical figure. Admiring biographers Milan Živanović and Miloš Bogićević depicted him as Serbia's predominant military figure (along with Marshall Putnik) between 1903 and 1917, involved positively in all key events, personally exemplary, heroic, even saintly. Apis' magnetic personality and the May Coup, claimed Živanović, transformed Serbia politically, economically, and militarily. 'Apis died like a hero in the knowledge he had always acted honourably and well,' concluded his nephew. Živanović agreed with Apis' own assessment that he had always acted on behalf of Serb and Yugoslav interests and should be ranked among the chief creators of Yugoslavia. Added the English scholar, R W Seton-Watson: 'Dimitrijević's enthusiasm for the achievement of the Yugoslav idea caused him to be remembered in every home in Serbia.'[56]

Lawyer Prvoslav Vasiljević, Apis' defender at the Belgrade Retrial of 1953, compared 'Black Hand' favourably with nineteenth century European nationalist organisations in seeking national liberation and unity. Apis' national views, affirmed Vasiljević, were broader and more progressive than those of his organisation. He had approached ever closer to the Yugoslav idea, working closely with Croat and other South Slav leaders. Apis 'was a progressive individual who...contributed to destroying the enslaving powers of Austria-Hungary and Turkey and liberating and unifying the Yugoslav peoples.'[57]

On the other hand, after the Retrial two leading Yugoslav scholars claimed that neither 'Black Hand' nor Apis had played a progressive role in Serbia. They characterised 'Black Hand' as a reactionary, chauvinist and militarist organisation; its official organ, *Piedmont*, had mouthed Apis' praetorian views derived from imperial Germany.[58] Dr Petar Opačić, a retired Yugoslav army officer, was critical of Apis' military expertise and his deep involvement in politics. As the chief 'Black Hand' leader, Apis had led a subversive military faction undermining army unity. As Chief of Military Intelligence, he had failed to gather full information about Austrian military plans in 1914. After 1906, affirmed Opačić, the ambitious Apis aimed to dominate the army and seize power. Since his behaviour was divisive and inexcusable, the Corfu regime had been justified to act against him.[59]

Apis and his associates, this author believes, were innocent of the charges brought against them at Salonika but were guilty of violating military regulations and conducting impermissible political activities. Convincing evidence is lacking that Apis sought to seize state power or create a praetorian regime in Serbia. However, his letters to his Skoplje colleagues in 1914 suggest that he favoured replacing some civilian officials in Macedonia with military officers. Had 'Black Hand' and Colonel Apis decided to seize power, they faced tempting opportunities in May 1903, May 1914 and December 1915, but on none of those occasions did they plan to act. Apis generally favoured strong, effective civil rule, not military control, nor did he share *Piedmont's* chauvinism after the Balkan wars. The evidence suggests that there was no attempt on Prince Aleksandar's life in August 1916. Certainly, Apis had no motive to strike down his former benefactor and commander-in-chief. Apis' strong patriotism excluded any betrayal of Serbia to the Central Powers or arranging a separate peace with Austria. His enemies' unprincipled and vindictive actions, as much as his own accomplishments, made Colonel Apis a unique historical figure.

Notes

1 The first numeral denotes the date according to the Julian calendar. The second numeral denotes the date according to the Gregorian calendar.
2 MacKenzie (1989), pp. 16-21. Old style dates have been used unless otherwise indicated.
3 Apis to Milan Živanović, 25 June 1917 in Dedijer (1978), pp. 338-339.
4 'Sestra o bratu', in Živanović (1955), pp 643-645, and 'Iz života Pukovnika D. D. Apisa' in Živanović (n.d.).
5 Živanović (n.d.), Papers of Pavle Popović, 'Oko veridbe i ženidbe'.
6 Živanović (n.d.), 1985, Papers of Pavle Panković.
7 Vasić (1925), pp. 54-55, and Jovanović (1929-31), Vol. II, pp. 351-352.

8 Živanović (n.d.), 'Uzroci majske zavere 1903 g.'
9 Živanović (1923-1925), Vol. IV, pp. 343-347.
10 Živanović (1923-1925), Vol. IV, p. 347.
11 Živanović (1923-1925), Vol. IV, p. 349.
12 Živanović (1923-1925), Vol. IV, pp. 329-330, 353-354, Vasić (1925), pp. 88-89, and Jovanović (1929-1931), Vol. II, pp. 367-370.
13 Živanović (n.d.), 718, 'Apis'.
14 Živanović (1923-1925) Vol. IV, pp. 334-335.
15 Živanović (n.d.), 617, Simić, B., 'Ujedinjenje ili smrt!', and 718, 'Apis'.
16 Živanović (n.d.), 617, Simić, B., 'Ujedinjenje ili smrt!', and 718, 'Apis'.
17 Popović (1927), pp. 397-398.
18 Ljubibratić (1964), pp. 34-35.
19 Živanović (n.d.), 3, 'Iskazi i odbrana Pukovnika Dimitrijevića-Apisa'.
20 Živanović (n.d.), 3289, 'Crna i Bela ruka'.
21 Živanović (n.d.), 3, 'Iskazi i odbrana Pukovnika Dimitrijevića-Apisa'.
22 Tartaglia (1928), pp. 26-28.
23 MacKenzie (1989), pp. 90-91.
24 Živanović (n.d.), 3289, 'Crna i Bela ruka.'
25 Jovanović (1962),p. 408.
26 Živanović (n.d.), 35, 'Rade Malobabić'.
27 Zec (1986).
28 Apis to General Staff, 8/21 June 1914 in Dedijer (n.d.), pp. 363-365.
29 Živanović (n.d.), 719, 'Konflikt 1914 g.'
30 Živanović (n.d.), 3, 'Iskazi i odbrana Pukovnika Dimitrijevića-Apisa'.
31 Nesković (1953), pp. 158-160.
32 Anon (1918), p. 172.
33 Živanović (1955), p. 219.
34 Živanović (n.d.), 3, 'Iskazi i odbrana Pukovnika Dimitrijevića-Apisa'.
35 Živanović (n.d.), 2091, 'Lične podatke o Apisu'.
36 Živanović (n.d.), 4019, 'Rad Organizacije "Ujedinjenje ili smrt!"'.
37 Živanović (n.d.), 35, Dimitrije Pavlović's reminiscences of Malobabić.
38 Apis to Salonika Court, 28 March 1917 in Wurlthe (1975), unpaginated.
39 Blagojević, Aleksandar in *Oslobodjenje* (Sarajevo), No. 2092, 17 June 1953.

40 Bogićević (1962), pp. 125-126.
41 Ljubibratić (1964), p. 163.
42 Ljubibratić (1964), pp. 153-164.
43 Jevtić (1924), Seton-Watson (1925), pp. 500-506.
44 Jovanović (1962), p. 410.
45 Marinković, Dušan, 'Jedan susret sa "Apisom" iz saslušanje kod ministra policije,' *Oslobodjenje* (Sarajevo), 16 May 1953, p. 5.
46 Živanović (n.d.), 716, 'Solunska afera.'
47 Vojno-istoriski arhiv (Belgrade), Popisnik Kutija, V., 483, f. 1, br. 12, 'Ocene za pukovnika Dragutin Dimitrijevića od strane Načelnika Štaba 3. Armije', 9 March 1917.
48 Arhiv Srbije (Belgrade), 'Solunski proces', F. 4, 2097, Interior Minister to War Minister, 12 December 1916.
49 Živanović (n.d.), 463, Colonel Pavlović to Supreme Command, 14 December 1916.
50 Živanović (n.d.), 3205, Diary of Captain Milan Stojković, entry of 8 March 1917.
51 Živanović (n.d.), 716, ' Solunska afera.'
52 Zec, Stevan, 'Protić Memoirs, III', *Duga*, June 1986.
53 Živanović (n.d.), 3205, Stojković, entry of 13/26 June 1917.
54 Živanović (n.d.), 1933, Apis to 'Vaše Kraljevsko Visočanstvo,' 30 March 1917.
55 Živanović (n.d.), 3205, Stojković, entry of 13/26 June 1917.
56 Seton-Watson (1922).
57 Vasiljević, Prvoslav, 'Organizacije Ujedinjeje ili smrt!', *Politika* (Belgrade), 5 July 1953, and 'Ispravka Prvoslava Vasiljevića', *Politika* (Belgrade), 29 August 1953.
58 Dedijer & Pavišević (1953).
59 Author's interviews with Dr. Opačić, 16 June 1986 and 11 December 1987.

References

Anon (1918), *Tajna prevratna organizacija, Izveštaj sa procesa u vojnom sudu za oficire u Solunu po beleškama vođenim na samom pretresu*, Salonika.

Bogićević, Miloš (1928), *Le Colonel Dragutine Dimitrijević-Apis*. Paris.

Bogićević, Miloš (1927), *Le proces de Salonique, juin 1917*, Paris.

Bogićević, Vojislav (1962), *Sarajevski atentat, Pisma*, Sarajevo.

Brehm, Bruno (1931), *Apis und Este (So fing es an)*, Munich.

Cassels, Lavender (1985), *The Archduke and the Assassins: Sarajevo, June 28, 1914*, New York.

Dedijer, Vladimir (n.d.), *Serbia, Dokumenti o spoljnoj politici Kraljevine Srbije 1903-1914*, Vol. VII, Book 2, Belgrade.

Dedijer, Vladimir (1978), *Sarajevo, 1914 I & II*, Belgrade.

Dedijer, Vladimir & Pavićević, Branko (1953), 'Organizacija "Ujedinjenje ili smrt!"', *Nova Misao* (Belgrade), July, 1953.

Gilfond, Henry (1975), *The Black Hand at Sarajevo*. Indianapolis.

Jevtić, Borivoje (1924), *Sarajevski atentat*, Sarajevo.

Jovanović, Slobodan (1929-1931), *Vlada Aleksandra Obrenovića*, 2 Vols., Belgrade.

Jovanović, Slobodan (1962) *Moji savreminici*. Windsor.

Ljubibratić, Drago (1964), *Mlada Bosna i Sarajevski atentat*, Sarajevo.

MacKenzie, David (1989) *Apis: The Congenial Conspirator. The Life of Colonel Dragutin T. Dimitrijević*, East European Monographs, Boulder.

MacKenzie, David (1991) 'The Black Hand and its Statutes,' *East European Quarterly*, Vol. 25 No. 2, pp. 170-206.

MacKenzie, David (1995) *The Black hand on Trial, Salonika 1917*. East European Monographs, Boulder.

Nešković, Borivoje (1953), *Istina o Solunskom procesu*, Belgrade.

Petrovich, Michael Boro (1976) *A History of Modern Serbia, 1804-1918*. 2 Vols., Harcourt Brace Jovanovich, New York and London.

Popović, Čedomir (1927), 'Organizacija "Ujedinjenje ili smrt!"', *Nova Evropa*, Vol. 15, No. 12.

Seton-Watson, R.W. (1922), 'Serbia Must Choose', *The New Europe*, 21 October, 1922.

Seton-Watson, R.W. (1925), 'Murder in Sarajevo', *Foreign Affairs*, Vol. 3, pp. 500-506.

Šavković, Dušan (1988) *Apis: Krv i bes*, Belgrade.

Tartaglia, Oskar (1928), *Veleizdajnik*, Split.

Vasić, Dragiša (1925), *Devetsto treća (Majski Prevrat)*, Belgrade.

Vucinich, Wayne (1954) *Serbia Between East and West: The Events of 1903-1908,* Stanford.

Wurthle, Fritz (1975), *Die Sarajewoer Gerichtsakten*, Vienna.

Zec, Stevan (1986), "Bele senke Crne ruke', *Duga*, June, 1986, Nos. 3-4.

Živanović, Milan (n.d.), *Zaostavština Milana Ž. Živanovića*, Arhiv Srpske akademije nauke i umetnosti, Belgrade.

Živanović, Milan (1955) *Pukovnik Apis. Solunski proces 1917.* Belgrade.

Živanović, Živan (1923-1925), *Politička istorija Srbije u drugoj polovini XIX veka*, 4 Vols., Belgrade.

4 King Petar I Karađorđević

MILE BJELAJAC

Introduction

Petar I Karađorđević was the constitutional monarch in the parliamentary Kingdom of Serbia from 1903 to 1918, and the first ruler of the Kingdom of Serbs, Croats and Slovenes from 1918 to 1921. He has been remembered by his people as a king-democrat and moderniser, as the 'Great Liberator', and, perhaps most significantly from the perspective of an assessment of his rule and his relationship to his people and vice-versa, as 'uncle Pera'. From a foreigner's perspective he was in Serb eyes one of their own, a peasant son by origin, whom they elected as king just as they elected their parliamentary representatives.[1]

Early Years

The future king of Serbia, young prince Petar Karađorđević was born on 29 June 1844 as the fifth child of Prince Aleksandar Karađorđević and Princess Persida.[2] Due to various circumstances he was not born at the Court, which was undergoing a renovation at the time, but at the house of the renowned merchant Miša Anastasijević. His birth was not specially celebrated, except in Valjevo, where the his mother's family (the Nenadovićs) lived, since Petar was the third son, and his elder brother Svetozar was the heir to the throne. It was only upon Svetozar's untimely death in 1847 that he became the heir to the throne.

Petar spent his childhood in Belgrade and Topola, from where the Karađorđević family originated. He received elementary education in Belgrade schools, never standing apart from other town children. Not only did he spend school classes with his classmates but they also played together in all the parts of the city they could reach. In this way he became acquainted with the life of ordinary townspeople, his peers from both rich and poor town families alike. During summer vacations in Topola he learned about rural life. There he played with peasant sons from the surrounding villages, frequented ordinary country homes and wandered through the landscapes of Šumadija.

At that time Belgrade was still both a Serb and a Turkish town, since the Turks kept a garrison there. The young Petar got acquainted with this world in various ways. With a host of his peers he fought with the Turkish 'hosts' in the fields outside the town. After one of these fights Nikola Hristić, a member of the town government, had to intervene using all his prestige and skill on Petar's behalf. But on the other hand, by paying visits to the Vizier's quarters with his mother Persida he learned about the manners and way of life of noble Belgrade Turks.

The Period of Exile

His departure to a college in Geneva in 1858 coincided with his father's dethronement. The Obrenović dynasty again ruled Serbia. An emigre life, constantly accompanied by financial difficulties, began for the Karađorđević family.

After four years in Switzerland, in 1861 Petar was taken to Paris and enrolled in College Sainte Barbe, located in the heart of Latin Quarter and founded as far back as 1430. A year later he entered the renowned military academy Saint-Cyr, where he stayed until 1864. After finishing the academy he continued to live in Paris for some time, where he passed his time engaged in photography and painting. His education was continued in Metz, where he entered the Higher Military School which he attended for almost two years (1866-1867).

When in 1870 Franco-Prussian war broke out he joined the Foreign Legion as Lieutenant Petar Kara, together with his relative Nikola Nikolajević. They belonged to the 15th Corps headed by General Martin Paggier. He fought at Orleans and at Villersexel in the difficult battle of 9 January 1871. His conduct there earned him a Legion of Honour award, but was soon thereafter captured. He managed to escape captivity and went back to the fighting. The story of his participation in the 1871 Commune of Paris is still covered by a cloak of mystery. What is known is that he took part with his friend and relative Vlada Ljotić.

When the Serbian insurrection against the Turkish rule in broke out in late June 1875 in the Hercegovinian town of Nevesinje, and later spreading into Bosnia, Petar decided to take an active part in it. On the territory of Banija and Kordun he gathered and organised a force of about

200 men. He spent almost all his money on the enterprise. Under the secret name Petar Mrkonjić he reached Dubica, in Bosnia, in August, where he contacted insurgent leaders. Instead of the expected welcome, he encountered mistrust, reserve, envy, calculation, cowardice, and even open hostility. There he also learned about the planned attempt on his life prepared by Prince Milan Obrenović. Obrenović believed that young prince Petar came to Bosnia with the intention of winning popularity and making contacts which would enable him to regain the throne in Serbia.

Battles in Bosnia did not go well for the future king. Defeated, he and his men had to withdraw back to Austrian territory. There, Austrian soldiers interned some them at the village of Bojna in Banija, and some in Glina. Petar escaped from detention and organised another group of men. He was present at assemblies of Serb leaders and received various couriers. He travelled to Zagreb and Vienna, and then went back to Bosnia, fighting until the end of May 1876. Young prince Petar's successes in guerilla warfare aroused the suspicion of the Belgrade government against him. As his involvement in the insurrection threatened to cause divisions among the insurrectionists between Prince Milan's followers, the young prince Petar's followers, and Austrian supporters, Petar Mrkonjić withdrew from Bosnia, disappointed and unhappy, impoverished, and his plans unfulfilled. Before leaving he wrote a letter to Prince Milan explaining his departure as being motivated exclusively being in the interests of the Serb people, expressing his willingness to work personally, if necessary, on eradicating, once and for all, the hatred between the two dynasties and their adherents.

Accusations against the young prince were still being spread from Serbia. In an attempt to prove his innocence and patriotism, he decided to come to Kragujevac and explain his attitude and conduct before the National Assembly. After the Topola Rebellion in 1877 he was accused of a conspiracy against the Prince and the Obrenović dynasty, as well as of collaborating with the Turks. In the summer of 1878 he illegally crossed the Danube into Serbia near Golubac, but with his escort he got lost in the Homolje mountains, where he hid from police persecution. He then returned to the Austrian side of the border, where he was arrested, and then interned at the family estate at Bokszeg. In late 1878 he was allowed to leave Bokszeg, from where he went to Budapest, and then to Paris. At all these places he was constantly watched by spies who reported on his movement and contacts.

In January 1879, whist he was in France, court proceedings in Smederevo were initiated against him and his companions, *in absentia*, on charges of high treason. The court sentenced him to goal. Thus, Petar was prevented from freely returning to his homeland.

In 1883 at the age of 39, Petar came to Cetinje, the capital of the other free Serb state of Montenegro. He came as a guest of Prince Boža Petrović, whom he had met in Paris. At the Saint-Cyr military academy he had met another Montenegrin, Stanko Radonjić, and now a minister in the government of Montenegro. While staying with Boža Petrović, he often called at the court of Montenegro's ruler, Prince Nikola, where he finally met Prince's eldest daughter Zorka. The idea of arranging, with Prince Nikola, a marriage to Zorka had been in Petar's before coming to Cetinje. This aroused great disquiet and concern in Belgrade, Vienna and St. Petersburg. The wedding, which took place in the summer of 1883, provoked a change for the worse in the relations between the two Serb courts at Cetinje and in Belgrade. The relations between Austria-Hungary and Russia, the chief rivals over influence in the Balkan region, also became strained.

When his father died in spring of 1885, Petar became the head of the house of Karađorđević and took the title of prince. However, his poor financial standing made him dependent, not only on his father-in-law, Prince Nikola, but also on Russia and his brother Đorđe. After the defeat suffered by the Serbian army and King Milan in the war with Bulgaria in 1886, Petar Karađorđević and his father-in-law Nikola Petrović devised a plan to make a raid on Serbia with the aim of toppling the Obrenović dynasty. But Prince Nikola abandoned the idea at the very last minute, leaving Petar feeling betrayed, and leading to a long-standing conflict between them. Nevertheless, he remained at Cetinje until 1894, devoting himself to the family. It was in Cetinje that his sons Đorđe, in 1887, and Aleksandar, in 1888, and daughter Jelena, in 1884, were born. His wife Zorka died at the birth of his last child on 4 March 1890. This was a great loss for Petar himself and the whole Karađorđević house. The lack of maternal care significantly affected the children which was manifested in their mutual relationships upon their return to Serbia. This was a general observation of all those who stayed at the Court or were close to the family. Petar strove to provide his children with a happy childhood and good education. They received their first education at Cetinje, particularly in the history of the

Serb people and its literature. After that the family moved to Geneva, to stay until their return to Serbia in 1903.

In the meantime, Petar travelled widely throughout Europe and Russia, sometimes meeting with opponents of the regime in Serbia. He helped their political activity and propaganda with modest contributions.

King of Serbia

During preparations, between 1901 and 1903, of the plot to replace King Aleksandar Obrenović, the conspirators decided in favour of Prince Petar Karađorđević at a meeting of officers and politicians in November 1901. Their attempts to get in touch with Petar were initially refused. He had no great trust in Serbian politicians and political parties. He finally agreed to meet their emissary Hadži Toma in Lucerne. He consented to be the candidate only after he was informed that officers he trusted were also taking part in the conspiracy. This was the only meeting between him and the plotters. Hadži Toma failed to inform the conspirators that Petar insisted that he himself would not take part in the conspiracy. He vigorously stipulated that he or his dynasty should come to the throne through the regular procedure, that is, by a decision of the *Skupština* (Assembly). Further contacts with the conspirators were made through his Vienna friend Jaša Nenadović. All news about the developing situation and the attitudes of Russia and Austria-Hungary toward the overthrow of the Obrenovićs came through Nenadović. On the eve of the 1903 coup which toppled the Obrenović dynasty, Petar was engaged in completely different matters, such as planning a journey to Russia and then to Romania, and meeting his children during vacation. This suggests the conclusion that he was ignorant about the putsch itself. In his first response to the cable sent from Vienna by Jaša Nenadović he expressed satisfaction, but also regret that bloodshed had occurred, 'which was not gentlemanly, nor worthy of 20th century'. After the assassination of King Aleksandar and Queen Draga, by a decision of the *Skupština* on 15 June 1903 he was called to assume the throne of Serbia.

Together with a deputation of the *Skupština*, he left Geneva for Belgrade via Vienna and Budapest. This journey was already organised as a royal one. In Vienna he was solemnly welcomed and sent off. He was welcomed by, amongst others, Serbian and Croatian students, and greeted as the 'first Yugoslav king'. He arrived in Belgrade on 26 June, after an absence of 45 years.

Coming to the Serbian throne gave King Petar the opportunity to apply his knowledge, beliefs and experiences acquired over the decades spent in European countries. There he had witnessed many changes, especially in France and Switzerland. He remembered particularly well the appearance of the rule of Napoleon III in France: formal democracy and formal liberties which the police and central government ignored as they pleased, accompanied by all sorts of corruption. He, however, also witnessed the rise of the freedom-loving opposition to this regime, which, for all the nations of Europe, demanded universal suffrage, freedom of the press, freedom of public meetings and freedom of association. Napoleon had to yield to such demands.

Petar had also been in contact with the free-thinking spirit among foreigners in Switzerland; the ideas of 'Ujedinjena omladina srpska' ('United Serb Youth'), founded in Novi Sad in 1866. The platform of this organisation stated that 'without freedom our people cannot progress', and it was completely accepted by Petar. Thus, it was no coincidence that Petar decided to translate into Serbian the work of the English economist and philosopher John Stuart Mill, *On Liberty.* The commitments of his youth were fully expressed in the preface that he wrote to the translation:

> 'Freedom opens a nation's eyes, so that it can learn its defects and correct them; freedom gives it an opportunity to know its virtues, develop them and turn them into deeds, whereby it hardens its strength, improves its spiritual and physical well-being, in order to participate, in cooperation with other nations, in bringing humankind closer to the goal set by God....All that today's knowledge is proud of,...all that has promoted and advanced today's sciences, all that has increased by a hundredfold, or been perfected, and invigorated the power of the people - all this is fruit brought by the freedom of man, by the freedom of the people!'[3]

The time Petar spent living in Montenegro and observing the rule of his father-in-law Prince Nikola, could only confirm the validity of his democratic beliefs. There he saw in real life, and often found out the hard way himself, what the arbitrariness and despotism of a ruler meant. He could see how honest and deserving people were humiliated and ridiculed for no reason, how the strongest of characters were broken, how virtuous patriarchal life was being penetrated by decay and corruption, and how, even if it were at the expense of the national interest and prestige, the highest positions were given over to people of poor qualities, but pleasing to the ruler.

He, thus, assumed the Serbian throne as a convinced democrat and enlightener, eager to see his country and his people advance as quickly as possible.

Facing the circumstances and state of affairs in Serbia, he strove to ensure that the necessary changes be adjusted to the traditional values of the Serbian society. Although he relegated home policy to political parties he always wanted to have close and direct contact with ordinary people, particularly peasants who comprised the majority of the Serbian population. In the summer of 1905 he uttered the little known, but highly significant, words: 'Without the people's love, worldly thrones are shaky'. On the same occasion he warned that the people's love could only be won by respecting the law.

When meeting peasants and their emissaries he always advised and instructed them. He urged them to work harder and more diligently, introduce new crops, but also to preserve their customs and values. He advocated better education for the young, better hygiene and better diet. He supported the development of industry, manufacturing and trade. He backed private initiative and all those who invested capital in new workshops and factories. On all occasions he urged manufacturers and merchants to accept modern business ways.

In the context of the contemporary international relations and plans for the forthcoming liberation of the Serb people outside the borders of Serbia, as the ruler and the commander-in-chief of the army, he paid special attention to its improvement and modernisation. Not surprisingly, the issue of supplying the Serb army with modern artillery from France was a major priority for Petar soon after becoming King in 1903.

The issues of providing the army with new equipment and of speeding up railroad construction - which was a prerequisite for general modernisation - were closely related to the condition of the state budget, and to the sensitive issue of relations with big powers as well. During his rule, and in spite of the Customs War imposed by Austria-Hungary in 1906, Serbia managed to balance its finances and make considerable advances in all areas within the competence of the state, thereby stimulating enterprise.

At this point, too, King Petar himself was setting the best personal example. Having come to Serbia burdened with his own and many debts, he lived sparingly within the confines of his state salary from which all expenditures of the Court were financed, including those for military personnel.

King Petar was a true believer and greater respected Church and Orthodox Christianity. He thought they should play an important role in the revival of the people and the state. He believed that the duty of the clergy was to fortify in the people their ancestral faith and the traditions stemming from St. Sava. The clergy were also supposed to inculcate patriotic sentiments into the people. With his European experience, he was extremely broad-minded and tolerant to other nations. Any excess or impropriety by clergymen was sharply criticised by him. One of his great wishes was to leave a religious monument behind him, in the manner of ancient Serbian medieval rulers. He chose Topola, the home of the Karađorđević family. On the Oplenac hill above the town of Topola he built St. Đorđe's Church and buried the remains of his forefathers there.

King Petar's national-political programme was shaped primarily by his firm belief that the liberation and unification of the Serbs of the Balkan region was necessary. This included Serbs from the Ottoman Empire in the provinces of Raška and Kosovo, the cradle of ancient Serbian statehood; the region of Macedonia, which contained the capital, Skoplje, of the medieval Serbian Empire of Emperor Dušan; Bosnia and Hercegovina, occupied in 1878 by Austria-Hungary, and subsequently annexed in 1908, where the Serbs were the majority population, despite the permanent emigration of many to Serbia during the nineteenth century; as well as Vojvodina, with its centuries-old Serb intellectual centres at Karlovci and Novi Sad. At the time when these legitimate national interests were being articulated Serbia was manoeuvring in an unfavourable international environment, so that national interests were combined with strategic ones, above all the aspiration to gain access to sea. This suggested close cooperation, or a union, between the two Serb of Serbia and Montenegro.

In his vision, Serbia was to become not only an attractive centre for gathering Serbs together, but economically and socially attractive for others as well - Croats, Slovenes, and Muslims. King Petar advocated 'cultural Yugoslavism' as a means of South Slavs getting to know each other and establishing closer mutual links. Thus, he was the sponsor and patron of many gatherings, congresses and exhibitions in Belgrade between 1903 and 1914. It was in Petar's time that Ivan Meštrović began his career of court sculptor and friend of the house of Karađorđević, earning generous sinecures, to be continued in the Kingdom of Yugoslavia.

Unfortunately, both the king's good intentions and the whole Karađorđević dynasty were overshadowed by what could be defined by just one word: 'conspirators'. These were the people who toppled the previous dynasty and thus enabled his return to Serbia. This group, made up mainly by officers, to whom Petar felt grateful and loyal, often abused his good will. Because of them the King came into conflict with other constitutional factors, but also with some foreign states, England in particular, which refused to recognise the new dynasty as long as 'the murderers of the King and the Queen' remained at large. This obstacle was only partially removed when in 1906 the senior conspirators were pensioned into retirement. Nevertheless, the conspirators - or, as they were often called, 'the army' - remained a prominent factor in domestic and foreign policy. The Government and the *Skupština* were incapable of containing this influence, and on some occasions looked upon them with benevolence.

The officers thought that when the grand battle for the nation was being prepared the actions of state institutions and parliamentary democracy had to be more efficient and speedier. This was not easy to achieve, because the necessary political culture and tolerance were lacking, and because political parties engaged each other in incessant quarrels, sometimes causing parliamentary crises. The senior military officials became dissatisfied and impatient, leading them to play, at times, a decisive role in state affairs. The importance of the military rose, and it become an institution for whose political support Serbia's political parties competed. The military's influence always grew with the escalation of internal crises, wars and diplomatic disputes.

The conspirators were also divided among themselves and in mutual conflict, drawing into these affairs the king's sons Đorđe and Aleksandar. In 1911 the most prominent circle of conspirators formed the secret organisation 'Ujedinjenje ili smrt' ('Unification or Death'), soon to be renamed 'Crna ruka' ('Black Hand') by its opponents. Its primary purpose was the realisation of the goal of Serb national liberation from Ottoman and Austro-Hungarian rule. The idea itself was shared by the sovereign, by civilian state officials and the most powerful political parties, but the way in which the conspirators meddled in these affairs in a complex international environment caused grave consequences, and compromised Serbia's parliamentary system of government. In the end, after the victorious Balkan

Wars, the relations between the military (conspirators) and the civilian authorities (the Radical Party) became so tense that the king was forced to withdraw, and on the very eve of the July crisis in 1914 he transferred the royal prerogative to his heir Aleksandar, whereby the latter became the regent. King Petar's actual rule came to an end.

King Petar experienced his greatest moments of glory and triumph during the Balkan Wars of 1912-1913. The victories of the Serbian army in the two wars sanctioned by subsequent peace agreements, greatly expanded Serbia's territory. Most of the territories, once belonging to the medieval Serbian empire but subsequently occupied by the Ottoman Empire, were now liberated and united with Serbia. A common border with Montenegro was established. The glory of these victories was shared with the army, and it was the clash between one faction of the army and civilian authorities that led to the king - The Great Liberator - to step aside in favour of his son Aleksandar.

World War I

In June 1914, just four days after he arrived in Ribarska Banja to have medical treatment and a rest, he received the news that the heir to the Austro-Hungarian throne, Archduke Franz Ferdinand and his wife Sofia were assassinated in Sarajevo. Realising the possible serious consequences this could mean for Serbia, he immediately sent a long letter to his son Aleksandar advising him that the government should disassociate itself from the assassination and condemn it officially. He recommended extreme restraint.

King Petar and *Vojvoda* Putnik were the only ones who possessed the keys to the safe where war plans were kept. Since Putnik was abroad, the king was urgently called to Belgrade so that the plans could be retrieved. He immediately returned Ribarska Banja, where he heard that military preparedness had been ordered. On that day he noted in his diary: 'This means the beginning of war with those barbarians - the Austro-Hungarians'. He followed the battle of Cer[4] from Vranjska Banja, and the September 1914 operations from Topola, where he supervised the building of his endowment, St. Đorđe's Church. He particularly worried for his son, Đorđe, who was in the midst of heavy battles in the mountains over the river Drina as a unit commander. When he learned that Đorđe was wounded on 19 September he immediately went to Krupanj to see him, and together they travelled on to Valjevo. From Valjevo he again went to Topola, frantically trying to speed up the work on the church so that it could be finished as soon as possible.

He felt much aggrieved about the news of the Serbian troops retreating from the Drina. The reports he was receiving from the Supreme Command on the difficult conditions in the army, particularly on the lessening of morale and desertion, made him decide to go to the front at once, to inspire morale into the troops again. This initiative of his was misunderstood by Regent Aleksandar and a very embittered exchange of cables took place between father and son. The Supreme Command and *Vojvoda* Putnik took the king's side, while the government ministers were opposed. Petar was proven to be right. His arrival belied Austro-Hungarian propaganda and raised morale in all the units he visited.

After the planned withdrawal of Serbia's government from Belgrade, Petar reached Kragujevac, the seat of the Supreme Command, on 1 December. The king was determined to appear among the soldiers at the front line. He ordered a horse readied for him, although his doctor had long ago forbidden him to ride. When warned not to move around and that his difficulties with keeping in the saddle would make the impression even poorer, he replied: 'Don't worry, I'll sit up.'

So, on 2 December 1914, a day before the famous Kolubara counter-offensive started, he showed up at the 2nd Army front. Having made a round of the most exposed posts, he addressed tired and cold soldiers with the following words: 'I'm here, and I'll stay with my sons to the end to defend the homeland. Who's afraid and doesn't want to fight, he's free to go!' His action was a significant boost to morale. For the ensuing few days he was constantly with the troops.

Some ten days later, when the fortunes of war changed completely to the Serbs' advantage, King Petar and his two sons were at the first fighting lines. Their adjutants had troubles stopping them and sheltering them in safer places. At the foot of the Avala the court car reached advanced infantry guards, almost stumbling into Austrian forward positions. For members of a dynasty in World War I, this was a unique behaviour. On the morning of 15 December, while battles in Belgrade itself and around it were still going on, King Petar set off to the town by car. Upon arrival in Belgrade the king first went to the main Serbian Orthodox Cathedral, notwithstanding nearby gunfire. The old Belgrade merchant Đorđe Radulović related later that he saw the King and couldn't believe his eyes, since Austrian patrols were still cruising the town.[5]

The great victory of the Serbian army in December 1914, known as the battle of Kolubara,[6] not only resulted in driving the occupier away from Serbia, but also ensured ten months of peace without war operations. Great joy spread over the country. King Petar, Regent Aleksandar, the Supreme Command and the Government were receiving congratulations from abroad. The King, in good humour, left Belgrade, to celebrate his family patron's day St. Andrija in Aranđelovac.

The time until October 1915, when the offensive of the Austro-Hungarian, German and Bulgarian armies against Serbia began, Petar spent at Vranjska Banja and Oplenac, supervising the building of his endowment. The great typhus plague which carried away about 30,000 soldiers and 100,000 civilians deeply shook him. War casualties and victims of the plague represented a great loss. He was worried about how these losses would be felt after the war.

The lull in fighting during 1915 saw significant diplomatic pressure being placed upon Serbia by the Allies, in which the King was involved. Intent on persuading Bulgaria to enter the war at the side of the Entente, the Allies demanded that Serbia give Macedonia over to the Bulgarians. In July 1915 a proposal was prepared according to which Serbia would not get Bosnia-Hercegovina and access to the Adriatic Sea unless it ceded Macedonia to Bulgaria. The proposal also envisaged an end to financial aid for Serbia as long as she agreed to the proposal. An ultimatum was handed to the Serbian government on 4 August 1915. At the same time, the king received personal letters from the Russian tsar, the kings of Italy and Great Britain, and the president of France. Regent Aleksandar immediately visited the king, and Nikola Pašić, the prime minister, did the same on 11 August. Pašić explained the motives of his visit by the need to warn the king not to reply to foreign rulers without the consent of the Government and Skupština. Pašić wanted to preclude the possibility of Petar replying in a manner contrary to the intentions of the Government and needs of the country. The king interpreted the Allies' note as a demand to revise the Bucharest Peace Treaty of 1913 and was against it as it made demands on Serbia with nothing in return.

After a secret session of the parliament on 15 August, Pašić came to Oplenac again to draft the reply with the king. Their views were similar. They put together an essentially negative reply, hoping to buy time in this way. The reply did not satisfy the Allies, while at the same time Bulgaria was already negotiating cooperation with Germany and Austria-Hungary.

In the face of the offensive of joint enemy forces from Austria-Hungary, Germany and Bulgaria, launched on 5 October 1915,[7] the Serbian army slowly withdrew, in heavy autumn weather, constantly fighting along the way, and expecting a more energetic assistance by the Allies from Salonika. Unfortunately, due to various circumstances, and above all, the conduct of Greece, such aid never came. The result was the complete withdrawal of the Serbian army and a mass of civilians across Montenegrin and Albanian mountains to the Albanian coast, and into uncertainty.

King Petar left Oplenac on 23 October, visiting the Supreme Command, headquarters of particular armies and the units. In Kruševac he saw that discipline was beginning to lapse, looting began, and the will to fight was dropping. The Serbian Supreme Command was successfully manoeuvring its forces, not allowing the enemy to surround its larger formations. The king had to retreat together with the army. Until 6 November he travelled in a car, and then moved to a cannon wagon. In this way he arrived in Prokuplje and then on to Priština and Prizren.

During the retreat, at a moment of widespread despair, in Regent Aleksandar's suite they realised nobody knew where the king was. It soon turned out that he was at the front, 'exposing himself in order to get killed, like in the battle of Kosovo'. Witnesses relate that he said he did not want to leave the country alive, so that people would call him a 'deserter', like Karađorđe. They had a hard time persuading him to come to Prizren.

When Bulgarian advance units came as close as eight kilometres away from Prizren, the local front commander General Petar Bojović most energetically demanded that the king leave, because robber bands were already prepared to start killing and looting in the town. On 28 November Petar set off to Ljum-Kula. The car ride was very short; he then went on a horse, and then on foot. The king was walking slowly, with a small escort of just a dozen men. Any Serbian soldier and refugee could see that he was sharing all the misfortunes just like they were - wrapped in a soldier's overcoat with no sign of rank at all, an officer's cap on his head, and a cane in his hand.

'King Petar was a great man. The coldest and most terrible night was on 30 November, my birthday; we spent the night in a demolished tower between Ljum-Kula and Spas. At Spas we found the old king, sitting all night long by the fireplace, so that the houses could shelter the refugees.

My wife made and served him a tea.' These were the words Regent Aleksandar's aide-de-camp Panta Draškić wrote down in his diary.[8]

The King seemed not to care about his personal safety. He was escorted by just four armed guards. He separated himself from both the Government and the Supreme Command which travelled toward Shkoder. He did not wish to take the same direction, turning toward Lješ instead. In this way he avoided a meeting with the Montenegrin king, Nikola, as well as heated disputes about the responsibility for the defeat which had sprung up between the government and the Supreme Command, and among members of parliament themselves. Along the way he met soldiers whom Esad Paša had sent to meet him. They accompanied him from Lješ to Tirana, though he expressed disapproval. The Government learned about him only on 9 December, when he was already in Tirana, a town controlled by the Serbian troops since the summer of 1915. Communications between himself and the government went through the Serbian consulate in Durres. He met with Esad Paša, visited Serbian troops and recruits that were retreating in this direction. He did not refrain from advising the government in Shkoder how best to prevent massive casualties amongst the soldiers.

In Durres and Vlore, towns which he passed on his road to exile, he experienced grave humiliations by Italian military representatives. This was the reason why, upon his arrival in Brindisi, he refused the hospitality of the Italian royal couple to continue his stay in Italy and spend some time in one of the royal cottages. Instead he took a boat to Salonika, where he arrived on 1 January. There he found parts of the army and other refugees in a miserable condition. Shaken, exhausted and sick, he boarded a French ship to the island of Edypsos, to the Eubea spa for recuperation.

He came back to Salonika in late December 1916. At that moment the well-known 'Salonika Process' was being prepared against the leading members of *'Crna ruka'*, including Colonel Dragutin Dimitrijević-Apis. In exile, while the Allies were losing ground on all fronts, the last act of a drama, that in a sense began on the night of 29 May, 1903, when King Aleksandar Obrenović and his wife were killed, took place. The manner in which this process was carried out, the accusations of 'preparing a rebellion in the army', and the allegations of planning the 'assassination' of Regent Aleksandar, had a long-lasting impact on the life of Kingdom of Yugoslavia after 1918. Regent Aleksandar allied himself closely with one group of officers, and this would greatly influence future military and political circumstances.

At all times prior to 1914, Petar protected the *'Crna ruka'* conspirators, just as did *Vojvoda* Putnik and the minister of defence Colonel Rade Bojović. The latter two men were both removed from office during the retreat through Albania. All the posts in the army crucial for carrying out the court process were filled by Regent Aleksandar's loyal men. Pašić, the prime minister, also supported the removal of *'Crna ruka'* members from the military, but through sending them to retirement. It was only later that he consented to the court process. The king was certainly not informed about the details of judicial preparations. Two days before Colonel Apis was arrested, Colonel Kostić, who was familiar with the preparations, was received by the King. It is a reasonable assumption that in their 20 minute meeting, Petar was informed about what was in the offing. On 27 December he noted in his diary: 'Last night they brought to Salonika Colonel Dimitrijević (Apis) whom they had arrested and charged with 'high treason'. Tomorrow I'll learn about the whole affair. They say they have a mountain of evidence' This obviously indicates they did not present him the actual bill of indictment, perhaps out of fear of a negative response. Between 25 to 31 December Petar received no visitors. Unfortunately, the most valuable source on Petar's actions and views on these events, his diary, stops at this point. We do not know whether he continued writing it or whether it was deliberately hidden after his death. Other sources only indirectly suggest his demeanour in the whole affair. The members of the tribunal visited him several times before the proceedings commenced. During the proceedings he also separately received Colonels Josif Kostić, and Petar Živković, who stood behind the whole process. The main promoters of the whole idea were certainly eager to win him over because he had the right to grant a pardon. Knowing this, Apis also addressed the king a letter, asking him to 'stop the whole thing'.

In May 1917 Petar received the internal affairs Jovanović and prime minister Pašić. After the tribunal's verdict and death sentences were delivered, he was again visited by Colonel Kostić. In the days when the pardon applications of the condemned were to be considered, Colonel Živković was the king's most frequent visitor. There are several subsequent testimonies to the effect that both the heir to the throne Aleksandar and Petar desired the death of the most prominent conspirators. Did the old father fear for his son's life and the future of the dynasty? He ignored their earlier service and their close relations with him. Neither he nor Aleksandar took into account the impact of the verdict on Allied public opinion and political circles, or even in the Serbian army, which was fighting outside the country. Prince Đorđe was also in Salonika during the process. He was of a different opinion, and he was shunned by the organisers of the process.

After the Salonika Process the King stayed for some time in Salonika, and then set off for Athens. Until the end of the war he stayed in the Athenian suburb of Kastela, in a nice villa at the seaside. Illnesses took their toll and Petar grew increasingly isolated from political and military events. He was most worried about the uncertain fate of his elder daughter Jelena in the tumultuous days of the Russian revolution.

It was in the spring of 1918 before Petar again became involved in events of the day. He closely followed the German offensive in France, and then the victorious end of the war. Precisely in those days of celebration he was overpowered by a grave illness which, together with the necessary recovery, postponed his return to Serbia.[9]

Abdication and Last Days

The king returned to his country in the summer of 1919, when he formally abdicated the throne in favour of his son Aleksandar. In July he arrived in Aranđelovac, a well-known spa near Topola and Oplenac. In September he arrived in Belgrade. He spent his last days in a villa on the Točider hill, where he died on 13 August 1921.

King Petar really was a person held in high esteem, apart from very rare exceptions, by his contemporaries. According to them he was, the embodiment of the love for freedom, a fighting spirit, persistent and always ready for sacrifice. He personified heroism, in the overall suffering and agony of a people, that sacrificed much for the realisation of national ideals - ideals believed in by generations from 1804 to 1918, and which Petar shared from his earliest days. A king elected, just like his father, by the *Skupština*, he strove to be a monarch within strict constitutional limits. He made mistakes, but also admitted them. He endeavoured to set his country on the road of genuine democracy and modernisation.

(Translated from the Serbian original by Ivana Spasić.)

Notes

1 Several commemorative publications and memorials on the life of King Petar I and the Karađorđević dynasty have been published in Yugoslavia and abroad. His personal diaries and memoirs have also been published. The most comprehensive account of his life and work is the three-volume study by Dragoljub Živojinović: Živojinović (1988), Živojinović (1990), Živojinović (1994). See also Pavlović-Krpa (1922), Vukićević (1924), and Karađorđević (1969).

2 The children of Persida and Prince Aleksandar were as follows: Poleksija (1833-1914), Kleopatra (1835-1855), Aleksa (1836-1841), Svetozar (1841-1847), Petar, Jelena (1846-1867), Andrija (1848-1864), Jelisaveta (1852- ?), Đorđe (1856- ?), Arsen (1859-1936): Mrđenović, Palavestra & Spasić (1987), p. 199

3 The translation of Mill's On Liberty was probably from a French translation of the original text. The translation was completed by the end of 1867, and printed in Vienna the following year. Of the 2,200 copies printed, Petar donated 2,000 to the fund of United Serb Youth in Novi Sad. A reprint of his translation appeared in Belgrade in 1911. See Živojinović (1988), pp. 56-60.

4 The Battle of Cer, in the north-west of Serbia, along the Drina and Sava rivers, was fought in August, 1914, with the decisive battle taking place in the Cer mountain between 16-19 August. This was a defeat for the Austro-Hungarian army and the first victory for the Allies in World War I.

5 Vukićević (1924), p. 49, Draškić (1990), pp. 103-105, and Živojinović (1994), pp. 40-41.

6 The Battle of Kolubara began on 6 November 1914 with the withdrawal of Serbian army forces from the Drina and the Sava to the Kolubara river. The defeat of Austro-Hungarian troops was great, but the Serbian army lost 150,000 men, including the dead, wounded, sick and captured.

7 The assault was started by the Austro-Hungarian and German armies under the command of Marshall Mackensen, while the Bulgarian armies attacked from the east on 13 October. The retreat of the Serbian army and part of its civilian population was completed on 26

January 1916, when the French helped them evacuate to the Greek island of Corfu and to Bizerta in Tunisia.

8 Draškić (1990), p. 128.

9 King Petar suffered from rheumatism, arteriosclerosis and a loss of hearing in one ear. In the autumn of 1918 he got pneumonia. The rheumatism was probably a legacy of the Franco-Prussian War of 1870-71 and the guerilla warfare in Bosnia in the 1870s. His condition worsened dramatically after the retreat through Albania.

References

Draškić, Panta M. (1990), *Moji memoari,* Srpska književna zadruga, Belgrade.

Karađorđević, Đorđe (1969), *Istina o mom životu,* Belgrade.

Mrđenović, Dušan, Palavestra, Aleksandar & Spasić, Dušan (1987), *Rodoslovne tablice i grbovi Srpskih dinastija i vlastele,* Nova Knjiga, Belgrade.

Pavlović-Krpa, Milorad (1922), *Priče iz života kralja Petra,* Belgrade.

Vukićević, Milenko M. (1924), *Kralj Petar, od rođenja do smrti,* Zagreb.

Živojinović, Dragoljub R. (1988), *Petar I Karađorđević, život i delo, u izgnanstvu 1844-1903. godine,* Bigz, Belgrade.

Živojinović, Dragoljub R. (1990), *Petar I Karađorđević, život i delo, u otadžbini 1903-1914. godine,* Bigz, Belgrade.

Živojinović, Dragoljub R. (1994), *Petar I Karađorđević, život i delo, rat i poslednje godine 1914-1921. godine* Bigz, Belgrade.

5 Radomir Putnik

DIMITRIJE DJORDJEVIĆ

Introduction

The lives and careers of two men are deeply embedded in the history of Serbia at the turn of the century and during the decade preceding World War I. They were nearly the same age and collaborated closely. One was a politician, the other a soldier. Nikola Pašić, the leader of the Radical Party, guided Serbian politics in the stormy international and domestic crisis before and during the war. Radomir Putnik, the patriarch of Serbian soldiery, prepared the army for the coming war and held the post of commander-in-chief during the victorious battles of 1912-1914 and the defeat suffered in 1915.

Both men shared exciting and turbulent careers, in accordance with the dynamic times in which they lived. The politician had the better fortune. Destiny allowed Pašić to witness the victorious issue of the struggle he waged. Fortune was less inclined to the soldier. Putnik started his career with a defeat in the war of 1876 and ended it in exile, after the 1915 invasion of his country. He died before the war ended and was unable to see the victorious result of the campaign to which he sacrificed his life.

However, the 'finest hour' of vojvoda Putnik was during the 1912-1915 battles in which he waged two wars: one for the survival of his country, the other for his own survival. The Serbian armies were fighting a desperate war to repulse the invader. Their commander, Putnik, orchestrated the strategy of defence and counter-attack from his bedside, terminally ill from emphysema and fighting for each breath of his paralysed lungs.

Both the army and its commander scored brilliant victories at Kumanovo, Bregalnica, Cer and Kolubara. They were both defeated in 1915. Serbia survived, Putnik did not.

Early Military Career

'Putnik' in Serbian means traveller. This was the name which the poor emigrant from Kosovo, Arsenije, gave to the Hungarian authorities at the end of the eighteenth century. Balkan people, pushed away from their homes by wars and famines, were true travellers. However, deeply attached to the old country, the Putnik family returned to Serbia in the early 1830s. The autonomous principality, recently emancipated from Ottoman rule, needed skilled people. Arsenije's son Dimitrije Putnik, got a job as a teacher in Kragujevac. The family had five children. The second son Radomir was born on 24 January 1847.[1]

For children of poor families, without land or money, schooling was the best, if not the only, option. Among the few schools in Serbia, the Artillery School, which became the nucleus of the future Academy, offered tuition-free education, lodging, food and even some pocket money. After obtaining basic education in Kragujevac, Radomir Putnik moved to Belgrade and joined the cadets.[2]

The Balkan man nurtured a respect for the army. History and self-protection taught him to keep a gun at home. The uniform symbolised power. The army was the instrument of national liberation.[3] The Serbian army, which Radomir Putnik joined, had originated in the 1804 uprising against the Ottomans and had a peasant character. The organisation of regular, standing army units started in the 1830s. However, it was only in 1861 that compulsory military service was introduced for the adult male population. This kind of 'armed people's' militia was finally modernised in 1883 and again at the end of the century.[4]

The Artillery school, which Radomir Putnik joined, had been founded in 1850.[5] Its first director, a Czech officer named Frantishek Zah, was under the influence of the French military doctrine, while his successor, Milojko Lešjanin, was a student of the Berlin Kriegsakademie.

Twenty-three cadets were enrolled in the same class with Putnik. Seventeen of them graduated in 1866. Putnik ranked eighth among them. Obviously the score was not brilliant. However, Napoleon ranked forty-second in a class of fifty-eight. Other distinguished Serbian military leaders proved a similar average: Vojvoda Živojin Mišić was twenty-first, and vojvoda Stepa Stepanović fourteenth in rank in their classes. In spite of the grades, Putnik's class was to produce eight generals of the Serbian army.[6]

Poverty in childhood often results in toughness during adulthood. The genes inherited from a peasant ancestry produce frugality and deep attachment to the native soil. Patriarchal society preaches the morality of the dominant male. Military training imposes subordination and discipline. All these traits can be found in the character of Radomir Putnik.

The majority of European military leaders and generals prior to World War I belonged to the aristocratic elite of their countries. Not so with the Serbian military, who were almost all of peasant, or nascent middle-class, social layers.

Radomir Putnik was one of these self-made men, deeply steeped in the Balkan environment. Only in his mid-thirties did he start learning foreign languages, in order to study European military literature. His professional training was obtained in Serbia, although it was strongly influenced by French and German military doctrines. Only once did he stray abroad, for a six months study of a military factory in Hotin, in Russia.[7]

The rigid atmosphere of the Artillery School might have contributed to the introverted character of Putnik. Chain smoking, which later caused a heavy emphysema, was a sign of inner tension, aggravated by intense work and total submission to duty. Even at a young age Putnik found himself alienated from the talkative and ebullient Belgrade society. His in-laws called him 'the grouch', and his subordinates referred to him as a 'chronic cougher' (*kašljavko*).[8] They respected him, but did not love him.

We do not know much about Putnik's personal life. In 1879 he married Ljubica Bojović, the daughter of a colonel of the general-staff. They had seven children, three girls and four boys. Three of them were educated in Russia; two boys attended military schools and a girl joined a finishing school at Smolni.[9] After his wife died in 1913, Putnik lived with his younger daughter, who stayed with him until he died in exile.

Life in Putnik's household was austere. His deputy, Živojin Mišić, described one of the rooms; it had a sofa, a table without a tablecloth and a couple of chairs - that was all;[10] like a room in the military barracks.

Remoteness and seclusion did not fit the turbulent political life of the young country, which went through dynastic conflicts and coups d'etat at the end of the century. Personal integrity could only aggravate the case. The newly promoted captain Putnik was punished with fifteen days of detention during the 1876 war when he clashed with his superior officer over the food supply for his unit. Putnik was pardoned only when his brave conduct on the battlefield was reported to general Cherniaev.[11] On two further occasions, in 1881 and 1883, Putnik was again punished with fifteen days of detention for 'using strong words' in correspondence with his superior.[12]

The most serious jeopardy to Putnik's career came from his disfavour into which he fell with both kings, Milan and Aleksandar Obrenović. A westerniser, charming but unstable, King Milan genuinely disliked the self-contained and austere young officer with didactical tendencies. The king expected his officers to comply with his requests, justified or not. When King Milan asked Putnik, a member of the officer's examination committee, to let one of his favourites pass, Putnik answered that the result depended on the candidate's performance. When this proved to be negative, Putnik failed the king's favourite.[13]

The conflict escalated. Putnik's name was stricken from the list of decorated officers. When King Aleksandar travelled in 1893 over the territory of the division under his command, Putnik sent his deputy to greet the monarch instead of doing it personally.[14] Both Milan and Aleksandar suspected Putnik of sympathising with their arch enemies, the Radical Party. The final break came when Putnik's name, accompanied with some code-like numbers, was found in the notebook of an arrested conspirator, accused of plotting against the dynasty. The irony of the entire story was that the arrested man was the owner of a quarry, from which Putnik ordered the stone for the monument to be placed on the grave of his parents. The 'secret numbers' were the specified size of the stone.[15] However, colonel Putnik was put in retirement in 1896, at the age of forty-nine.

The conflict between King Milan and Putnik harmed both of them, but mostly the Serbian army. King Milan devoted all his energies during the two last decades of the century to organising and modernising the Serbian army. Military budgets were augmented, modern arms were purchased abroad, the standing army was enlarged and numerous manoeuvres were held. A man of Putnik's experience and capacity would have been invaluable to the king in these endeavours. On the contrary, in the best years of his life, Putnik was forced to watch, inactive, the development of the army to which he dedicated his entire life.

Through three decades of service, from 1866 when he graduated from the Artillery School until 1896 when he was forced to retire, Putnik was promoted from sub-lieutenant to colonel.[16] During this time he held important posts. In 1880 he became deputy commander of the only standing army division in Serbia, and got the same duty in 1883 with the newly formed Danube division. Putnik passed the exam for general-staff officers and became the chief of the Intelligence Section of General Headquarters. Promoted in 1888 to Chief of the Operational Department of the General Headquarters, he became deputy chief-of-staff in 1890.[17]

One event largely contributed to Putnik's prestige in the army. From 1886-1887 and from 1888-1895 Putnik was a professor of the Military Academy. During this time eight classes of general-staff officers, among them the most prominent future Serbian war commanders, were his students. According to Putnik's own saying, he knew personally all Serbian officers above the rank of battalion commander.[18] With his students Putnik crossed the country during military manoeuvres. The story that he was acquainted with all the innkeepers along the roads in Serbia was close to the truth. Gifted with a phenomenal memory, Putnik knew so well the geography of his country that he was able to dictate orders during the 1914 campaign without consulting the map.[19]

During the forced retirement, Putnik returned to writing and private teaching in order to supplement his modest pension, insufficient to support his large family. Already in 1883 he had published a manual, 'Artillery in the War of Siege', based on Belgian studies and the system of detached block-houses in the chain of city fortifications. In 1890 Putnik published the manual, 'The General Staff Service in Times of Peace', and the second volume dealing with the service in times of war, in 1899.[20] The two volumes totalled 1344 pages. Based on French and German military literature, they remained textbooks in the Military Academy as late as 1927. Along with his writing, Putnik was privately preparing at home young officers for the examinations to join the general-staff service.

The seven years from 1896 to 1903 spent in retirement were the most trying in his life. After the 1899 assassination attempt against the life of King Milan and the spectacular trial of Radical Party leaders, Putnik briefly moved out of the country to avoid eventual persecution. All seemed grim and bleak. Lonely, rejected and disappointed, Putnik lived the life of a misanthrope, locked in his home and distant from the public.

Suddenly, as in the old Greek tragedies, fortune smiled on the unhappy soldier. The bloody 1903 military coup in Belgrade took the lives of King Aleksandar and his wife, and King Petar I was returned to the throne. A period of democracy in domestic policies, and dynamic nationalism in foreign affairs, was awaiting Serbia. Under the new regime Putnik was reactivated, promoted to general and appointed Chief of the general staff. This title was changed during the 1912-1918 wars into that of Chief of the Supreme Command Headquarters. Putnik was to keep this position for twelve and a half years, interrupted only when he was on duty as the minister of national defence.[21]

Through fifty years of active military service Radomir Putnik participated in six wars: two campaigns in 1876 and 1877 against Turkey, the 1885 Serbo-Bulgarian war, the two Balkan campaigns in 1912 and 1913, and World War I, whose end he did not live to see.

Captain Putnik started his war career with a defeat suffered in 1876 in the war with Turkey.[22] His own brigade sustained heavy losses at the first encounter with the Turks, at Kalipolje.[23] Through these events the young officer obtained invaluable experiences. He learned that real war was different from the one he found in textbooks. In a letter addressed to his old friend and schoolmate, the physician Vladan Đorđević, Putnik described the dichotomy between theory and practice:

> 'The concentration of troops is done fast and easy on paper. With few strokes of the pen they are already at the desired location...Only personal experience can tell about the strains and obstacles the soldiers have to face...In fact, these are long, exhausting marches through the icy rain, over mud up to the knees, and snow storms.'[24]

The defeat also taught Putnik not to be overconfident. It contributed to his already cautious nature. Later in his career, when he had to assume the post of commander-in-chief, Putnik proved to be an extremely cautious strategist. He was much better in winning the battle than in exploiting the victory. The memory of 1876 would stay hidden in his subconscience during the 1912, 1913 and 1914 campaigns.

The next war with Bulgaria in 1885 went beyond the 1876 defeat; it was a disaster for Serbia. Putnik witnessed an inefficient and uncoordinated command, as well as an unpopular war whose cause was rejected by the Serbian population.[25] The catastrophic result of the 1885 war offered to the young chief-of-staff of the Danubian division further lessons in the art of warfare. He learned about the importance of a unified command, able to evaluate the situation and to concentrate forces at the right moment and in the right place. He wrote about this in his later published volume on the general-staff activity in war: '...to direct all the forces toward the strategic target in such a way that all of them act simultaneously in regard to timing, location and effectiveness.'[26]

Putnik also learned about the importance of the initiative in carrying out military operations, which the Serbian command lacked at the battle of Slivnica. But more than these technical lessons, Putnik learned that one cannot keep the discipline of an army by beating retreating soldiers with sabres. The worst effect on soldiers' discipline is caused by exhaustion, over-extended marches and confused orders. Under a determined and effective command, wrote Putnik 'the army soon becomes aware of the skill of the people who determine its destiny.'

Through the defeats Putnik learned about two factors which determine the issue in a war: the effectiveness of the High Command and the confidence of the soldier in his leadership in fighting for a just cause.

Chief-of-Staff

All that happened before 1903 seems to be only the prelude in the life of Radomir Putnik. During that time he obtained the skills, experience and wisdom for the events that awaited him and his country in the first two decades of the twentieth century. The activity of Putnik in these times was aimed at preparing the Serbian army for the coming wars and preparing Putnik himself to command over this army during the conflicts. Essentially, the job assigned to Putnik was of a three-fold character: military, political and diplomatic.

Immediately after being appointed chief-of-staff, Putnik started reorganising the Serbian army. He restructured the peace- and war-formation of the army, added to it five new divisions of the second call-up, and made personnel changes by retiring old, and promoting young, officers. Putnik fortified the southern frontiers of the country towards Turkey and ordered the planning of strategic alternatives for an eventual war. Old plans for the war with Turkey, made in 1898 and 1903, were revised under his supervision. On the eve of the 1912 Balkan war the General Staff had at its disposal four of such alternate plans.[27] They each included the strategic targets, the forces to be engaged and the initial direction of war operations. The crisis created by the Austro-Hungarian annexation of Bosnia and Hercegovina in 1908-1909 hastened plans for the war with the Habsburg monarchy, as well as with Bulgaria.[28] During these years Putnik prepared in total seven variants of war plans: four of them were against Turkey; two with Austria-Hungary; and one with Bulgaria. The plans against Turkey were offensive, while those against Austria-Hungary and Bulgaria were defensive.

Putnik was not alone when he undertook this huge task. In accepting the post of Chief-of-Staff, he conditioned it by obtaining colonel Živojin Mišić for deputy.[29] The two men collaborated closely and made a good balance: while Putnik was rational, cool, and cautious, Mišić was ebullient, imaginative and emotional. Sporadic frictions that erupted were appeased by Putnik, who highly praised his assistant.

The Serbian constitution forbade politics to the military. However, the high office he held in the army, as well as his participation in governments as minister of defence, inevitably engaged Putnik in politics. Two issues precipitated his involvement: the purchase of arms connected with a foreign loan, and the split in the Serbian officer corps between the 'conspirators', participants in the 1903 putsch, and their opponents, the so-called 'counter-conspirators'.

The question of armaments had a threefold aspect: political, financial and technical. The choice of French, German or Austrian artillery carried in itself the political affiliation of Serbia with one of these countries. The purchase was linked to a loan which was to impose a heavy financial burden on the poor country. Finally, experts were to decide which one among the offered European cannons was of the best quality.[30] Over these complex questions the two largest political parties in Serbia, the 'old' and the 'independent' Radicals, split in 1904. Heated discussions in the parliament and a crisis in the cabinet followed. Because of the rejection of the Austrian arms, the customs war with the Habsburg monarchy started in 1906.

In the 'gun question' Putnik supported the 'old' Radicals and the government of Nikola Pašić who turned to France for money and arms, looking towards Paris as a potential ally in the anticipated conflict with Austria-Hungary. Finally, the guns were purchased in 1906 from the French factory Schneider Creusot, when Putnik was in the office of the ministry of defence.

The conflict in the army betweeen 1903 conspirators and their opponents also had diplomatic, political and technical aspects. The British conditioned the re-establishment of diplomatic relations with Serbia, severed after the 1903 putsch, on the punishment or retirement of the regicides. Their leaders, entrenched for some time in the royal palace, refused to comply, provoking a political crisis which echoed in the parliament. The rest of the military split into two camps, for and against the conspirators.

The conflict among army ranks threatened military discipline and the reforms Putnik was trying to introduce. He faced the crisis with tact, impartiality and firmness. The decision was not easy to make. As a matter of principle, Putnik opposed politics stealing into the army. He was loyal to his monarch and to the government. On the other hand, it was the putsch in 1903 which made the main change in his life and brought him back to the army. As a soldier, Putnik highly esteemed the professional qualities of many officers among the conspirators. The historian Slobodan Jovanović testified about the high regard which Putnik had for colonel Dragutin Dimitrijević-Apis, one of the leaders of the regicides.[31]

The question was solved in 1906 with acceptance of the modified British requests. During the crisis, Putnik supported the government, mediated between the conflicting parties, and tried to appease the ebullient mentalities of the officers. His main goal was to restore the unanimity of the officer corps, profiting from the authority and prestige he enjoyed in the army.[32]

The negotiations for the Balkan alliance, which started in 1911, introduced Putnik to diplomacy as questions of military importance were approached. He assisted the government in negotiations with the Bulgarians and insisted that Ovče Polje in Macedonia be assigned to Serbia, due to its strategic importance.[33] During 1912 Putnik was directly involved in negotiations with Bulgaria, Greece and Montenegro concerning collaboration of the Balkan armies in the forthcoming war with Turkey.[34]

The First Balkan War

The Serbian plan for the war with Turkey was based on the expectation that the decisive battle would be fought at Ovče Polje (the Skoplje-Štip-Veles line). The three Serbian armies were deployed in accordance with this assumption.[35] The frontal attack was assigned to the First Army, while the two other armies had to outflank the Turks at Kosovo and Bregalnica in order to join together at Ovče Polje for the final stroke.

The strategy conceived in Putnik's plan did not materialise. Nizam Paša, the recently appointed Ottoman commander-in-chief and disciple of French offensive-war doctrine, decided to push forward as fast as possible on the Vardar front, defeat the Serbs and then turn against the Bulgarians.[36]

On 23 October the advanced detachments of the First Serbian Army, under the command of Regent Aleksandar, quite unexpectedly collided with the main Turkish forces at Kumanovo, much further to the north of Ovče Polje. The encounter took the Serbs completely by surprise. Putnik and the Supreme Command had no chance to participate during the first day of the battle. The main burden was placed on the Danube Division that was directly engaged in the battle, and on the stubborn charge of its soldiers.

Assuming that the First Army was facing only the advanced elements of the Turkish army, Putnik ordered the First Army on 24 October to take the offensive, without waiting for coordination with the two other armies, scheduled to concentrate on Ovče Polje.Thus, the Kumanovo battle was planned by the Turks and was a complete surprise to Putnik. However, the Seventh Turkish Army Corps was completely annihilated during the two-day battle.

Putnik was later criticised for stubbornly sticking to the idea of deciding the war issue at Ovče Polje. However, in grouping his armies, Putnik reinforced the First Army to the extent that, by itself, it was able to wrestle with the Seventh Ottoman Corps.

Turkish haste, incomplete mobilisation and concentration, combined with inept command, facilitated Putnik's job. Criticism was appropriate only to the point that Putnik, still expecting the main encounter at Ovče Polje, missed the chance to exploit the victory at Kumanovo. Instead of throwing his armies into the pursuit of the defeated enemy, Putnik cautiously regrouped them, expecting the main encounter was still to come, and lost precious time preparing for it.[37]

However, in Putnik's favour one could quote his own statement made previously in 1876: 'It is easy to philosophise and propose actions when the event is known and closed.'[38] The victory at Kumanovo brought to Putnik the rank of 'vojvoda', the highest military rank and, at that time, a unique one in Serbia. After all, in spite of wrong predictions, this army that won the victory was the child to which he dedicated his life.

The 1912 war was resolved for Serbia with the victory obtained in the battle at Bitolj on 16-18 November. To support the Bulgarian campaign in Thracia, Putnik dispatched two divisions to Edirne. The Adriatic expedition, which in November and December brought Serbian troops to the seacoast of Albania, proved to be a failure. Under international pressures orchestrated by Austria-Hungary, the Serbian detachment had to withdraw from the littoral.[39] Putnik was criticised for not opposing the Adriatic expedition. However, one must have in mind that Putnik followed the demands of political authorities.

The Second Balkan War

The 1913 conflict with Bulgaria,[40] caused by the Serbian request to revise the alliance treaty, placed Putnik in a delicate and awkward position. Personally in favour of the treaty revision, Putnik refused to join the group of army officers who pressured the government to provoke a war with the Bulgarians. His strategic initiative was thoroughly weakened by the government's instruction to stay on the defensive and leave the surprise advantage to the enemy. Under such circumstances his main task of protecting the long frontier with Bulgaria and Albania became extremely vulnerable.

In such a situation, Putnik put his hopes on collaboration with the Greeks. His army commanders, whom Putnik summoned on 1 June 1913 at Skoplje, expressed the opinion that Serbia could save her chances in the war with Bulgaria only if she immediately attacked or synchronised her defence with Greece.[41]

The night of 30 June wasa stormy one in the Serbian Supreme Headquarters. On the eve of that day Putnik went to bed relaxed, only to be awakened in the middle of the night by the news of a Bulgarian surprise attack at Bregalnica. Further news obtained the next day was more cheering: the Greeks were subject to the same attack.

At that moment Putnik faced the dilemma of either withdrawing from Bregalnica and organising the counter-attack from the secondary defence line at Stracin, or accepting the battle at Bregalnica with the initiative on the side of the assailant. All the army commanders, except one, supported the first option. The one in favour of taking the risk at Bregalnica was Putnik's Deputy Chief-of-Staff, General Živojin Mišić. A retreat from Bregalnica could revive the memory of the 1885 defeat at

Slivnica, damage the morale of the troops and discourage Romania and Turkey from joining the war against Bulgaria.[42]

After some hesitation, Putnik sided with his deputy, Mišić.[43] This risky decision resulted in the Serbian victory over Bulgaria at Bregalnica.[44] However, Putnik failed to exploit the victory, in the same way he did at Kumanovo. Shaken by the news of a partial Bulgarian success on the southern part of the front, and by the offensive which Radko Dimitriev - the newly appointed and energetic Bulgarian general - started in the north, Putnik proceeded to indecisive measures which enabled the Bulgarian Fourth Army on the central front to escape the catastrophe.[45] The Romanian declaration of war on Bulgaria on 13 July, followed by similar Turkish action, sealed the fate of Bulgaria in the second Balkan war.

World War I

An incident almost prevented Putnik from participating in World War I. Suffering from acute bronchitis and exhausted by the two Balkan wars, the old soldier left for a cure in the Austrian spa of Gleichenberg, accompanied by his daughter. The July 1914 crisis found him in Austria-Hungary.

When the ultimatum was presented to Serbia on 23 July, he was asked to return home immediately. On the way back Putnik and his daughter were detained in Budapest and locked in a hotel room, after a mob insulted them at the railway station. The incident was resolved by the personal intervention of Franc Conrad von Hotzendorf, chief of the Austro-Hungarian general staff. Putnik and his daughter were allowed to return to Serbia via Romania.

However, on the way to Turnu Severin Putnik contracted pneumonia, which delayed his arrival in Serbia for eight days.[46] He reached the headquarters on 5 August, when the war was already in full swing. In the meantime two of his adjutants had to blow up the safe containing mobilisation and concentration plans, the keys of the safe being with Putnik in Gleichenberg.[47]

Coming back home, Putnik offered his resignation to King Petar I, justifying it by reason of poor health. The king refused his request, asking him to decide only on the main strategy and conduct of battles, leaving details to younger officers. Putnik accepted: the army needed his name and experience in these crucial moments.

The strategy which Putnik carried on in 1914 was based on ideas expressed in his manual, 'The War Service', published in 1911:

> 'The defence has the goal of inflicting on the enemy as much damage as possible. At the same time it has to prepare conditions necessary to switch to a counter-attack. A passive defence means defeat. However, the initial conduct of operations is not definite, because the intentions of the enemy are not yet known. This is the reason why the main body of the army has to be deployed in depth, in order to be flexible in synchronising its reaction to the attack.'[48]

This was exactly what Putnik and Mišić had in mind for the war with Austria-Hungary. Their expectations concerning the conflict with the Habsburg monarchy were based on one correct and one wrong assumption. They rightly foresaw that Russia would not abandon her little brother in the Balkans. But they erroneously expected the invasion to come from the north, across Danube and through the valley of Morava.

However, the error did not have far-reaching consequences. The 'concentration in the rear', which assigned the main force to the centrally located Second Army provided for reaction to attacks coming from both the north and northwest. The deployment of the three armies was structured for initial defence. At the moment when the direction of the main invasion became clear, the defence was to switch into a counter-attack.[49]

Instead of coming from Danube, the Austro-Hungarian invasion of Serbia started from the Sava-Drina rivers, to the northwest of the country. On 12 August the so-called Balkan Streit Armee, under the command of Feldzeugmeister Oskar Potiorek, crossed both rivers in order to engulf Serbian armies in the Sava-Drina triangle, push along the Jadar valley and cut the country in two. Under such circumstances, Serbia would be forced to capitulate.[50]

During these initial days of the invasion, Putnik and his staff in Kragujevac had to answer two essential questions. The first was to discern the intention of the enemy, and the direction of his main attack. The second was to respond to the invasion and to switch to counter-attack.

At his desk, Putnik was comparing and evaluating the confusing reports coming from the fronts. They indicated the main attack was coming from the west, instead of the expected one over the Danube. But what if it was a bluff, a diversion to distract attention from a forthcoming blow in the north? The time was pressing, the answer could be revealed too late. If Kutuzov in 1812, supported by the vast Russian spaces, could rely on patience and time, Putnik was unable to profit from these. He had to choose between his reason, which pointed to the Danube, and his instinct of a trapped beast, which turned his fears towards the news coming from the west. Slowly and cautiously, step by step, Putnik started moving his central Second Army towards Drina and Sava. Finally, during the night of 14-15 August, the decision was made. Two of Putnik's closest collaborators, General Mišić and Colonel Pavlović, rushed out of his room: 'Huh! The die is cast: the vojvoda made up his mind!' The Serbian divisions turned at a ninety-degree angle towards the west.

The decision essentially meant a switch to a counter-offensive. Now that the intentions of the enemy were read, the second stage of Putnik's strategy could be applied. While the Third Serbian Army had to stop the enemy's advancement through the valley of Jadar and towards the city of Valjevo, the Second Army was to attack the left flank and rear of the Potiorek's forces on the mountain of Cer. The Third Serbian Army would stay in reserve.[51]

The execution of this plan was assigned to General Stepa Stepanović, commander of the Second Army. He engaged his divisions in a four-day battle, from 16-19 August, with the pivot on the mountain Cer. Seasoned in previous Balkan wars and staunchly defending their native soil, the Serbian soldiers successfully carried out the counter-offensive. The invading forces were defeated and repulsed. The battle of Cer marked the first victory of the Allies over the Central powers in World War I. General Stepanović, the architect of the victory, was promoted to the rank of vojvoda.[52]

Pushed by the Western Allies, who were fighting German armies marching towards Paris, Putnik launched an offensive which aimed to outflank the Austro-Hungarians on the rivers Drina and Sava by penetrating into Srem and Bosnia. It started on 6 September, the same day as the Battle of the Marne in France. However, the Serbian troops were exhausted by the previous campaign and unprepared for a larger offensive. After some initial success obtained in taking Zemun and penetrating into Srem the expedition ended in a catastrophe. Detachments of the 2nd army lacked pontoons in crossing the river Sava at Mitrovica. They were seized with panic, trapped and annihilated.

The penetration into Bosnia also proved to be a failure: Serbian and Montenegrin troops, advancing towards Sarajevo, were stopped and thrown back over the Drina. Aware of the failure, Putnik ordered the withdrawal of all forces back to Serbia, but met the opposition of Regent Aleksandar. However, the directive was carried out when Putnik threatened the Regent with his resignation.[53]

Indeed, Putnik had good reason to worry. Storm clouds were covering the horizon on the Drina. On 7 September Felzeugmeister Potiorek started an offensive with his regrouped and resupplied armies on the central part of the Serbian front. A fierce battle, known as the battle on the Drina, was fought for almost two months.[54]

Facing a long front line from Belgrade to the upper Drina, Putnik organised the new command for the defence of Belgrade and turned the other three armies toward the west. Like a wounded tiger, he was retreating, counter-attacking, trying to outflank the enemy in Mačva and to stabilise the shaky front. Bloody Serbian counter-attacks at Gučevo and Mačkov Kamen brought heavy casualties on both sides,[55] but failed to produce the effect Putnik expected. Finally, both sides, exhausted and entrenched, tried to catch their breath before the final blow that would decide the fate of the campaign.

The long war, the attacks and counter-attacks, not only decimated the Serbian army but depleted ammunition and arms. Fighting for their own survival, the Western Allies were unable to help; Romania and Bulgaria proclaimed neutrality and banned the transit of arms from Russia. At the end of October, on the eve of the Austro-Hungarian final offensive, the situation for the Serbs worsened: the artillery had only 160-200 shells available per gun. Desperate, the commander of the Second Army, vojvoda Stepa Stepanović, offered his resignation in a dramatic phone conversation with Putnik: 'I cannot fight without ammunition!' At that moment of general distress the authority of Putnik restored the balance. 'Courage, my friend, courage!' roared Putnik into the phone. 'If we don't have guns, we shall fight with rifles.'[56]

While encouraging his subordinates, Putnik warned the government and the Allies about the desperate situation and the danger of his army melting and disintegrating. Putnik, too, was at the end of his own energies. Suffocated by emphysema, almost paralysed, he was trying to reach the impossible - to pressure his government and the Allies for help, to stimulate his commanders, and to coordinate a helpless defence.

Clearly, Putnik was approaching the end of his own rope. On 7 November he sent to the government a desperate message: 'Remember that nothing is endless. I refuse to take responsibility for the fatal consequences that might occur.'[57] Shocked by the dispatch, Prime Minister Pašić summoned the next day a joint meeting of the cabinet with the Supreme Command. 'Without ammunition,' Putnik told the participants at the meeting, 'any further resistance of our army has minimal prospects. Under such conditions we face only two possibilities: separate peace or capitulation.'

It is not quite clear whether this request was sincere or whether it aimed at blackmailing the Allies to come to Serbia's assistance. Pašić rejected Putnik's proposal, but transmitted it immediately to Russia. Satisfied, Putnik left the conference room saying: 'Well, we have to fight even if we are cornered in Đevđelija.'[58]

Putnik did not exaggerate in his evaluation of the situation. The battle on the Drina was lost. The enemy was penetrating through the confused and defeated country. The Serbian army withdrew at first on the Kolubara-Valjevo line. Then, failing to organise a counter-attack, Putnik retreated further, leaving the city of Valjevo. At the beginning of November the entire Serbian front seemed to be on the verge of collapse.

At the crucial moment no one was aware that Putnik was on the eve of the most brilliant victory in his military career. Several factors contributed to the dramatic switch in the fortunes of war.

During the second half of the month of November the Allies were finally able to dispatch to Serbia, via Greece and the Danube, the badly needed ammunition. By retreating, Putnik was able to shorten the line of the front. Most painful was Putnik's decision to abandon Belgrade. At the general outcry which this decision provoked, Putnik growled: 'It is not my fault that the capital city is placed there, where a frontier blockhouse had to be!'[59]

The Serbian retreat extended the supply lines of the Austro-Hungarian army, over muddy roads, rivers swollen by autumn rains, and over a devastated country.

This time it was not Putnik but General Živojin Mišić who prepared the counter-offensive and chose the moment for attack. On 14 November Mišić replaced the wounded General Petar Bojović as head of the First Army. He realised the destructive effect on the morale of his soldiers, caused by the constant fighting-in-retreat strategy. On 28 November in a dramatic telephone conversation with Putnik that lasted over two hours, Mišić asked for permission to further withdraw his army to Gornji Milanovac, in order to consolidate the regiments in disarray, rest them and prepare for a successful counter-offensive.

The request for further retreat put Putnik in a terrible dilemma. The move of the Mišić army inevitably meant further withdrawal of the two other armies. More than that: the eventual loss of Gornji Milanovac could open the heart of Serbia to the enemy and cut the country into two pieces.

On the other hand, Putnik knew well his former deputy, Mišić, and trusted his judgement. A counter-offensive was what Putnik had urged from the beginning of the war.

Backed to the wall, Putnik applied his usual tactic in reference to his commanders. At the beginning he opposed them, to let them persuade him with the validity of their arguments. When refused, the ebullient Mišić threatened the vojvoda with his resignation. Finally Putnik gave in and issued the necessary orders for the synchronised retreat of the two other armies.[60]

Mišić was right. The short interval gained by the retreat provided time to recuperate and reorganise the troops. On 3 December there began a smashing Serbian counter-offensive, known as the battle of Kolubara, which turned defeat into victory.[61]

Military historians discussed later the role which Putnik and Mišić played in the battle of Kolubara. Some of them credited the vojvoda, the other, his general, for the victory. From the beginning of the war the two men worked as a team. Putnik was the architect of the general strategy and the coordinator of activities. Mišić was the army commander with the intuition to grasp the right moment, to take the risks and to carry out the counter-attack successfully.

After the defeat of the Fifth Austro-Hungarian Corps at Kolubara, the center of the battle was transferred to the north. Potiorek's Fifth Army Corps threatened to penetrate from Belgrade towards the south, in the rear of the Serbian armies. Cautiously manoeuvring with his exhausted and decimated troops, Putnik redirected divisions of the Second Army towards the north.[62] Some historians blamed Putnik later for not sufficiently exploiting the results of the Kolubara battle. But he was less concerned with chasing the defeated enemy at Kolubara than removing the threat coming from the north and liberating Belgrade. Indeed, on 15 December the old commander-in-chief was able to report to King Petar I that on that very day, there was not one free enemy soldier left on the soil of Serbia. This was not only the most glorious, but also the last victory of vojvoda Radomir Putnik.

After the 1914 campaign, the Serbian front was calm during the winter and spring of 1915. The Russian offensive in the Carpathians, the Dardanelles expedition, the entrance of Italy into the war - all these combined to remove the pressure from Serbia. But the country was caught by an epidemic of typhoid fever, cholera and dysentery. All this, together with losses suffered during the 1914 campaign, forced Serbia into passivity, except for one brief intrusion into Albania.

The situation turned worse for Serbia during the summer and early fall of 1915. After his military success in Galicia, General Falkenhayn decided to break down Serbian resistance in order to establish a direct territorial contact with Turkey. When the Bulgarian king decided in September to join the Central powers, the fate of Serbia was sealed.

Putnik had no illusions about a war waged over the 900-km-long front line.[63] The only hope he had was based on two wrong expectations: co-operation with Greece, like the one in 1913, and the arrival of the Anglo-French expeditionary corps from Salonika. In such a case Putnik would be able to deploy all his forces on the north, in a kind of replay of the 1914 campaign. When the Bulgarians proclaimed their mobilisation on 22 September Putnik urgently asked the government either to prevent it by diplomatic means, or to allow him a pre-emptive attack on Bulgaria. The first possibility was unrealistic, the second was rejected for reasons of international politics.

In such a situation, Putnik's strategy could rely only on defence, losing the initiative for a counter-attack. The deployment of Serbian armies in 1915 was completely different from the one in 1914. They were now stretched along the northern and eastern frontiers and deprived of a strategic reserve. The only possible task of the Supreme Command was to 'mend the wholes' in the cracking front line.

On 5 October General August von Mackensen launched the invasion of Serbia.[64] A storm of steel covered the long front. In two days Belgrade was hit by 30,000 artillery shells. On the same day the Greek monarch forced Venizelos to resign and Serbia was informed that the *casus foederis* in case of a Bulgarian attack was not applicable. *The coup de grace* was inflicted on 13-14 October when Bulgaria entered the war. Bulgarian soldiers were met in Niš with slogans 'vivent les alliees', prepared for the expected French troops.[65] The Anglo-French detachments in Salonika insufficiently equipped, were not able to offer any help.

During these days Putnik was fighting his own last battle. He was overtaxed, exhausted and hit by a severe case of influenza which bound him to bed. The Italian war correspondent Ferry Pisani described him as a 'run-down man, with tremulous gestures and staggering steps'. 'The illness almost erased the features of his face', wrote the journalist, 'only the eyes were left, like steel, together with an indomitable soul...Each moment seemed to be his last.'[66] Doctor Archibald Reiss, the Swiss professor and criminologist, when meeting Putnik, got 'the impression of an old and very ill professor...who found in his unlimited patriotism the resource to fight death'.[67]

Obviously in such a state, Putnik was unable to take part in directing military operation, but could only supervise the main decisions. Not much could be done anyway. When Von Mackensen dislodged the Third Serbian Army from the Danube, the entire concept of defence was compromised. Defending every inch of the country, Putnik supervised the successful escape from the pincer which Von Mackensen tried to close upon the Serbian army at Kragujevac. When the Bulgarians entered Kačanik, Putnik withdrew the eastern part of the front to the left bank of the South Morava river in order to shorten the line and preserve its continuity.

The goal Putnik had in these days was to pull out his armies from the strangling loop and to keep open the avenue of retreat toward the Kosovo plain and Albania. The indomitable Mišić, constantly yearning for a counter-attack, suggested a counter-offensive against the advancing Germans in western Serbia, a replay of the Kolubara battle. However, in a heated conversation he had with Putnik on 27 October, his proposal was rejected. The situation was hardly like the one in 1914, nor was Putnik the same man. He ordered Mišić to protect the retreat toward Kosovo.[68] The commander of the First Army did so successfully and prevented Mackensen from engulfing his divisions at Kraljevo.

The situation became desperate when the Bulgarian Second Army occupied Skoplje and cut off direct Serbian contact with Salonika. On 4 November the cabinet held a joint meeting with the Supreme Command at which it was decided to continue resistance as long as possible, and to withdraw the troops over the Kosovo Plain, into Albania, toward the Adriatic.

By taking the cities of Niš and Skoplje, the Central Powers achieved their strategic goal of establishing a territorial connection with Turkey. The German Command started pulling out its troops gradually from the Balkans. This offered a slim chance for an attempt to break through this encirclement, toward Skoplje and Salonika. All in vain: after a brief local success at Leskovac, the counter-offensive was repulsed.[69]

For fifty days the Serbian soldiers, with sombre faces and blurred eyes, exhausted and pursued, waged a desperate struggle. The army and the government, accompanied by a mass of civilian refugees, were finally encircled, cut off from the Allies and driven toward the Albanian mountains. The option was to capitulate or to risk an exodus through the icy passes and over the rocky peaks of the Albanian mountains, ill-equipped for a winter campaign and in the middle of a hostile Albanian population.

Exile and Last Days

On 25 November Vojvoda Putnik issued his last and most painful command to the army. The troops were ordered to start the march through Albania, towards the Adriatic shores, to meet the Allies. Recuperated and reorganised, they would continue to fight. Unable to be carried over the Albanian trails and mountain peaks, the artillery was to be dismantled and buried in the ground. 'The State did not lose its being - it still exists', Putnik reminded his soldiers.[70]

Unable to walk, Putnik was carried over Albania by four young soldiers in a kind of improvised sentry-box, supplied with a chair. The old King Petar I joined him in an ox-cart. The 115-km-long trip was covered in eleven days. The day after his arrival at Skutari, on 8 December, Putnik got a five-month's leave of absence for reasons of health. Accompanied by his daughter and a private physician, Putnik left for Brindizi, but soon returned to Corfu, where the remainder of the Serbian army, some 150,000 men, were stationed before being transferred in 1916 to the Salonika Front.

Obviously Putnik's military service was over. During his last days, personal misfortune was to join the misfortune of his country. As often happens after the defeat, the question of responsibility surfaced. In an atmosphere of mutual recrimination, the government, in order to justify itself, blamed the military. Actually, responsibility for the tragic issue of the 1915 campaign should have been shared by all the elements which took part in deciding on Serbian politics and strategy. Under the circumstances, Putnik did the best he could to avoid the annihilation of his army from a superior adversary. The error he committed, together with the government, was to rely too much on the expected support from the Allies. A retreat planned in due time towards the Adriatic, through Montenegro, would have saved the Serbian army from the tragedy of the exodus over Albania.

Be that as it may, the scapegoat was found. In January 1916 the entire Supreme Command, including Putnik, was relieved from duty. The vojvoda learned about his replacement from the cashier who delivered him his salary without the commander-in-chief's supplemental amount. Embittered, the vojvoda moved to Nice, where the French government received him with honours and offered a comfortable villa in the suburbs of the city. Bronchitis and emphysema finally took their toll: on 17 May 1917 Putnik died at the age of seventy.

Among Serbian military leaders in the twentieth century wars, vojvoda Putnik was the most distinguished, but also the most tragic figure.

His main achievement was the preparation of the Serbian army for the coming wars. Putnik trained brilliant commanders - Stepa Stepanović, Živojin Mišić, Petar Bojović and Živko Pavlović. They worked as a team under his guidance and supervision. His authority dominated their temperaments; his judgement and decision were the final ones.

The strategy which Putnik applied in the 1912-1914 wars was flexible and adapted to the requirements of the specific situation. In 1912 he applied the offensive strategy, in 1913 he switched from defence to attack. This strategy, which he called 'active defence', was best developed in the 1914 campaign. The concentration of the main forces in the rear, and their use in a counter-attack, proved to be successful.

Obviously, as in everyday life, a bit of luck is necessary in war and politics. Putnik profited from the inept Turkish command, the megalomaniac policy of the Bulgarian King Ferdinand and the Russian intervention in 1914, which confused the Austrian plans to invade Serbia. But in 1915 the attacks coming from all sides by far superior invaders turned the fortunes of war against Putnik.

In spite of all, history was sympathetic to the soldier. At the climax of the battle of Kolubara Putnik had dissuaded King Petar I from visiting the front: 'The only thing you will learn there is how the soldier curses you and me.' However, since Putnik's remains were returned to Belgrade in 1926, the chapel in which they were buried carries the inscription: 'To Vojvoda Putnik, the grateful fatherland'.

Notes

1 For accounts of Putnik's life see Belić (1938), Ranković (1936), Pavlović (1934), Mićić (1924), Ćirić (1924), Stanojević (1928), and Skoko (1984).
2 On Putnik's family and childhood see Skoko (1984), Vol. I, pp. 19-20, and Belić (1938), pp. 7, 10.
3 Djordjević (1982), pp. 317-318.
4 Grujić (1879).
5 Mitrović (1958), and Ekmečić (1978).
6 Ranković (1926), p. 34, and Skoko (1984), Vol. I, pp. 32-33.
7 Belić (1938), p. 17, and Skoko (1984), Vol. I, p. 115.
8 Mišić (1981), p. 307.
9 The older son Dimitrije served during World War I in the Russian army. After the revolution in Russia he joined, together with his brother Vladimir, the Serbian army at the Salonika Front. Promoted colonel in the Yugoslav army after 1918, he served as a military attache in Moscow during World War II. After the war he refused to return to communist Yugoslavia, lived and died in 1962 in France. See Skoko (1984), Vol. I, pp. 120-122.
10 Mišić (1981), p. 242.
11 Belić (1938), p. 21, and Skoko (1984), Vol. I, pp. 80-81.
12 Skoko (1984), Vol. I, pp. 116-119.
13 Ranković (1926), p. 111, and Belić (1938), p. 22.
14 Skoko (1984), Vol. I, pp. 190-192.
15 Mišić (1981), pp. 194-196.
16 Promotions were regular: lieutenant in 1971, captain and major during the 1876-1877 wars with Turkey, lieutenant-colonel in 1884 and colonel in 1889. See Belić (1938), pp. 35-38.

17 Skoko (1984), Vol. I, pp. 115, 119, 190.
18 Belić (1938), pp. 25-26.
19 Skoko (1984), Vol. I, p. 185, and Ranković (1926), p. 118.
20 Skoko (1984), Vol. I, pp. 186-187.
21 Putnik was a member of the government in 1904, 1906-1908 and 1912. See Ranković (1926), p. 48.
22 On the 1876-1877 campaigns see Đorđević (1907) and Popov (1981), pp. 381-421.
23 Skoko (1984), Vol. I, p. 73.
24 Đorđević (1907).
25 On the 1885 campaign see Đorđević (1908), Popov (1983), pp. 76-86, and Jovanović (1990).
26 Putnik (1899).
27 The first volume was written by Putnik himself. See Skoko (1984), Vol. I, p. 219.
28 Belić (1938), pp. 52-53.
29 Mišić (1981), p. 231.
30 Đorđević, Dimitrije (1962), pp. 46-48, 221-223, and on Putnik's role in the crisis at pp. 65-66, 76, 82, 211.
31 Jovanović (1962), p. 45.
32 Belić (1938), pp. 43, 56-59. On the conflict between military and civil authorities in Serbia see Vučković (1963-1965).
33 Đorđević (1959), pp. 477-478.
34 Skoko (1984), Vol. I, pp. 237-238.
35 In 1912 Serbia mobilised 345,000 soldiers, 57,000 horses and 42,000 oxes. The first and second call-ups formed 10 infantry and one cavalry divisions. The units were armed with 288,000 rifles, 230 machine-guns, 544 artillery pieces and 10,000 sabres. See Skoko (1984), pp. 245-246.
36 On the 1912 campaign see Lazarević (1931), Đurišić (1960), and Stanojević (1928a).
37 On arguments in favour of Putnik see Skoko (1984), Vol. I, p. 287.
38 Putnik's 1976 letter to Stanojević is cited in Skoko (1984), Vol. I, p. 94.
39 Đorđević (1956), p. 160.
40 On the 1913 operations see Skoko (1968), and Lazarević (1955).

41 Skoko (1984), Vol. I, pp. 3441-342. The military convention with Greece was signed on 1 June 1913.
42 Skoko (1968), pp. 338-362.
43 Skoko (1984), Vol. I, p. 354
44 Maksimović (1926).
45 Skoko (1984), Vol. I, pp. 378, 380.
46 This incident as well as the strategy of the Serbian High Command in the campaign of 1914 is discussed in Djordjević (1986).
47 Skoko (1984), Vol. II, p. 33.
48 Putnik (1911).
49 Belić (1938), pp. 108-109, and Pavlović (1924), pp. 65-66.
50 On Austrian war plans against Serbia see Gleize-Horstenau (1930), 99. 91-97, 102-103, and Pavloviđ (1924), pp. 68-73.
51 Pavlović (1924), pp. 101-102.
52 Stanisavljević (1927), and Radenković (1953).
53 On that occasion Putnik said to Regent Aleksandar: "The constitution relieves you from responsibility, but not me!' See Belić, (1938), p. 23.
54 Đurišić (1969).
55 Both Prince Đorđe, the oldest son of King Petar I, and General Petar Bojović, the commander of the First Army, were wounded in the firing line.
56 Skoko & Opačić (1981), pp. 401-403.
57 Skoko (1984), Vol. II, p. 137.
58 Putnik warned the government that the artillery was useless without ammunition, and that the army had to retreat from Gučevo because of the lack of ammunition. The divisions lost half of their men during the campaign, as well as approximately half of the commanding staff. See Skoko (1984), Vol. II, p. 143.
59 Skoko (1984), Vol. II, p. 182.
60 Skoko (1984), Vol. II, p. 368, and Mišić (1981), p. 372.
61 Radenković (1959), and Pavlović (1928-1930).
62 Pavlović (1922).
63 Skoko (1984), Vol. II, pp. 230-231.
64 Pavlović (1968), and Zelenika (1954).
65 Mišić (1981), p. 401.

66 Cited in Ranković (1926), p. 51.
67 Cited in Skoko (1984), Vol. II, p. 146.
68 Skoko (1984), Vol. II, p. 266, and Mišić (1981), pp. 397-398.
69 Bojović (1922).
70 Skoko (1984), Vol. II, p. 278. Not all army commanders were willing to admit defeat. After vojvoda Putnik left for the Adriatic coast, vojvoda Mišić summoned the remaining army commanders and proposed a counter-offensive starting from Kosovo. However, after a heated debate during six meetings, at which chances for such an enterprise were analysed, the majority decided to follow Putnik and the government. See Skoko & Opačić (1981), pp. 521-524, and Mišić (1981), pp. 404-405.

References

Belić, Vladimir (1938), *Putnik*, Belgrade.

Bojović, Petar (1922), *Odbrana Kosova polja i zaštita odstupanja srpske vojske preko Albanije i Crne Gore*, Belgrade.

Ćirić, Đ, (1924), 'Vojvoda Radomir Putnik', *Vojnički Glasnik*, No. 16-18.

Djordjević, Dimitrije (1982), 'The Role of the Military in the Balkans in the Nineteenth Century' in Karl Otmar Freiherr von Aretin (ed), *Der Berliner Kongress*, Wiesbaden, pp. 317-147.

Djordjević, Dimitrije (1986), 'Vojvoda Putnik, the Serbian High Command and Strategy in 1914' in Bela K Kiraly & Nandor Dreisziger (eds), *War & Society in East Central Europe: East Central European Society in the First World War*, East European Quarterly, New York, pp. 569-589.

Đorđević, Dimitrije (1956), *Izlazak Srbije na Jadransko more i konferencija ambasadora u Londonu 1912*, Slobodan Jović, Belgrade.

Đorđević, Dimitrije (1959), 'Pašić i Milovanović u pregovorima za Balkanski savez 1912. godine', *Istorijski časopis*, Vol. 9-10, pp. 467-486.

Đorđević, Dimitrije (1962), *Carinski rat Austro-Ugarske i Srbije 1906-1911*, Istorijski institut, Belgrade.

Đorđević, Vladan (1907), *Srpsko-turski rat, Uspomene i beleške iz 1876, 1877 i 1888 godine, I & II*, Belgrade.

Đurišić, Mitar (1960), *Prvi balkanski rat 1912-1913*, Belgrade.

Đurišić, Mitar (1969), *Bitka na Drini 1914*, Belgrade.

Ekmečić, Milorad (1978), 'Srpska vojska u nacionalnim ratovima od 1876 do 1878', *Balcanica*, No. 9, pp. 97-129.

Gleize-Horstenau, Edmund (1930), *Oesterriech-Ungarns letzter Kreig 1914-1918, Vol. I, Das Kreigsjahr 1914*, Vienna.

Grujić, Sava (1879), *Vojna organizacija Srbije*, Belgrade.

Jovanović, Slobodan (1962), *Moji savremenici*, Windsor.

Jovanović, Slobodan (1990), 'Srpsko-Bugarski rat' in Radovan Samardžić & Živorad Stojković (eds), *Sabrana dela Slobodana Jovanovića, Vol. 2*, Bigz, Belgrade, pp. 455-581.

Lazarević, Milutin (1931), *Naši ratovi za oslobođenje - srpsko-turski rat 1912, I, II & III*, Belgrade.

Lazarević, Milutin (1955), *Drugi balkanski rat*, Belgrade.

Maksimović, Vojin, *Bitka ba Bregalnici 17-25 juna 1913*, Belgrade.

Mićić, R. (1924), *Četiri bojne vojvode*, Belgrade.

Mišić, Živojin (1981), *Moje uspomene*, 3rd ed., Bigz, Belgrade.

Mitrović, J.D. (1958), 'Organizacija i oprema narodne vojske I kneževini Srbiji 1854 godine', *Vesnik Vojnog Muzeja JNA*, Vol. II, No. 5, pp. 183-204.

Pavlović, Živko (1922), *Beogradska operacija (Oslodođenje Beograde) Novembra 1914*, Belgrade.

Pavlović, Živko (1924), *Bitka na Jadru 1914*, Belgrade.

Pavlović, Živko (1928-1930), *Bitka na Kolubari, I & II*, Belgrade.

Pavlović, Živko (1934), 'Vojvoda Radomir Putnik', *Godišnjica Nikole Ćupića*, Vol. 43.

Pavlović, Živko (1968), *Rat Srbije sa Austro-Ugarskom, Nemačkom i Bugarskom 1915*, Belgrade.

Popov, Čedomir (1981), 'Srbija u istočnoj krizi 1875-1878' in Vladimir Stojančević (ed), *Istorija srpskog naroda, Vol. V, No. 1, Od Prvog ustanka do Berlinskog kongresa 1804-1878*, Srpska književna zadruga, Belgrade, pp. 369-421.

Popov, Čedomir (1983), 'Nemirne godine i vezivanje za Austro-Ugarsku' in Andrej Mitrović (ed), *Istorija srpskog naroda, Vol. VI, No. 1, Od*

Berlinskog kongresa do ujedinjenja 1878-1918, Srpska književna zadruga, Belgrade, pp. 50-94.

Putnik, Radomir (1899), *Služba Đeneralštaba, II Deo*, Izdanja Ministartsva vojnog, Belgrade.

Putnik, Radomir (1911), *Ratna služba*, Belgrade.

Radenković, Milan (1953), *Cerska operacija*, Belgrade.

Radenković, Milan (1959), *Kolubarska bitka*, Belgrade.

Ranković, Živan (1926), *Vojvoda Radomir Putnik, Njegov život i rad*, Sarajevo.

Skoko, Sava (1968), *Drugi balkanski rat*, Belgrade.

Skoko, Sava (1984), *Vojvoda Radomir Putnik, I & II*, Bigz, Belgrade.

Skoko, Sava & Opačić, Petar (1981), *Vojvoda Stepa Stepanović*, Bigz, Belgrade.

Stanisavljević, Živko (1927), *Cerska bitka*, Belgrade.

Stanojević, Stanoje (1928), 'Radomir Putnik', *Narodna Enciklopedija*, Zagreb, p. 608.

Stanojević, Stanoje (1928a), *Srpsko-turski rat 1912 godine*, Belgrade.

Vučković, Vojislav (1963-1965), 'Unustrašnje krize u Srbiji i prvi svetski rat', *Istorijski časopis*, Nos. 15-16, pp. 175-229.

Zelenika, Milan (1954), *Rat Srbije i Crne Gore 1915*, Belgrade.

6 King Aleksandar I Karađorđević

BRANISLAV GLIGORIJEVIĆ

Introduction

To date little has been written in Yugoslavia about King Aleksandar Karađorđević. It is doubtful that there has been any similarly significant person so persistently ignored and wiped from historical memory. Nor has such a giant in Serb history been the subject to so unfavourable judgements without any real examination of the facts. The greatest mockery of history is that he, who did more than anyone else to save the Serbian army whilst retreating into Albania in World War I and who erected monuments and memorials in honour of his fallen fighters, has had his name erased from the inscriptions on those monuments.

King Aleksandar was a national king in a sense that cannot be applied to any European monarch going back centuries. He was of pure Serb blood on both sides of his family, proud of his peasant origins and in close contact with the widest spectrum of his people. If one was to choose a single word that would in most general terms describe his life that word would be 'struggle'. His life was a gigantic struggle in which he opposed two empires that had lunged out to destroy Serbia and then sought to diminish internal conflicts in the new state of Yugoslavia which had been created on very unstable foundations.

Early Life

Aleksandar Karađorđević was born on 17 December 1888[1] in a modest home in Cetinje, opposite the Montenegrin royal palace. His father was Prince Petar Karađorđević and his mother was Princess Zorka, the eldest daughter of King Nikola of Montenegro. He was one of five children, only three of whom survived infancy. He received his name at baptism where his godfather was the Russian Tsar Aleksandar III. His name was of Byzantine origin and was very popular in Russia and Serbia, and gaining in popularity in Europe. The name denotes a person as 'protector of the people'.

The single most important factor affecting Aleksandar's development as a child was that he was left without a mother who died just after the birth of her last child and when Aleksandar was just eighteen months old. Aleksandar was left with no memories of his mother. Of frail health and without the love of a mother, he was raised by a stern father who was unprepared to spend any great amount of time with his children. His elder brother Đorđe, a nervous child, was consistently rough with Aleksandar. For tenderness Aleksandar turned to his grandmother Princess Milena, and her daughter Jelena, who was later to marry the Italian king and became Aleksandar's political opponent. the departure of his father into exile from Montenegro, following disagreements with King Nikola, was a painful turning point in Aleksandar's life. He attended school in Geneva with ordinary children before moving to St Petersburg where he studied at the Pravovedenije School in preparation for a career in the diplomatic service. His life's path was completely altered in 1903 following the assassination of the Serbian royal couple Aleksandar Obrenović and his wife Draga. The assassinations, organised by a conspiracy of military officers, led to the fall of the Obrenović dynasty in Serbia and the return to Serbia of his father as king.

The return of the Karađorđević dynasty to Serbia in 1903 was a turning point in Serbian history. However, establishing the prestige of the dynasty was difficult and painful process. King Petar was not the forceful personality needed by Serbia as it confronted the events that were to unfold. The conspirators that enabled Petar to assume the Serbian throne assumed control of the army and meddled in Serbia's political affairs, especially in foreign policy matters. The leaders of Serbia's political parties were dissatisfied with Petar even though he did not interfere greatly in parliamentary matters. Both the military and political circles began contemplating the removal of the Karađorđević dynasty and its replacement by an appropriate English prince. The dynasty's problems were exacerbated by the conduct of Petar's eldest son and heir, Đorđe, a psychologically unstable personality. His propensity to physical violence was a cause of public scandals.

Growing up in such an environment, Prince Aleksandar withdrew into himself, devoting his time to study and personal improvement. His first tutor in 1904, Lujo Vojnović, observed that Aleksandar was a talented student with a quick mind, able to quickly grasp the essence of things, and with a special interest in art and music.

Events in Serbia influenced his further education and determined his future in the armed forces. At the age of fifteen he enlisted as a private in the Sixth Regiment of the Serbian Army, with his father, King Petar, wanting his son be in the service of "the sacred aims of every Serb" with ordinary soldiers. The major impact on his development was his education over a period of ten years in Russia.

The Balkan Wars

In 1909 Prince Aleksandar's education in St Petersburg had to be interrupted. He was called back to Serbia to assume the position of heir to the throne after his elder brother Đorđe renounced that position. Prince Đorđe's abdication was triggered by a serious incident in March 1909 when he physically assaulted a servant. The injuries to the servant were of such severity that the servant died. This event occurred at a time of political complexity in Serbia. In the previous year Austria-Hungary annexed Bosnia-Hercegovina. The Balkan countries responded by seeking closer mutual relations with the aim of resolving on their own, and thus bypassing Europe, the so-called Eastern Question, by seeking their liberation from the centuries long enslavement under Turkish occupation.

Following his proclamation as heir to the throne, the dynamic nature of Aleksandar's personality came to the fore. He exhibited great flair in communicating with people. His Court became a meeting place for scientific workers, writers, artists and painters. In a short time he toured the whole of Serbia and got to know the towns and villages and the people in them. He talked to ordinary peasants about their everyday concerns and established contacts with the prominent local leaders whom he invited to visit him. The trip enabled Aleksandar to assess the mood of the populace as it awaited the coming armed struggles. Aleksandar then spent a lengthier period in the army's barracks and garrisons on military exercises, thereby enabling an examination of the country's military readiness. He also visited Serbia's Balkan neighbours where his forthright personality did much to alleviate tensions and remove obstacles to the creation of alliances between them.

In the First Balkan War, Aleksandar was entrusted with the most important task of commanding the First Army, which, in turn, was assigned the role of breaking through Turkish positions. In the important Battle of Kumanovo Aleksandar showed himself to be a cool and composed leader under difficult circumstances. On the first day of the battle the left wing of his forces suffered losses and Aleksandar's Chief-of-Staff proposed retreat. Aleksandar instead responded with successful a counter-attack the following day, which led to a victory which was decisive for the outcome of the First Balkan War. Following a triumphant entry into Skoplje and the capture of Bitolj, the First Balkan War came to an end after a month's fighting. The outcome of the Second Balkan War against Bulgaria which soon followed was determined at the Battle of Bregalnica where again Aleksandar commanded Serbia's First Army. The Second Balkan War was a war for prestige in the Balkans, and Serbia emerged from the war as its leading power. Upon his return to Belgrade after the Balkan Wars Aleksandar was hailed by the masses as the 'avenger of Kosovo'. His modest response was that he was not a great leader, but that he led in war a truly great people.

History favoured Aleksandar Karađorđević most as a warrior and soldier. By his upbringing and his conduct in life he revealed himself to be above all a soldier and warrior. Seven years of his life was spent in wars where he endured all the privations and sufferings of war just like any soldier. Unlike other European rulers who spent wartime well away from the battlefield and only received reports of battles, Aleksandar was on the site of the battlefield and often exposed to enemy fire. In the First Balkan War during the liberation of Bitolj he was in positions showered by enemy fire. In World War I similar situations arose on a number of occasions, and on one such occasion he suffered minor injuries from an exploding grenade. His adversaries could point to the fact that he had not completed his studies at the Military Academy. However, war is not an exact science and military success depends more on natural abilities and reasoning than on formal education. Prior to World War I no European military leader had been engaged in war excepting minor skirmishes with the native tribes of their colonies. On the other hand Aleksandar gained considerable experience in the bloody Balkan Wars, especially in the battles at Kumanovo, Bitolj and Bregalnica where he was in command. Circumstances, especially the advanced age and illness of his Chief-of-Staff Vojvoda Radomir Putnik, saw him making crucial decisions, not only in the context of the specific battles but also for the outcome of the whole military campaign.

World War I

Following the assassination of Austria's heir to the throne Franz Ferdinand in June 1914 at Sarajevo, Vienna issued an ultimatum to Serbia. Given the absence of Serbia's Prime Minister Nikola Pašić and Vojvoda Putnik, Aleksandar was the first to take the position that the ultimatum could not be completely accepted. Perhaps he was the only person who was convinced that irrespective of Serbia's reply to the ultimatum, Austria was determined for war against Serbia. In the war that followed Aleksandar organised the Headquarters of the Supreme Command, perused war plans and supervised the mobilisation. He took a concern in all aspects of planning, down to distribution of food for the soldiers, which was crucial in Serbia's first victory in the war in the Battle of Cer.

In the autumn of 1914, at the time of the Battle of Kolubara, Aleksandar resolutely opposed the views of Vojvoda Putnik, who suggested that, because of her hopeless military position, Serbia should cease resistance and sue for peace. Aleksandar's leadership at this time enabled the Serbian army to turn matters around and counter-attack. During the spring and summer of 1915 he persistently resisted Allied pressure that Serbia's tired army undertake a risky offensive towards the west with the aim of joining up with the Italian army. Threats of withdrawal of financial and military aid arrived from Paris and St Petersburg if the planned offensive was not undertaken. The Allied demand would have led to the Serbian army finding itself in the vicinity of Vinkovci where it would have been caught in between a coordinated attack from the Austrians, Germans and Bulgarians with no chance of escaping the enemy encirclement. Capitulation would have been the only option.

Both Pašić and Aleksandar made their greatest mistake of the war in believing the empty promises of Allied military aid. When in the autumn of 1915 this aid was not forthcoming, Aleksandar agreed to the crucial decision on the exodus of Serbia's army from Serbia. The exodus south through Kosovo and Montenegro came at a heavy price both as to lives lost and the fall in army morale. However, Aleksandar maintained his composure and his belief that all was not lost. The exodus meant that he had to temporarily renounce the services of his favourite military leader, Vojvoda Živojin Mišić, who opposed retreat and proposed a counter-offensive, which if it failed would leave Serbia with no choice but to seek an armistice.

Aleksandar's role in the rescue of the withdrawing Serbian forces which found themselves on the Albanian shores of the Adriatic in a truly hopeless position, exposed to illness, starvation and cold, was perhaps his greatest deed. Pašić feared that the army would have to surrender just to save lives. This was also Aleksandar's greatest fear. A stream of petitions were sent to the Russian Tsar, the French President, and the English and Italian monarchs, all expressing his bitterness, protest and pain, but at the same time his belief that his army could endure and help, not only Serbia, but the Allies as well. His appeals found a favourable response in the Russian court. Russian intervention eventually led to French and Italian ships arriving with food and then evacuating Serbian soldiers to the island of Corfu. Aleksandar, at that time, succumbed to illness and underwent a serious groin operation. Not withstanding his loss of weight and lack of strength, he refused evacuation to Italy, preferring to stay with his soldiers. In the retreat across Albania he walked part of the way, but because of exhaustion he was carried the rest of the way by stretcher or, when passing through swamps, on the back of his aide-de-camp.

In the summer of 1916 on the Salonika Front Aleksandar's efforts were concentrated on strengthening the front by increasing the efforts of Allied forces to undertake the speediest offensive possible. An extensive collection of his letters, proposals and petitions of the time bear witness to the importance to Aleksandar of a breakthrough on the Salonika Front. By 1916 Aleksandar had persuaded Allied statesmen and leaders that the war would end where it had started - in the Balkans. Aleksandar argued for the importance of a breakthrough on the Salonika Front on strategic and psychological grounds. Strategically, it would halt the German forces and with an attack towards the east, make it impossible for supplies to reach German forces. Psychologically, the Salonika offensive would enable the now ready Serbian army to attack, rather than remain inactive and far from home. However, for a long time the Allies disagreed with these arguments, insisting that the war would be won on the Western Front. British Prime Minister Lloyd George was later to concede that the war would have finished earlier had Allied forces been sent to the east rather than perish in vain on the Western Front. Allied dithering only came to an end when, in the summer of 1918, French General Depere arrived at the Supreme Command on the Salonika Front and advised Vojvoda Mišić that the moment had come to 'fulfil the longtime wish of your heir apparent'.

The breakthrough itself and the pursuit of enemy forces fell mainly to Serbian forces, while French and British troops followed in the rear as observers of Serbian operations. Poor coordination of French and British troops meant that the Serbian forces advanced so far ahead of their allies that there remained the possibility that they could be cut off from the rear. Although the Supreme Commander General Depere advised that they wait until an Allied breakthrough on the flanks, Aleksandar was eager that his forces continue into the Vardar Valley and thus separate the German and Bulgarian forces. Aleksandar gave orders for the offensive to continue and it was successfully completed. Approaching Niš Serbian forces were faced with a combination of a German and a Bulgarian divisions. General Depere again cautioned against further advancing so as to avoid risking the success of the entire campaign. Despite this warning and the reserve of Vojvoda Mišić, Aleksandar, again inspired by the moment, ordered his army to continue attacking. The First Army of Vojvoda Petar Bojović conquered Niš. These two courageous decisions by Aleksandar were critical to the successful conclusion of the war. Bulgaria capitulated and with the emergence of Allied forces at the Danube, Germany soon sought an end to hostilities. The German emperor was bitter, asking his commanders how a small army of some 60,000 men could emerge victorious against so many other armies and so contribute to the final outcome of the war.

During the course of World War I Aleksandar was also concerned with important, but non-military, decisions. One of the most difficult decisions was to give his consent to the court-martial proceedings against a group of officers of the so-called 'Black Hand', led by Dragutin Dimitrijević-Apis. The conspirators that had brought the Karađorđević dynasty back to power in 1903, had firstly attained complete control over the military - the nomination of the Army minister and the head of the General Staff depended on their approval. Secondly, they interfered in the political affairs of the country, especially in foreign affairs. In 1911 this group founded the secret organisation 'Unification or Death', known as the 'Black Hand', with the aim of uniting, by revolutionary means and terrorism, all Serbs in one state. Within Serbia members of the organisation endeavoured to control all spheres of society. In 1914 they attempted to organise a coup. Aleksandar strongly resisted this effort and became a bitter opponent of 'Black Hand'. During the war Aleksandar was targeted by Apis' supporters, who threatened him with 'a final settling of accounts'. In the summer of 1916 an attempt was made on Aleksandar's life, with 'Black Hand' suspected as being the organiser of the attempt. An investigation was initiated, which uncovered the existence of 'Black Hand' as a terrorist organisation that had planned, *inter alia*, assassinations of foreign statesmen. When later, Apis admitted that he was involved in the organisation of the Sarajevo assassination in June 1914 of Archduke Franz Ferdinand which in turn led to Austria's declaration of war against Serbia, this was sufficient for a Military Court in Salonika to bring down a sentence of death against him. The Military Court verdict led to the execution of Apis, Major Ljubomir Vulović and Radeta Malobabić in mid-June 1917.[2] Aleksandar denied clemency to the three on the ground that they wished to replace the democratic constitution of Serbia with an autocratic military regime. Aleksandar's actions effectively liquidated the terrorist organisation that sought to influence Serbia's national policies, and enabled much needed unity to return to the armed forces. This unity was exhibited in the conduct and success of Serbia's army in the Salonika Front operations.

As to Aleksandar's political views during the war, he was most preoccupied with the idea of freeing all Serb territories as an immediate national goal. As Supreme Commander he had to be pragmatic and to indicate to his soldiers exactly what they were fighting and dying for, and that could only be that the struggle was for their homes, their fatherland and for their fellow Serbs. Thus, the majority of Aleksandar's proclamations addressed to the army called for the 'liberation of all Serbdom' and the creation of Great Serbia. Aleksandar approached Yugoslavism cautiously and did not care much for the activities of the Yugoslav Committee around Ante Trumbić, although he did not openly oppose them. On this issue he was in complete agreement with Pašić.

At the end of the war, when armistice negotiations with Hungary had commenced, Aleksandar sent a note to General Depere, who was conducting the negotiations on behalf of the Allies, that he (Aleksandar) 'is most interested in territories in which Orthodox Serbs dominate because it is our historical right, and also because it is their aspiration to unite with Serbia'. In November 1918 he authorised his delegate Colonel

Dušan Simović to convey to the members of the National Council in Zagreb that, with the signed armistice with Hungary, temporary borders had been determined going from Đakovo in the north to Cape Planka in the south, and that outside this territory the Croats should decide either to go with Serbia or form a separate state. By that time the Serbian army had liberated Bosnia and Hercegovina, Dalmatia, Srem, parts of Slavonia and Vojvodina. Aleksandar told British Admiral Truebridge that these regions were 'now in our hands and they have to enter into a future state with Serbia. In relation to the Croats we are unconcerned. If they wish they too can join with us'. The creation of the Yugoslav state union in 1918 was not a primary aim of Aleksandar's. Rather, it was but one possible alternative. He accepted the Yugoslav solution for national-strategic reasons, because it would have been difficult to maintain a single Serb state surrounded by Catholic states (especially Italy), at a time when Serbia would not have had the support of an Orthodox Russia.

The Kingdom of Serbs, Croats and Slovenes (1918-1929)

The Kingdom of Serbs, Croats and Slovenes that attained full legality with the adoption of the Constitution of 1921 was, in terms of its population and size, the most powerful state in the Balkans and southeast Europe. However, the state did not have an internal national consensus. The majority of Croats and Slovenes were against the Constitution, which had been adopted by a simple majority of delegates to the constituent assembly. Amongst the Serb political parties there was a general consensus that the Yugoslav state had resolved the Serb national question and that the state had to be defended by a strong central government. In this belief, demobilisation was effected and the state's authorities left to take care of national interests. Otherwise Serb political parties presented a variety of national programmes. An all-Serb view was promoted by the Radical Party, whilst the Democratic Party presented a Yugoslav programme. With these national ideologies both parties opposed each other and contested elections to the Parliament in a robust manner. On the other hand the Croat and Slovene parties increasingly achieved national homogenisation.

The greatest resistance to the new state carne from the Croats who insisted on a confederalist or dualist government structure with two states, one Serb and one Croat. The Croats refused to renounce their aim of a separate Great Croatia in which a significant number of Serbs would be found. Up to 1924 Croat deputies boycotted the Parliament's work. A change occurred in 1925 when Croat leader Stjepan Radić, under pressure of accusations of high treason because of his party's membership of the Peasant International (a branch of the Comintern), recognised the 1921 Constitution. For a while his party cooperated in a coalition government with the Radicals, but the coalition disintegrated at the beginning of 1927. Thereafter, Radić's party was in opposition. A new crisis in relations with the Croats arose suddenly following the assassination attempt in Parliament on Radić by Puniša Račić on 20 June 1928. The assassination attempt occurred in an atmosphere of heated verbal and physical confrontations between the deputies of Radić's Croat Peasant Party and government parties. Two Croat deputies were killed and Radić was wounded. He died a few months later from the injuries, the effects of which were complicated by his diabetic condition.

Even though the crime in Parliament was the act of a psychologically unstable personality, Croat politicians laid the blame on Serbia and its people. Deputies from the Peasant-Democratic Coalition, founded in 1927 as a coalition of the Croat Peasant Party and the Independent Democratic Party led by Svetozar Pribičević, boycotted the work of Parliament. They rejected the 1921 Constitution and sought a new government structure based upon the full recognition of national and state individualities. Parallel to this there was, from Zagreb, a flow of propaganda, extolling its more advanced 'western culture', and on the Drina river as the border between Croatia and Serbia. A 'social boycott' ensued in which the aim was the prevention of all political and economic contacts with people from Serbia. The crisis reached its climax with reports that a Croat Parliament would be constituted in Zagreb to proclaim the secession of Croatia from Yugoslavia. A crisis meeting of the government, chaired by Aleksandar, had on its agenda a proposal to 'amputate' Croatia from Yugoslavia. Provisional borders were drawn up but the 'amputation' option was abandoned following statements from Zagreb that Croat demands did not extend outside the framework of Yugoslavia. However, the crisis remained as the new Croat Peasant Party leader, Vlatko Maček, requested that Yugoslavia be restructured along the lines of a commonwealth united in the person of the Crown.

In early 1929, Aleksandar held consultations on possible ways out of the crisis. Maček, in an audience with the King, proposed the division of the state into seven units, with a Croat unit being the largest and with the strongest legal status. The noted Serb legal scholar and historian, Slobodan Jovanović, suggested a union of states along the lines of the former Austria-Hungary. Aleksandar was displeased with Maček's suggestion given the size of the Croat unit envisaged by Maček. When his Minister of State, Dragomir Janković, suggested that he should come to some agreement with Maček, the King angrily replied that he could not accept Maček's plan. He said: 'Am I supposed to look from Kalemegdan on the Croatian flag in Zemun[3] as Maček requests?" The next day, on 6 January 1929, Aleksandar, by Royal Proclamation, revoked the 1921 Constitution and dissolved Parliament, claiming that the affairs of state could no longer be conducted as they had been to that date. This act marked the start of Aleksandar's personal rule over Yugoslavia.[4]

Aleksandar's Personal Rule (1929-1934)

Three basic factors influenced Aleksandar's revocation of the 1921 Constitution and introduction of his personal rule. The first and most important was the threat, by the end of 1928, of the state's disintegration in the wake of secessionist demands by Croat politicians. Second, although the communist movement as such did not represent a serious threat, an alliance of communist forces with extreme Croat forces represented a serious potential danger to Yugoslavia's integrity. Following the 1927 transfer of the headquarters of the Central Committee of the Communist Party of Yugoslavia (CPY) from Belgrade to Zagreb, the course of the CPY's politics was increasingly influenced by Croat cadres who advocated the dismantling of Yugoslavia. The third factor was the general paralysis of the Yugoslav Parliament which, according to the existing constitution, was unable to function effectively.

Events immediately following the Royal Proclamation amply demonstrate that the coup was not a carefully planned event, but rather was provoked by the events that preceded it. However, the question remains as to whether Aleksandar's action was the only option. A politician of Pašić's calibre would certainly have found other ways out of the crisis. But Pašić was no longer on the scene, and there was no other politician of his standing around who could have advised the King to act otherwise than he did.

According to the principles of monarchical power and supreme governmental administration, the King is the source of all power within a state. Aleksandar's regime revoked all civil rights previously in force, including the freedom to express an opinion, the right of association and the right to gather and confer. According to the Law of Public Security and Social Order, all political parties were banned, and the establishment of new parties based on religious or 'tribal', that is national, origins was precluded. In the early years of his rule Aleksandar did not face any serious opposition to this situation. His authority within the country was crucial in this process, and the new regime did have significant support within the ranks of the pauperised peasantry. The other significant source of support came from Croat and Slovene commercial circles whose interests were served by Yugoslavia's free market economy. In the first government under Petar Živković Croat members included the president of the Zagreb Stock Exchange, a representative of Croat industrialists, a Croat agricultural expert and a Croat legal representative of major business firms.

The temporary state of affairs of Aleksandar's personal rule lasted until September 1931 when a new Constitution was promulgated. A new constitutional structure was thus put in place. The 1931 Constitution provided for a form of parliamentary monarchy with the introduction of popular representation to two chambers, the National Assembly and the Senate. The Assembly was elected by direct vote, but a later law provided that voting be public. In the Senate half the members were elected and half appointed by the King.

The major feature of Aleksandar's personal rule was the idea of national unitarism with the proclamation of Yugoslavism as official ideology and the prohibition of all activities and opinions that opposed this ideology. It was this ideology that had inspired the change in the name of the state to Yugoslavia on 3 October 1929, and which now saw the country reorganised into nine administrative territorial units called *banovine*.

The divisions of the state into the nine *banovine* was made according to economic and geographic criteria, and aimed at preventing the grouping of the various nations of Yugoslavia. Even though the policy of integral Yugoslavism was aimed at the fracturing of national territories, in some cases it was impossible to do so. Thus, the Drava *banovina* was overwhelmingly Slovene in composition and the Sava and Primorje *banovine* were dominated by Croats. A concession to the Croats was also made in the choice of the word *banovina* as the name of the new administrative units. The word *banovina* was from the Croat national heritage. The Vardar *banovina* was heavily populated by Macedonians. The major changes to territorial boundaries occurred within what had been the former Kingdom of Serbia, in Bosnia-Hercegovina and Vojvodina. The territorial restructuring there was aimed at preventing any Muslim dominated unit. Of the nine *banovine*, six had populations in which Orthodox Christians were at least an absolute majority.

However, it was a mistake on Aleksandar's part to think that the assimilation and unification of the various national groups into one 'indivisible Yugoslav nation' would be accelerated by means of a Royal Decree. The policy of integral Yugoslavism, rather than internally consolidating the country, served only to sharpen nationalist sentiment. Rather than breaking the earlier passive resistance policy of the Croats, the Croats emerged more powerful and stronger than before. Maček achieved a greater degree of unity within the Croat nationalist movement by attracting the support of a group of *frankovci* (Frankists). He also gained the support of the Catholic Church, and formed an alliance with the prominent dissident Democratic Party member Svetozar Pribičević, which was used to neutralise the Serbs in Croatia. With this strengthened position, Maček was able to make demands that went towards the creation of a Great Croatia. In November 1932 the Maček-Pribičević alliance adopted the so-called Zagreb Resolutions calling for a return to the situation as it existed in 1918 and for a new organisation of the state in which the peasantry should be the foundation of organised public life.[5] The Zagreb Resolutions were supported by Serb politicians in Croatia, but the views of the masses were never sought. The Zagreb Resolutions led to Maček's imprisonment for a term of three years. Pribičević who was then abroad began an intense campaign against the personal regime of Aleksandar, sending messages to Serb opposition politicians urging them to accept, if ultimately necessary, the creation of a Croat state outside the framework of Yugoslavia, notwithstanding that many Serbs would be found in such a state.[6]

While the Croat and other national movements were getting stronger and aspiring to their own national states, the Serbs were increasingly becoming prisoners to Yugoslavia. The Serb national idea became weaker and weaker as it absorbed itself into Yugoslavism.

Aleksandar had hoped that Serb national elements would be strengthened in the country, but the result was the destruction of Serb political and party life to such an extent that no similar comparisons can be drawn from recent Serb history. Serb political parties crumbled. Parts of them joined with Aleksandar's governments, whilst other parts went into opposition. The latter formed, in Belgrade, a second strong centre of opposition to Aleksandar. However, the Serb opposition was focussed on the struggle for the establishment of a democratic social order, while the Zagreb opposition was focussed on the nationalist and territorial goals of the Croats. The Serb opposition had as a priority the preservation of the Yugoslav state. For Maček the primary goal was the establishment of a Croat state.

King Aleksandar himself eventually realised that his personal rule did not bring the results he had expected. State consolidation remained elusive and the people did not 'get to love Yugoslavia'. He conceded to a prominent member of the Serbian Orthodox Church, Metropolitan Gavrilo Dožić, that the circumstances and political life within Yugoslavia entitled the people to say that he, as King, ruled by himself and as he wished. He accepted as a great mistake, not only his personal rule but also the governmental structure founded on the policy of integral Yugoslavism and the negation of national identities of his peoples, especially the Serbs and Croats. To Metropolitan Gavrilo, on the eve of his fateful journey to Marseilles in October 1934, Aleksandar outlined his ideas for a complete restructuring of the country upon his return. With the support of the Serb opposition leaders, as well as that of Slovene and Muslim, representatives he planned the return of parliamentary democracy and a reorganisation of governmental structures to reflect the demands of Yugoslavia's individuals peoples. He planned that the Croats should be granted self-rule, excepting in the domain of foreign affairs, the military, finances and transport. He was not prepared to allow secession or confederation. Serb national interests mitigated against such actions. The Serbs outside Serbia would not want to separate from Serbia, nor allow the partition of Bosnia and Hercegovina. It was because of Bosnia and Hercegovina that Serbia and Montenegro had entered World War I and had paid a high price with the loss of the best and brightest of a generation of Serbs. For Aleksandar it would a catastrophe to abandon policies that were traced back to the days of Ilija Garašanin.[7]

In contrast to his lack of success in internal matters, Aleksandar displayed skill and flair in the conduct of foreign policy. He managed to maintain Yugoslavia's international standing and independence, with Yugoslavia becoming a central factor in maintaining Balkan and Central European stability. He staunchly defended the European international order created after World War I. In the early 1930s the revisionist states in Europe began to group. On such grouping was initiated by fascist Italy, which had ambitions to its east, in particular in Yugoslavia. Within these groupings there was discussion of a new rearrangement for Europe, one plan being the restoration of the Austro-Hungarian empire, or its extension within the framework of a Danubian Confederation, which would include, after the 'expected' disintegration of Yugoslavia, Vojvodina, Croatia, Bosnia and Hercegovina and parts of Slovenia. In 1933 Italian leader Benito Mussolini's plan for a new Balkans and Central Europe was announced: Hungary would acquire Vojvodina, Austria would acquire Kranjska with Maribor, Croatia would become independent, and Dalmatia, Hercegovina and Montenegro would become an Italian protectorate. In 1934 a formal alliance between Italy, Hungary and Austria was formed, and it was anticipated that Croatia would eventually join this Catholic bloc.

Great Britain and France did not openly oppose this grouping of revisionist states, but rather focussed their concerns on Adolf Hitler and Germany. Faced with the threats emanating from Rome and Berlin, Aleksandar undertook independent defensive action. Following Hitler's rise to power Aleksandar, in 1933, went about strengthening the Little Entente, raising this alliance of Yugoslavia, Romania and Czechoslovakia, to the level of a strong military, political and economic bloc. Permanent joint authorities of this bloc were established, including a Council of Foreign Affairs Ministers and a Council of Commerce, thereby resulting in Europe's first political and economic community which had a territorial area greater than that of any individual European power.

In 1934, Aleksandar initiated talks that led to the formation of the Balkan Pact between Yugoslavia, Romania, Greece and Turkey. Friendly relations were established with Bulgaria and there was even talk of the two countries uniting into one state. At this time Aleksandar's stature as a statesman was at it greatest. He was seen by many as the master of the destiny of the Balkans and Europe. However, Aleksandar's international prominence also raised concerns of those forces that had aggressive intentions towards the Balkan states. Many of them were obsessed by the thought that the removal of this 'strong man' of the Balkans would lead to Yugoslavia's disintegration, and thus open the way for their aggressive goals to be realised.

One of the internal enemies of Aleksandar were the Ustaše, an extremist Croat organisation led by Ante Pavelić. In the early 1930s Mussolini supported the Ustaše. The Ustaše publicly declared their intention to assassinate Aleksandar. Pavelić appointed Eugen Kvaternik to organise and lead a terrorist group for this purpose.

In the meantime, closer relations between Italy and France had provoked tensions in relations between France and Yugoslavia. French policy was understood to be motivated by the need to present a joint Franco-Italian opposition to Germany's desires to incorporate Austria. On the other hand the dangers were that this would lead to Italian hegemony in Central Europe, leading to either the restoration of the Austria-Hungary or the creation of a Catholic bloc of states dominated by Mussolini and supported by the Vatican.

Assassination

Ustaše plans to murder Aleksandar, and thus facilitate the dismemberment of Yugoslavia, were set to be carried out in 1933. In December of that year, during a visit to Zagreb, an Ustaša operative who was designated to kill Aleksandar was arrested. The trial of the would-be assassin was given great publicity in an attempt to expose Italian support for the Ustaše terrorists. Attempts by France to defuse Italo-Yugoslav relations were looked upon with suspicion by Aleksandar, and it was in this environment that he planned a visit to France in October 1934. Prior to departing Aleksandar indicated his policy to his foreign minister Bogoljub Jevtić. He stated that he did not wish to hinder closer Franco-Italian relations, but only if Yugoslavia's integrity was assured.

At the time of his departure for France, Belgrade authorities warned their French counterparts that an attempt would probably be made on Aleksandar's life. They requested an increase in security for the visit. The French took little notice of the warnings. The security arrangements for the King's arrival at Marseilles were minimal. On the other hand it was in the King's nature to defy death. On occasion he had told friends that he did not expect to die of old age. Prior to disembarking he was advised that an attempt on his life would be made by Croat terrorists, and that he should disembark elsewhere. Aleksandar refused because it was in Marseilles that he wished to pay his respects to the French soldiers who had died on the Salonika Front during World War I.

On 9 October 1934 after disembarking at Marseilles Aleksandar, in full military uniform, and French foreign minister Louis Barthou, were assassinated by Veličko Kerin, acting on Ustaše orders.[8] The inadequate security made the assassin's task relatively easy as he stood on the footrest of the automobile driving Aleksandar and Barthou and at virtual point-blank range fired the fatal bullets. Yugoslavia was outraged by the tragedy. Army Minister Voja Marinković complained bitterly of the 'terrible negligence' of the French.

The murder of King Aleksandar was the first step towards the destruction of the post-World War I European order. It opened the way to the emasculation of the Little Entente and Balkan Pact, and to the dismantling of Czechoslovakia and then to the German attack Poland in 1939 which ignited World War II. Yugoslavia increasingly found itself at the mercies of the great European powers without a strong defender of its independence and national integrity.

(Translated from the Serbian original by Melanie Petranović)

Notes

1 A number of biographical accounts of the life of Aleksandar have been written. See Eylan (1935), Graham (1939), and Gligorijević (1996).

2 For a detailed coverage of the trial see MacKenzie (1995).

3 Kalemegdan is an old fortress from Ottoman times in Belgrade on the bank of the Sava river. Zemun is a town across the Sava river from Belgrade.

4 For an account of Yugoslav politics in the 1920s see Gligorijević (1979).

5 On the Zagreb Resolutions see Dragnich (1983), pp. 93-95.

6 Pribičević's campaign against Aleksandar led to him writing a book in 1933. See Pribičević (1990). On his period in opposition see Boban (1973).

7 Metropolitan Gavrilo's recording of his discussions with Aleksandar in September 1934 are found in Džaković (1974), pp. 121-159.

8 On the Marseilles assassination see Roberts (1970). On the international reaction to the assassination see Pacy (1970).

References

Graham, Stephen (1939), *Alexander of Yugoslavia, The Story of the King Who Was Murdered at Marseilles*, Yale University Press, New Haven.

Boban, Ljubo (1973), *Svetozar Pribičević u opoziciji (1928-1936)*, Institut za Hrvatsku povijest, Zagreb.

Dragnich, Alex N. (1983), *The First Yugoslavia, Search for a Viable Political System*, Hoover Institution Press, Stanford.

Džaković, Mitar M. (1974), *Memoari patrijarha srpskog Gavrila*, Editions Richelieu, Paris.

Eylan, Claude (1935), *La Vie et la Mort D'Alexandre I Roi de Yougoslavie*, Bernard Grasset, Paris.

Gligorijević, Branislav (1979), *Parlament i političke stranke u Jugoslaviji (1919-1929)*, Institut za savramenu istoriju, Belgrade.

Gligorijević, Branislav (1996), *Kralj Aleksandar I Karađorđević, I*, Bigz, Belgrade.

MacKenzie, David (1995), *The 'Black Hand' on Trial, Salonika, 1917*, East European Monographs, Boulder.

Pacy, James S. (1970), *Hungary, The League of Nations and the Assassination of King Alexander of Yugoslavia: A Study of the Resolution of an International Political Crisis*, Unpublished Doctoral Dissertation, The American University, Washington.

Pribičević, Svetozar (1990), *Diktatura kralja Aleksandra*, Globus, Zagreb.

Roberts, Allen (1970), *The Turning Point, The Assassination of Louis Barthou and King Alexander I of Yugoslavia*, St Martin's Press, New York.

7 Prince Pavle Karađorđević

SRDJA TRIFKOVIĆ

Introduction

Prince Pavle of Yugoslavia is a figure both unique, and uniquely tragic, in modern Serb history. His was the story of a perennial outsider: a sophisticated art-lover thrust into the murky world of Balkan politics; an incorrigible Anglophile forced into unsavoury deals with England's enemies; a gentleman in the world of perfidious rogues. Always at pains to square the demands of personal integrity with those of 'the art of the possible', he was ultimately unloved in Belgrade, mistrusted in Berlin, and scorned in London.

At a personal level it would be interesting to trace the development of this abandoned child, from the loveless austerity of his uncle Prince Petar Karađorđević's all-male household in Geneva to the quiet self-confidence of a cosmopolitan aesthete moulded in the best tradition of Europe's upper crust. It would be curious to trace the impulse which induced young Pavle to ask to go to Oxford in 1912, instead of the traditional Serb student destinations, Paris or St. Petersburg.

This chapter's focus, however, will be on Prince Pavle's impact on Yugoslavia's turbulent politics, and especially diplomacy, during the six-and-a-half years of his regency. This was the crisis-ridden period during which the Prince was forced to take the central role in his country's political life following the assassination of his elder cousin, King Aleksandar, in Marseilles in October 1934. For this he was not prepared either by temperament or by experience.

His personal predicament was similar to that which had awaited his close personal friend, the future King George VI, but Prince Pavle's political challenges were infinitely greater. As Regent until young King Petar's coming of age, Pavle was expected to provide much more than merely a symbolic role reserved for the Crown in a well established constitutional monarchy and a functional state. He was supposed not merely to symbolise the state, but to keep it together from within, and protect it from without.

Unsettled Prince in an Unsettled Kingdom

The Yugoslav state built by King Aleksandar was a far from stable edifice. It rested on nineteenth century notions of South Slav unity, which fitted uneasily into the realities of twentieth century Europe. The Unification (*Ujedinjenje*) of the South Slavs occurred at least fifty years too late: the differences among them had developed too highly for an exercise in *Gleichschaltung* from above to be successful.

Serbia's dynamism in the decade preceding Europe's suicide of 1914 had, for its unstated objective, the unification of all Serbs, rather than the 'liberation of all South Slav brothers'. The Dual Monarchy perceived it as a threat which should be neutralised at source. With a blank cheque from Berlin, Austria-Hungary decided to attack Serbia in the wake of Sarajevo in July 1914, and by doing so it activated the system of European alliances which duly ignited the continent.

The Entente in World War I did not envisage the creation of Yugoslavia. Until the very end, there was no intention even to dismember the Habsburg Monarchy. Secret treaties (with Italy 1915, and with Romania 1916) certainly provided for the Monarchy's reduction in size, but the British prime minister, Lloyd George, said as late as January 1918 that the Allies did not intend to break it up. Even President Wilson's Fourteen Points envisaged autonomy for the Monarchy's nationalities, rather than sovereignty outside its framework.[1]

The rushed and improvised unification, proclaimed on 1 December 1918, was based on an *ad hoc* deal between two unrepresentative elites: the coterie around Aleksandar (then still Serbia's Regent, but acting with full royal prerogative), and a group of Croat, Slovene and Serb politicians from the Habsburg lands. The resulting edifice remained an unhappy and inherently unstable union throughout the seven turbulent decades of its existence. The legacy of different cultural, political and religious traditions, of uneven economic development and different aspirations, could not be overcome by a centralist constitution and slogans. Such differences were at the root of the political conflict in the country.

Prince Pavle was not only too young, but also too emotionally detached to be involved in the process of Serbia's unprecedented self-liquidation in the name of Yugoslav integralism. His formative experiences, including an unhappy decade of schooling in Belgrade (1903-1912), combined with his temperament to produce a man neither imbued with the strong nationalist spirit typical of that age in the Balkans, nor given to soldierly exploits. Except for two brief and undistinguished spells of military service (November 1914 - May 1915, and January - April 1917) he spent most of the war in Oxford, London and Scotland, where the names of his friends and associates included many of Britain's landed gentry, politically powerful, wealthy and influential.

The Yugoslav dilemma was essentially an issue of the Jacobin state versus the old Habsburg constitutional complexity of historic units. The Serbs were inclined to view the new state as a continuation of pre-1914 Serbia, and advocated centralism on the premise of national unity. The Croats knew pacts, agreements and contracts, with an external source of authority - Vienna or Budapest. The institution of parliamentary democracy, well known to Serbia prior to 1914, did not provide an adequate venue to those Croat politicians whose early political grooming, under the Habsburgs, had been in the art of obstructionism.

A Prince in Search of a People

During the painful early years of the Kingdom of Serbs, Croats and Slovenes Pavle's visits to Belgrade were infrequent and prompted by obligation. His life was centred on London, where in 1919-1923 he was a regular guest at parties in town, or shoots in the country. He only returned to his native land in January 1924, having married Olga, an impoverished Greek royal princess of exceptional beauty who had been previously engaged to - and then inexplicably abandoned by - a Danish prince.

Unresolved domestic arrangements within the royal household, unsuitable living quarters, and the general tedium of life in a Balkan capital - after the buzz of London - was 'like beginning lessons on Monday morning, only worse' for the young couple. But the change of lifestyle was not the only worry. Prince Pavle's cousin, the King, was not an easy man. His unpredictable nature sometimes made him appear cruel and inconsiderate, although he was on the whole a kind man. He enjoyed Pavle's conversation, his breadth of vision and his cool intellect; but he did not appear to have any role in mind for Pavle, who had hoped for a clear definition of his duties and his position

In the beginning of 1924 it seemed that the King would install Prince Pavle in some vice-regal capacity in the major Croat city of Zagreb. The project, although never clearly stated by the King, nevertheless captured Pavle's imagination, who believed that Croat commitment to the new state would be enhanced if its individuality were recognised in some form. Although careful not to make any statements on the subject, Pavle felt uneasy with the way the King sought to turn Yugoslavia into a more or less centralised, unitary state modelled on pre-1914 Serbia. He implicitly recognised that the response of the Serb establishment to Croat unhappiness with the centralist solution failed to take into account the differences conditioned by history, culture and geography.

King Aleksandar evidently changed his mind, and Prince Pavle remained at the gloomy old palace at Dedinje, without a role and without a sense of self-fulfilment. The word in Belgrade had it that Aleksandar was apprehensive not only of the impact Pavle's presence might have on a strongly nationalist Croats, but also of their impact on Pavle's highly developed sense of duty in the old, Edwardian sense. As Pavle's biographers have noted:

> If the King feared that his cousin, given the governorship, might take up the cudgels against his own, essentially Serbian, system of government in Belgrade, he may have known Pavle better than anyone then imagined. Pavle's approach to such a constitutional duty might turn out to be naive; but it would thereby be more ruthless.[2]

Throughout the 1920s Prince Pavle was uncomfortable with the way many Serb politicians behaved: as if the Croat discontent would be somehow weathered all by itself, as if the Croat Peasant Party (CPP) leader, Stjepan Radić, were merely an opposition leader in the mould of pre-1914 Serbia. Pavle may have understood better than his regal cousin that both sides in the Yugoslav equation were hostages of responses learned in earlier times and under different circumstances. But his very ability to develop an independent viewpoint outside Aleksandar's narrow terms of reference seems to have assured that he would have neither a clear role nor a regular duty to perform.

Prince Pavle found his solace in his many friends and contacts abroad, his expanding art collection, and his family. By the late 1920s his home in Yugoslavia was moved to a lovely Alpine villa in Slovenia, where he could feel both physically and spiritually closer to the places where he felt more at home in every respect. He exploited every opportunity to travel to London, Paris, Munich, Florence, Rome or Vienna, wherever there was an exhibition or a picture to be seen or studied. His time there was spent mainly reading, fishing and hunting.

In the meantime, the country's chronic instability caused by an unconsolidated constitutional order escalated into an acute crisis of the state. After a decade of attempts to develop a viable political system, the tensions exploded into bloodshed, when Radić and several other Croat deputies were shot by a Serb deputy from Montenegro in the *Skupština* (Assembly) in 1928. The parliamentary system finally collapsed in January 1929, when King Aleksandar proclaimed personal rule.

Unresolved domestic issues were coupled with an unstable international environment. The boundaries of the Kingdom of Serbs, Croats and Slovenes, determined in Paris after a long and arduous dispute with Italy, theoretically provided it with a viable basis for existence. At the same time, they did not bring longed-for stability to the Balkans region. As a 'beneficiary' of Versailles, the Yugoslav state eventually had to cope with an alliance of the discontents from within (Croat separatists, Macedonian 'autonomists') with the revanchists abroad (Italy, Hungary, Bulgaria).

In the years prior to Hitler's emergence on the scene, Prince Pavle was only informed of major diplomatic decisions; he was not to influence what turned out to be his international legacy. Yugoslavia's foreign policy was effectively conducted by King Aleksandar, even during the brief period of parliamentary system.

During this time Italy's relentless irredentism forced Belgrade to gravitate towards France, which was grimly determined to make the Versailles order as stable as could be expected in the absence of a meaningful balance-of-power system. Restraining Italy became the first item on the agenda of Belgrade's diplomats, and it could be achieved only by cultivating a 'special relationship' with France. With Russia and America out of the picture for domestic reasons of their own, and Britain unwilling to underwrite a *pax Gallica* predicated on Germany's permanent exclusion from the circle of 'legitimate' great powers, Paris had to look to Belgrade, Bucharest, Prague and Warsaw for support. The resulting weak and unstable system could linger on only as long as there was no major challenge to it from Berlin.

Mussolini found himself during this period in the contradictory role of supporting and sponsoring Yugoslavia's enemies on the one hand, and remaining staunchly anti-revisionist on the other (on the issue of the Brenner frontier, or Austrian independence). His ambitions across the Adriatic - his expansionist Albanian policy and the apparent increase in the influence of the implacably irredentist 'Julian lobby' at the Italian foreign ministry from April 1926 on - marked the end of a potentially fruitful phase in Italy's diplomacy, when it could hope to expand and cement its influence in the Danubian basin. The ensuing policy of pro-revanchist restlessness 'ran contrary to almost all of Italy's true interests and inexorably led to the Axis and a German triumph in the Balkans that could not stop short of Trieste'.[3]

While relations with Italy preoccupied successive governments in Belgrade to a great extent in the first decade of the new state's life, the second key foreign policy concern was the containment of revisionism in neighbouring states and the connected issue of the prevention of a Habsburg restoration. Even before the end of the World War I, the project of drawing Balkan and Danubian nations together to secure peace and the new order had been on the agenda.[4] After 1918 it was narrowed to the three states which had most to fear from Hungarian revanchism and a Habsburg revival: Yugoslavia, Romania and Czechoslovakia. Futile attempts by the former emperor and king, Charles, to return to the throne in Hungary speeded up the creation of the Little Entente, as the alliance between Belgrade, Prague and Bucharest came to be known.

The third major foreign policy concern of Belgrade in the 1920s was security in the Balkans. This aspect gained in prominence following the deterioration of relations with Italy, and some progress had been made; but the four Balkan Conferences (1930-1933) and the ensuing 'Balkan Pact' fell short of creating a firm entente in the region which would also embrace a revisionist-minded Bulgaria. But increasing links among Central European and Balkan states caused further resentment in Rome. Italy responded by the Rome Protocols (17 March 1934) on 'future coordination' of foreign policy between Italy, Austria and Hungary.

Mussolini thus became more closely identified with the revisionist camp in the Danubian basin.[5]

It is probable that Mussolini's move was also inspired by apprehension of the newly-arrived revisionist par excellence - Adolf Hitler. From January 1933 on, neither Yugoslavia, nor Italy, nor - indeed - any European country could omit the German factor from its foreign policy considerations.

King Aleksandar's Personal Regime

Prince Pavle's eventual domestic inheritance was no less problematic. The collapse of the parliamentary system in Yugoslavia in 1929 coincided with the period of growing political radicalism throughout Europe and the beginning of a world-wide economic crisis. King Aleksandar's personal rule was proclaimed in the name of safeguarding 'national unity and the integrity of the state'. He suspended the Vidovdan Constitution of 1921, abolished political parties and dismissed the *Skupština.* For almost six years, Yugoslavia was run on authoritarian lines in an effort to develop *from above* a feeling of national unity which would transcend ethnic particularism. In the process, many civil liberties were suspended, the press (exceptionally free from control until that time) was subjected to censorship, and numerous actual or potential opponents of the regime were arrested or interned. The king's power was exercised principally through the civil service, with the army not too far in the background.

In its first two years Aleksandar's dictatorship resembled the absolutist regime of Prince Miloš in Serbia a century earlier. It also reflected something of Europe's *Zeitgeist* in the stress on order, discipline, state authority and anti-Communism. It was hardly Fascist, though, contrary to the 'monarcho-Fascist' label attached to it by some post-1945 Communist historians in Yugoslavia. There was no mass movement to force the king to act in 1929. The crisis was that of the political system, not of the class structure. There was no ideology to provide the basis for the dictatorship, and a return to a parliamentary system was stipulated as the final goal from the beginning. The only 'ideology' Aleksandar tried to develop was that of integral Yugoslavism, and not an '-ism' of his personal rule *per se.*

By instinct and personal development Prince Pavle was averse both to autocratic rule and to militarism. His overall outlook was essentially sympathetic to a decentralised model - however vaguely defined at the time - and an understanding between Belgrade and Zagreb. He was also unhappy with the entourage of advisers with which King Aleksandar had surrounded himself. To Pavle they were all men who encouraged and played upon the rigid, authoritarian side of Aleksandar's personality.[6]

Increasing Croat opposition to Aleksandar was invigorated by his formal change of the name of the state to 'Yugoslavia' and the introduction of the administrative system of nine *banovine* (provinces), which cut across traditional historic and ethnic lines. This and a renewed insistence on the concept of the 'Yugoslav nation' were seen as further steps away from the form of federalism which would respect the individuality of the Croats. Even though some CPP members (including one of its vice-presidents, Karlo Kovačić) entered the cabinet of Aleksandar's prime minister, General Živković, in 1930, there was no hint of a real split within the party ranks.

This was in sharp contrast to the political parties in Serbia, which - although generally antipathetic to Aleksandar's personal regime - were in a state of disarray, divided among themselves and unable to find a common language with Maček, the new leader of the CPP. The leader of the CPP kept aloof from them anyway. All approaches to sounding him out over the possible formation of a united opposition front were met with the demand that prior commitments be made about the extent of a future Croatian unit in the reorganised state, and an indication of the powers of its autonomous institutions.[7]

There was a fundamental discrepancy at work between Maček and the rest of the opposition. To him, the Croat question was everything. All links with other parties, or with the Crown, have to be examined through that prism. Politics was but a means of achieving national objectives. On the other hand, to the fragmented Serb opposition (and to the Slovene People's Party of Mgr. Anton Korošec) the chief issue was political, rather than national. The re-establishment of democratic institutions and parliamentary life was seen as a prerequisite of any long-term reform of the state. In other words, the Croat opposition to the King's regime was *national,* while the Serbian opposition to it was *political.* If Aleksandar's chief objective had been to enhance the unity of the state, the attempt ended in failure. It only disoriented the Serb parties and consolidated the Croat party.

The Prince Regent

The King was killed in Marseilles on 9 October 1934 by a pro-Bulgarian Macedonian terrorist. The assassin was acting in agreement with the Croat separatist organisation known as *Ustaša* (insurgent), led by an implacable opponent of any agreement with the Serbs, Ante Pavelić. His host in the French port city, foreign minister Louis Barthou, was also killed. The attack had taken place shortly after the destroyer *Dubrovnik* - on which the King had arrived from Split - landed there.

On that day Prince Pavle was restless, although he never claimed that he had any 'premonition' of the looming tragedy. In late afternoon he received a telephone call with the news. Pavle took it calmly: his cousin had prepared him, in his own way, at least for this one eventuality. On two occasions when attempts were made on the King's life it was hinted to Pavle that he would have to pick up the reins. Although he had never been explicitly told that he would become regent in the event of Aleksandar's death, the King instructed him what to do in such an emergency.

Accordingly, Prince Pavle immediately proceeded to the palace at Dedinje, and summoned Prime Minister Uzunović and the Commander of the Royal Guard, King Aleksandar's confidante General Živković, to meet him there. Together they opened the King's last will, which stipulated that Pavle was to act as the first regent - the Prince Regent - until King Aleksandar's eldest son Petar came of age in September 1941. The other two regents, Ivan Perović (a bureaucrat) and Radenko Stanković (a professor of medicine and Aleksandar's fellow Freemason) were on the whole insignificant figures whose presence was to prove purely ceremonial.

At least one immediate source of concern for Pavle was temporarily removed from the agenda. Pavelić's small Ustaša group had originally found refuge and assistance in Italy and Hungary, where it was provided with weapons and training facilities. The ensuing international outcry and the results of French police investigations compelled Hungary to liquidate the Janka Puszta training camp for Croat terrorists. There was a general clampdown on Croat terrorists throughout Europe, notably in Belgium where their front organisation was disbanded and its activists expelled. More importantly from Yugoslavia's viewpoint, Mussolini decided to intern the entire Ustaša group on the island of Lipari. Subsequently, as a result of the overall improvement of relations between Italy and Yugoslavia under the premiership of Milan Stojadinović, the Ustaša camp was liquidated and its members dispersed throughout the peninsula.

It was odd for Italy to start changing posture towards Yugoslavia almost immediately after aiding and abetting an act of terrorism against its monarch. Mussolini's motives for returning to a policy of detente with his Adriatic neighbour is found in his understanding of the menace which the new regime in Berlin posed to Italy's position in the Danubian basin in general, and in particular to its long-term hold on the former Austrian lands in the north-east of the country. An associated objective could have been to detach Yugoslavia from her traditional alliances (France, the Little Entente), and thus alter the political map of South-East Europe in Italy's favour.

Stojadinović's Prime Ministership

The shift in Italian attitudes coincided with the appointment of Dr Milan Stojadinović as Yugoslavia's prime minister in June 1935. Stojadinović, a dynamic former finance minister, was initially selected by Pavle primarily for domestic reasons: as a man who could take the country out of the constitutional straight-jacket tailored by King Aleksandar without changing the Constitution, and, in particular, who could strike a deal with the Croats. Stojadinović's predecessors, Nikola Uzunović and Bogoljub Jevtić, were deemed by Pavle to be unimaginative specimens of the old guard, neither able nor willing to think imaginatively or act boldly in the trying times ahead.

But in order to get rid of Jevtić Prince Pavle had to indulge in an exercise in Machiavellian politics, an experience which he found personally distasteful, yet necessary in the milieu within which he had to operate. With Stojadinović's and Živković's connivance he assented to an artificially induced government crisis to bring down Jevtić, which cleared the way for his appointee.

It must be remembered that Pavle's freedom of action was limited. He may have wanted to act boldly and restructure the state in a federalist manner, but he felt duty-bound to see his seven years through without altering the existing centralist constitution of 1931. His major dilemma was that he perceived his role as Regent as that of a caretaker, not a reformer, while the pressure of events both at home and abroad demanded a fundamental restructuring of Yugoslavia's internal politics and external relations.

Stojadinović was invited to form a cabinet in June 1935 for reasons of domestic politics, but he also had a foreign policy agenda of his own. In 1934, as finance minister, Stojadinović had displayed eagerness for closer economic ties with Germany. Eventual reliance on Germany as its chief trade partner turned out to be an important feature of Yugoslavia's strategic position in the ensuing years. In his overall shift to a policy of neutrality and equidistance *vis-a-vis* Yugoslavia's traditional allies and totalitarian neighbours, Stojadinović acted in agreement with the ultimate mastermind of the country's foreign policy after King Aleksandar's death, the Prince Regent.

It was Prince Pavle's firm belief that good relations with Berlin were an insurance policy against the restless and ever dangerous neighbour Italy.[8] After a period of indignation after Marseilles, Yugoslav diplomacy detected fresh tones in Mussolini's posture and sought improved relations with Italy. The Regent's task was facilitated by the fact that he was encouraged by Yugoslavia's traditional allies - notably France - to seek an understanding with Rome.

Both Yugoslavia and France amassed solid evidence of Italian official involvement with the Ustaša. However, French diplomacy under Pierre Laval pressured Belgrade not to accuse Italy alongside Hungary at the League of Nations for the murder of King Aleksandar. Laval went out of his way to impress on Stojadinović the need for reconciliation with Italy, when the new Yugoslav prime minister visited Paris in September 1935.[9] At that time France sought support of Italy in face of the rising threat on the Rhine, and Laval even vaguely hinted at France's possible support for Mussolini's ambitions in Abyssinia.

Prince Pavle, the inveterate Anglophile, deemed it personally important to find approval in London, too, for his new course. It was duly given by Orme Sargent at the Foreign Office, whose advice was both cynical and pragmatic: 'If any foreign country is to be implicated in the assassination it is better on the whole that it should be Hungary rather than Italy'.

Detente With Italy

The emergence of Stojadinović as the strong man in Belgrade, able and willing to undertake bold new foreign policy initiatives with the Prince Regent's consent, impressed the Italians. Furthermore - ironically - just as France advised the Yugoslavs to seek accommodation with Italy, Germany advised Italy to do likewise: Hitler spoke to Ciano at Berchtesgaden in October 1936, and pressed on him the need to improve relations with Yugoslavia.[10]

For once, everyone seemed to be interested in improved relations between Belgrade and Rome. The French were worried about Germany, and wanted to reconcile their old ally, Yugoslavia, with Laval's newly-won friend Italy. The Germans were eager to offer Mussolini a compensation for, and a distraction from Austria, and pointed at the Balkans as his 'sphere of influence'. The Italians were apprehensive of German ambitions in the South-East and sought to establish links designed to block an eventual German advance; if this were to be accompanied by a weakening of Yugoslavia's traditional links, so much the better. As for Prince Pavle, he understood that *Anschluss* was merely a matter of time, after Mussolini had announced the creation of the Rome-Berlin Axis in Milan on 1 November 1936. To him, enhanced security on the western border was an urgent necessity.

Having received encouraging Italian signals, Prince Pavle authorised Stojadinović to dispatch an envoy to Rome in December 1936, to work out the details of a proposed treaty with Italy.[11] Mussolini's foreign minister Ciano appeared positively eager to reach a major agreement. The Yugoslav negotiator's final report contained a perceptive characterisation of Ciano's personality, and of the style of Fascist diplomacy: 'I have the impression that Ciano is very keen to come to Belgrade and create a sensation. It looks to me he wants to perform that visit in a 'hussard' style: he'll fly in and out, he'll stun the whole world.'[12]

Before the end of March, Ciano indeed went to Belgrade, where he and Stojadinović signed (on 25 March 1937) the Italian-Yugoslav Treaty. The negotiations were kept discreet, and the treaty came as a surprise to world opinion, just as Ciano seems to have desired. The gist of the political agreement was that common frontiers would be respected; if one side were to become a victim of unprovoked attack by one or more third parties, the other side would refrain from any action favouring the aggressor. The two sides reiterated their determination not to resort to war in bilateral relations, and to resolve all disputes by peaceful means. They also undertook 'not to tolerate on their territory nor to aid in any manner' any activity which would be directed against territorial integrity or established order of the other, thus spelling the end of all Ustaša activity.

The Italians made no secret to their Yugoslav counterparts that their readiness to compromise was partly based on their apprehension of Germany. This sounded like a far cry from the Axis principles, announced by Mussolini only four months previously. Ciano was very blunt:

> I am a friend of Germany, but - between us and confidentially - Germany is not only a dangerous adversary to her enemies, but also a difficult friend to her friends. I do not think that we need to organise against Germany now, but a man must bear in mind that your and our position in relation to Germany will be improved if we stick together. Our 42 million and your 15 million will mean more together than apart. Do not understand me wrongly. I don't think we should turn against Germany, but we must - between ourselves - organise our cooperation with her.[13]

Such statements presented Prince Pavle with a dilemma: how much was there of a discrepancy between Mussolini's pro-Axis rhetoric and Ciano's misgivings? They illustrated the fundamental - and ultimately fatal - contradiction in Italy's foreign policy in the 1930s. Germany had arrived, and was on the march. Hitler's categorical and repeated renunciation of South Tyrol demanded Italy's acceptance of the *Anschluss*. But even if Alto Adige was safe for Italy, what about the Danubian area and the Adriatic, which was a legitimate concern if Italy was not to abdicate its role as a great power? This had far-reaching consequences for Yugoslavia, too: Hitler wanted an alliance with Italy, but sought the expulsion of Italian influence from the Danubian basin and Italy's compensation in the Mediterranean.[14]

In early 1937 Mussolini felt compelled to try and make a friend, and even an ally, of Yugoslavia - previously regarded as an inferior heir to the Austrian legacy as Italy's rival in the Adriatic. The looming German colossus concentrated his mind, which made the change more palatable and positively attractive to both sides. As Ciano put it, 'Once the *Anschluss* is an accomplished fact, all those countries who must oppose the German descent towards the Adriatic or along the Danube valley will polarise around the Rome-Belgrade axis. This bloc which will arise will be such as to dissuade the Germans from any mad attempt.'[15]

On balance, Prince Pavle's and Stojadinović's agreement with Italy was favourable to Yugoslavia. It settled disputes which had been on the agenda for almost two decades. Italy could derive satisfaction from the fact that the agreement implied a shift in Yugoslavia's foreign policy, away from France and the Little Entente.

Prince Pavle's diplomatic gambit greatly alarmed the French diplomats and military in mid-1937, and led to visits by General Gamelin, in September 1937, and by Foreign Minister Yvon Delbos, in December 1937, to Belgrade to try to halt the drift in Yugoslav Foreign policy. But Stojadinović explained the shift to the French charge d'affaires in Belgrade in terms of Realpolitik: 'France in particular could not do a great deal for the Little Entente as she has no means of communication, in view of the fact that Italy - by definition - would be at war with her.'[16]

It was at this point that Stojadinović's enthusiasm for a 'Belgrade-Rome Axis' started going too far for Prince Pavle's liking. The Prince wanted to create a strong and independent Yugoslavia, and in the first two years of his government Stojadinović had acted in full accord with him. But the prime minister was beginning to act too much as his own man, which aroused Pavle's suspicions about his ultimate ambitions. His predecessor, King Aleksandar, had looked to France for protection, but by the mid-1930s France was no longer a reliable friend: she had acted ambiguously over Abyssinia, and her sense of a power vacuum in Eastern Europe induced her to sign a pact with the USSR. Nevertheless, while new diplomacy was needed, Prince Pavle was not prepared to allow Stojadinović to take the country too far into the fold of Rome and Berlin.

Italian enthusiasm for Stojadinović only strengthened the Prince's doubts. Ciano's own impression was that the Belgrade agreement represented but a first step towards the alliance 'which Stojadinović considers natural and inevitable'.[17] Echoing Ciano's openly stated apprehensions of Germany, the Yugoslav prime minister started talking in terms of the Belgrade-Rome Axis which would halt the German descent to the south. When Stojadinović proceeded to express his misgivings about the League of Nations in Geneva, his hopes for expanded trade with Italy, and his contempt for England's 'bluffs', Ciano delightedly concluded that 'Stojadinović is a Fascist', and 'Yugoslavia now had a profound knowledge of the Italian language and culture. Italy will shortly be able to take the place in Yugoslavia of France herself'.[18]

Relations With Germany

King Aleksandar's legacy gave Prince Pavle considerable room for manoeuvre on the German front, too. For all his ostensible Francophilia, the King was not *a priori* hostile to Hitler's rise to power, apparently regarding it as a possible counterweight to Italy's ambitions in the South-East. He said that he would prefer a German-Austrian customs union, and Germany as a neighbour, rather than Italy.[19] There are indications that on the eve of his fateful trip to Marseilles the King passed a message to Berlin with his assurances that Yugoslavia would never enter into any agreement which would attempt to bypass Germany in solving Central European issues.[20]

Prince Pavle realised that a more open policy toward Germany could strengthen his position vis-a-vis France, obtain concessions from her, and prevent any French-Italian agreement - inspired by the need to contain Germany - which would be obtained at the cost of French appeasement of Italy's aspirations in the Adriatic. He shared his cousin's readiness to accept the *Anschluss* because it would cut away a vital link in Italy's attempt to encircle Yugoslavia from the north and north-west (Italy-Austria-Hungary). It would also put an end to the perennial fear of a Habsburg restoration.

For his part, Hitler wanted to break up the Little Entente and to exclude French influence from Central Europe. He also appeared willing, from his earliest days in power, to cultivate Yugoslavia, rather than to seek its destruction. This was in contrast to his policy towards other 'Versailles creations', the despised Czechoslovakia and hated Poland. He correctly perceived that the cement keeping the Little Entente together, and its members close to France, was fear of Hungarian revisionism. Therefore, Budapest needed to be restrained, and its energy channelled in the desired direction.[21] Hitler's Balkan policy was based on the premise that Yugoslavia and Romania should be brought into Germany's sphere of influence - in the first instance primarily by economic means. A trade agreement between Berlin and Belgrade was swiftly concluded in 1934, ensuring an outlet for Yugoslav farm produce at prices above world markets, in return for German industrial goods. The agreement, favourable to Yugoslavia, represented an instance of Germany's readiness to subordinate its short-term economic interests to larger geo-strategic goals.

Accordingly, German ministries were told that Italy's pre-1937 policy of subversion of Yugoslavia was detrimental to Germany's interests. This was to be countered by the policy of friendship with Belgrade, which would act as a barrier to Italy's designs in the Danubian basin. The theme of a strong Yugoslavia, friendly to Germany, as the key to Berlin's policy in south-eastern Europe, was a salient feature of German diplomatic documents in the 1930s.[22]

Stojadinović's visit to Berlin in December 1937 was a success from the German point of view. The Yugoslav prime minister told Hitler that Yugoslavia would not join any bloc, or accept any obligations against Germany. This could only please Hitler, who had sought for years to break up the Little Entente by 'unequal treatment' of its members, that is, by the isolation of Czechoslovakia and the cultivating of Romania and Yugoslavia. Germany's economic penetration of the Balkans was also proceeding vigorously and swiftly. By 1936 it was taking a greater share of the Balkan countries' exports than all the other great powers combined.

Italy's rapid and irreversible estrangement from Britain and France, resulting from the Abyssinian crisis, fitted neatly into Hitler's plans. He was the chief benefactor: when Germany afforded Italy an opportunity to weaken France, Mussolini seized it. Mussolini's to see in the German reoccupation of the Rhineland the *casus foederis* stipulated by Locarno was 'gratuitously matched' by a relaxation of the vigilance on the Brenner.[23] Mussolini's ensuing visit to Germany, Italy's accession to the Anti-Comintern Pact and withdrawal from the League of Nations marked its final abandonment of the Europe of Versailles. But the Italians' shift to Berlin was not totally wholehearted - as evidenced in Ciano's confidences to Stojadinović - and fear of Germany's rising power necessitated the definition of an exclusively Italian sphere. By becoming reconciled to the *Anschluss*, Italy fell back on trying to shore up a zone of influence south of the area soon to become part of the Reich.

Hitler was only too pleased to oblige. His often stated respect for the Brenner frontier was reiterated in the strongest possible terms in March 1939. He perceived that, to Mussolini, Italy's status as a big power was at stake. Hitler accordingly stated his disinterest in the western Balkans. He knew that it was imperative to flatter and reassure the Italian leader. Ribbentrop's letter to Ciano of 20 March 1939 was worded accordingly, including an unequivocal statement that 'in all Mediterranean questions the policy of the Axis is to be determined by Rome'.[24]

The Fall of Stojadinović

The eventual fall of Stojadinović in February 1939 placed Mussolini's line of retreat in doubt. His 'Belgrade-Rome Axis' hinged too much on one man. Germany's seizure of the rump of Bohemia and the proclamation of an independent Slovakia - only a month later - were received in Rome with alarm. Hitler's reiteration of Italy's Mediterranean primacy admittedly averted the crisis in Axis relations, but it also acted as a substitute for comprehensive long-term analysis of the two powers' common interests. The strategic community of interests remained unclarified, with far-reaching consequences later on. The events of 1935-1939 created ideological solidarity between two totalitarian regimes, while their will to expand drew them together against forces devoted to the maintenance of the existing order.

Italy's subsequent return to the policy of subversion of Yugoslavia and territorial expansion along the eastern Adriatic could be interpreted as an attempt to secure the strategic 'rear' vis-a-vis its overbearing ally, Germany, rather than an element in a coherent long-term strategy of territorial expansion. The issue of Yugoslavia - insofar as it did not touch on the Italian interests in Albania - was a distraction, even from the limited task Mussolini had set for himself, namely, the removal of barriers that kept Italy confined to the Mediterranean.

Milan Stojadinović acquired a fairly bad name after his fall. To the Communists he was a reactionary exponent of 'big capital', and a friend of the Axis powers; to the Croats he was an inflexible 'greater Serb'; and in London he was viewed no better than a common fascist - and treated accordingly during the war by the British. When Prince Pavle appointed him in 1935, Stojadinović was regarded as an opponent of the dictatorship and the person likely to reintroduce normal political life. Indeed, the press grew considerably freer, and reported statements unfavourable to the government. At first Stojadinović also hinted at his readiness to solve the Croat question. After almost four years in office, however, he had not succeeded in doing so.

Stojadinović's freedom of manoeuvre, he later claimed, was limited by Prince Pavle's decision not to change the 1931 Constitution until young King Petar II came of age.[25] Furthermore, the Croat leader Vladko Maček was not ready to compromise yet. He expected the rising tension in Europe to work in his favour by making Belgrade readier to grant concessions. Within the CPP, extremist voices were heard with greater frequency, accusing Maček of 'softness' and insufficient radicalism. He responded to such pressures by making inopportune or unreasonable demands.

Maček had political and constitutional grounds to regard Prince Pavle as a more suitable partner for negotiations than the prime minister. Maček had stated on more than one occasion that he only recognised the Crown and the state, while everything else was open. When the Prince Regent eventually accepted the role of the interlocutor in the spring 1939, Maček had no qualms about making a deal over the heads of his Serbian opposition 'partners'. But what frustrated the Prince was that the Stojadinović years had turned into a period of stagnation in the resolution of the Croat question.

If in 1938 Maček did not seem to be in a hurry. Stojadinović was not too eager either. He was not impressed by the pressures of international events, because the treaty with Italy seemingly neutralised the only power which could offer some hope and comfort to the Croat cause. Cultivated by Germany, friendly with Italy, still (nominally) allied with France, and still allowing the fiction of the Little Entente to continue, the Yugoslav prime minister believed he was building a fairly strong external position.

While Maček had to contend with increasing radicalism in his ranks, from separatist quarters, Stojadinović was similarly targeted from the Serb side. This became obvious in 1937 with the dispute over ratification of the concordat with the Holy See. Although the concordat was King Aleksandar's idea, Pavle's and Stojadinović's opponents - which by now included the influential General Živković - claimed that it would give undue privileges to the Roman Catholic Church at the expense of the Serbian Orthodox Church. The Prince and Stojadinović were accused of pushing for its passage through the *Skupština* in order to gain personally, or score points with the Italians.

Prince Pavle supported the concordat, apparently unaware of the depth of sentiment it aroused in the Serb body-politic. He only stopped Stojadinović from proceeding with the potentially disastrous *Skupština* debate after the crisis point had been reached - when the police brutally dispersed a procession through the streets of Belgrade led by the clergy, and rioting broke out. The Prince's defeat left him embittered. Terence Shone, first secretary at the British legation in Belgrade and a personal friend, noted Pavle's complaints about 'Serbian politicians in general, maintaining that they were hidebound and tactless and that but for them he would have reached agreement long ago with Dr Maček on the Croat question'.

The dispute over the Concordat was a sign of deeper restlessness among the Serbs, which was further aroused by the new direction in Yugoslavia's foreign policy. During his tour of the European capitals in late 1937 Stojadinović was impressed by the contrast between the stale atmosphere of London and Paris, and self-confident dynamism of Rome and Berlin. To many of his compatriots, Stojadinović's instincts increasingly smacked of fascism. He introduced green-shirted youths and shouts of 'Leader, Leader' at his rallies, which could not impress a people tired of a decade of dictatorship and authoritarianism.

The new, increasingly neutralist foreign policy orientation, for all its pragmatism, was unappealing for the Serbs, who less than a generation earlier had fought a bloody war against the Austro-Germans, and who exhibited strong Francophile affinities. Stojadinović's idiosyncrasies went beyond Prince Pavle's concept of foreign policy which sought greater equidistance vis-a-vis rival European power blocs, but was decidedly inimical to any alliance with either fascism or nazism.

Prince Pavle's decision to replace Stojadinović shortly after the election of December 1938 - which the ruling government party, made up of Radicals, Bosnian Muslims and Slovenes, won, albeit narrowly - was due to several factors. The Prince was genuinely concerned that Stojadinović's policy of friendship with the Axis powers went too far, illustrated by events such as the premier's confidential *tete-a-tete* with Ciano in January 1939, when the forthcoming occupation, and possible Italo-Yugoslav partition of Albania was on the agenda.[26] Stojadinović failed to brief the Prince of this part of his talks, and Pavle was furious when he learnt of it from Ciano himself.

By this time Prince Pavle was inured to political methods which ill-suited his values and temperament, but which were considered normal *modus operandi* in the Balkan milieu. So he devised a scheme for Stojadinović's removal which was remarkably similar to the stratagem used to install him in power in 1935. On the clumsiest pretext possible -

a parliamentary debate which could have been construed as reflecting some differences of opinion within the governing party on the Croat question - the Prince demanded the resignation of Stojadinović's government. On 4 February 1939 Stojadinović resigned. The Prince then selected Dragiša Cvetković, a government minister, but nationally little-known, as Stojadinović's successor. The foreign ministry was entrusted to Aleksandar Cincar-Marković, a former ambassador in Berlin.

The fall of Stojadinović came as a surprise to the Italians, and it was seen as a blow to their policy. 'With the removal of Stojadinović', Ciano wrote, 'the Yugoslav card has lost for us 90 percent of its value'.[27] (Only two years later Mussolini and Ciano were to make the same error of basing their policy on one man in the case of the Ustaša leader Pavelić, to whom Mussolini referred as 'the only trump card we have in Croatia'.) New circumstances induced Rome to accept even such overtures by Croat separatists which would have been unthinkable only a few months previously. From March 1937 until the fall of Stojadinović Italy had regarded Yugoslavia as a friendly country and discouraged any Croat separatist activity. By the end of spring of 1939 the pendulum in Italy's attitude to its eastern neighbour had made another swing. For the final twenty-two months of Yugoslavia's existence the attitude of Italy remained inimical.

The Serb-Croat Agreement

Any 'philo-fascist' leanings and Stojadinović's increasing megalomania aside, a more pressing reason for the Prince to replace him was domestic: his inactivity on the Croat question. Stojadinović's self-confidence apparently increased after the December 1938 elections, and in a letter to the Prince he openly rejected any notion of a speedy compromise with Maček.[28] This was the last straw for Pavle. In order to reach an agreement with Maček - which he regarded as ultimately inevitable, and a matter of pressing importance - Prince Pavle knew he needed to find someone other than Stojadinović, not least because Maček demanded Stojadinović's removal as a *conditio sine qua non* for formal negotiations.

While Cvetković was known to be an advocate of agreement with Maček, his lack of authority and independent power base vouched to Prince Pavle that the new prime minister would not be too much his own man. Unfortunately for the Prince and for his new prime minister, it also meant that the government lacked credibility among most Yugoslavs, and especially among the Serbs.

Prince Pavle's insufficient contact with Serbia's traditions and political culture made him unaware that the looming European storm demanded not only determined, but also strong leadership. He failed to grasp that without undisputed legitimacy, and without a clear mandate, its many and difficult tasks ultimately became impossible.

Cvetković formally announced his intention to negotiate with Maček in his speech in the *Skupština* on 10 March, 1939. He recognised the individuality of Croatia as a fact predating Yugoslavia, and declared he was ready to go to Zagreb and negotiate with Maček immediately. He arrived in Zagreb on 3 April, not only as the Prime Minister, but - significantly - also as Prince Pavle's envoy. His talks with Maček proceeded smoothly, and a tentative agreement was reached quickly. It was short and simple: an autonomous Croat *Banovina* was to be created. It would enjoy wide autonomy; defence and foreign affairs would remain in Belgrade with the Crown. A joint government would be formed to see the *Sporazum* (Agreement) through. The agreement was to be legally based on Article 116 of the 1931 Constitution, which provided for emergency measures in case of a threat to the country's security.

Much to Prince Pavle's chagrin, this draft encountered massive opposition from very different political quarters, not all of them Serb. The sticking point concerned areas to be subjected to plebiscite on the boundaries of the Croatian *Banovina*, and the way it would be carried out.[29] Strong resistance came from the Bosnian Muslims, led by Mehmed Spaho, and from the military, which regarded the proposed solution as detrimental to the defence capability of the country. Any further negotiations were temporarily ended.

This domestic setback coincided with the rapidly worsening international situation. Italy's invasion of Albania in April 1939 affected Prince Pavle very deeply. Given to a pessimistic outlook at best of times, he came close to a breakdown: On 11 April he decided to send his children back to England. That night, feeling isolated, helpless and frustrated, he broke down and wept. The Regent was also facing a dilemma concerning the future of young King Petar. Prince Pavle was deeply hurt by the resignation of Petar's tutor Cecil Parrott in March, who in his letter reproached the Prince for neglecting the development of the heir to the throne. Many years later, the Prince gave an account of his state of mind in the spring of 1939, which was summarised, as follows, by his biographers:

> Behind the bitter tears of the Prince Regent...lay the years of struggling to preserve his country's unity and independence, and the realisation of the horrors which the next few months looked certain to bring to Europe, to his country and to his family. Pavle looked back on his years as Regent: on the obstinacy and corruption of the politicians; on the intransigence of the army chiefs and the deviousness of the Church leaders; on the lack of interest or assistance from his fellow regents; on the persistent intrigues and hurtful rumours; and on his own, inevitable, separation from his dearest friends. All this for a people who gave him little thanks and for a nephew who he was now accused of having neglected.[30]

During his visit to Berlin in June 1939 Prince Pavle became convinced that the war in Europe was unavoidable and imminent. He therefore resolved to revive the talks with the Croats without delay. Some contact between Cvetković and Maček had been maintained through intermediaries, and formal negotiations resumed by the end of June. The agreement was reached very quickly, and resolution of several finer points was entrusted to a team of legal and financial experts of both sides. The text was submitted to Prince Pavle for approval on 24 August. He signed it immediately.

The *Sporazum* opened with the statement that 'Yugoslavia is the best guarantee of the independence and progress of Serbs, Croats and Slovenes'. Such a declaration of principle by the CPP reaffirmed its acceptance of the Yugoslav state. However, as the only Yugoslav unit constituted on the principle of nationality, and named after the nation which comprised a majority within it, the *Banovina* of Croatia came close to resembling a nation-state.

The *Sporazum* was similar in spirit to the Austro-Hungarian *Ausgleich* of 1867. Such a deal would have most probably satisfied Radić two decades earlier. However, by 1939 it was seen as too little (or too much), too late. To the separatist-minded Croats the *Sporazum* was a sellout by Maček. Many Serbs thought that by 'solving' the Croat question Prince Pavle helped create the Serb question. Everyone knew that the *Sporazum* was imposed on the Prince and Maček by the pressure of external events. It was an emergency political measure meant to unify and strengthen the country on the eve of a new European war. For that it was too late.

King Aleksandar's legacy burdened Prince Pavle with an impossible task. In 1939 the CPP, led by Maček, could still legitimately claim the leadership of the Croat nation. On the Serb side the King's personal rule prevented the emergence of a healthy political structure, capable of providing legitimacy to the Prince's attempt to prepare the country for the European storm ahead. The authoritarian figure of Stojadinović was replaced by a government that was perceived as weak and without authority, and yet it was the only way open to him to try and square the circle of Serb-Croat relations.

On the whole there had been no 'Serb' (or even narrowly Serbian) political line on the central issue of the state - the Croat question - either before or after 1929. Prince Pavle sought to fill the vacuum in Serb minds and deeds. It was a notable achievement to get Maček to express his devotion to Yugoslavia and - especially - to the person of Prince Pavle. Dark mutterings of extreme separatists in Zagreb notwithstanding, the Croat mainstream political establishment regarded the *Sporazum* as an imperfect and incomplete, but nevertheless important step towards solving the Croat question within Yugoslavia.

Skirting the European Storm

After the change of leadership in Belgrade Hitler and Mussolini agreed that Yugoslavia should be induced to accept a more explicit pro-Axis policy.[31] Prince Pavle's diplomats attempted to give suitable assurances to Berlin and Rome, without making commitments. The foreign minister, Aleksandar Cincar-Marković went to Rome on 22-23 April, and told Ciano that in case of war Yugoslavia would be neutral, while continuing to provide economic support to Italy and Germany. Yugoslavia also accepted the *fait accompli* of the Italian occupation of Albania, which had been a major issue between the two countries in King Aleksandar's lifetime.[32]

From Rome Cincar-Marković proceeded to Berlin, where he conferred with Ribbentrop and Hitler on 25 and 26 April. He repeated Yugoslavia's desire to remain neutral under all circumstances, and reiterated her parallel determination to avoid any arrangements directed against the Axis.[33] His efforts may have paid off; at the meeting between Ciano and Ribbentrop in Milan on 6 and 7 May they agreed on their countries' joint interest in preserving the *status quo* in Yugoslavia.[34]

The following week Prince Pavle visited Italy (10-15 May). His overriding impression was that the alliance between Hitler and Mussolini was unbreakable, and that Mussolini was not to be trusted.[35] If the Prince was apprehensive of Italian intentions, Ciano also took a dim view of his visitor. When he went to Berlin a week later to sign the Pact of Steel, Ciano expressed his distrust of Pavle.[36] Ciano suggested that during the Prince's forthcoming visit to Berlin the Yugoslavs should be asked to leave the League of Nations and join the Anti-Comintern Pact. On 30 May, Mussolini prepared a confidential memorandum for Hitler in this vein.[37] He wrote that the Axis powers should not be satisfied with promises of neutrality and professions of friendship, but should occupy the entire Danubian basin and the Balkan peninsula as soon as war broke out.

Ciano's comments in Berlin and Mussolini's memorandum to Hitler heralded a new phase in Yugoslavia's relations with the Axis powers, which would last almost two years. During this period Italy reverted to its anti-Yugoslav posture of the pre-Stojadinović years, while Germany restrained Mussolini and effectively vetoed any action against Yugoslavia.[38]

Germany sought to bring Yugoslavia into its orbit by political pressure. During their visit to Berlin in June, Prince Pavle and Cincar-Marković were treated to an impressive display of German might, including a parade that contained an entire tank division. Hitler was determined both to impress and to intimidate his visitors. The French foreign minister, Georges Bonnet, later described the eight-day visit as a truly regal occasion, 'worthy of the mightiest of monarchs. Nothing was missed to create the impression of popular enthusiasm and to provide evidence of value that the Reich attached to Yugoslavia's friendship. But the Prince remained true to his promises, given to our Minister prior to the trip to Berlin, and he refused to make any concessions to Germany'.[39]

Prince Pavle nevertheless resisted German pressure to quit the League of Nations, or to join the Anti-Comintern Pact.[40] Germany put a brave face on the slim results of his visit, which the Wilhelmstrasse called 'mutually completely satisfactory'.[41] Hitler took a decidedly dim view of Pavle, however, describing him as 'slippery as an eel'. For Prince Pavle the most enduring impression was that a general war could not be avoided. He also became convinced that Hitler was literally mad.[42] His subsequent visits to France and Britain (in July) were aimed at explaining to the Western allies - with whom, it is generally assumed, his heart had truly lain all along - why it was inevitable and essential that Yugoslavia should remain neutral in case of war.

Prince Pavle was delighted to be back in Britain that last summer before another storm engulfed Europe, and enjoyed being lavishly entertained by his old friend, King George VI, who made him a Garter Knight. He was also concerned by the apparent complacency of his political interlocutors in London. He warned Prime Minister Neville Chamberlain of his particular suspicion that Russo-German negotiations were in progress, but the Prime Minister did not take this seriously.

The Prince was not surprised at the outbreak of war in September 1939, which was duly followed by Yugoslavia's declaration of neutrality. He was aware that the long-term prospects for such a status depended less on him and his government, however, than on the course of war itself and the designs of the great powers in the Balkans.

In the first months of the war Yugoslavia's neutrality was accepted by both belligerent sides with some satisfaction. Germany's focus was elsewhere, and her supplies of food and raw materials, needed for the war effort continued to arrive as before. Even though nobody in Berlin had any doubt about Prince Pavle's intimate sympathies, Germany had little reason for concern. Her quick victory over Poland, while the Allies remained passive, created a deep impression on the ruling circles in Yugoslavia and on the country's public opinion. Talking to Ciano on 1 October 1939 Hitler calmly said that 'for the time being nothing new is going to happen in the Balkans'. The Western allies were satisfied by Yugoslavia's neutrality for the simple reason that they could not expect more.[43]

Italy Plots Again

Italy's position was more ambiguous. Even though Mussolini decided against attacking Yugoslavia, after toying with the idea in the summer of 1939, he became markedly more aggressive, and decided to revive his Croat proteges, the Ustaše. Prince Pavle's suspicion of Italy was fuelled both by the evidence of Pavelić's renewed role, and by Mussolini's overall policy in the Balkans after the outbreak of the war. (High quality intelligence on both subjects was provided by an efficient intelligence network which the Yugoslavs had built in Rome and in the Vatican.)

Mussolini's policy was inconsistent and unpredictable, and increasingly expansionist. On several occasions in early 1940 Mussolini appeared determined to take specific steps against the Yugoslavs. He ordered that General Gambarra be recalled from Spain, so that he could take command of Italian troops which would 'march into Croatia'. Ciano's diary entry also mentions that Mussolini circled 'a day in early June' in his calendar.[44]

Italy's entry into the war on the side of Germany in June 1940 resulted in yet another postponement of any action against its trans-Adriatic neighbour. Only three days after circling a day in June, on 13 May 1940, Mussolini was sufficiently impressed by the German offensive in the West to confide to Ciano that he would not be attacking Yugoslavia after all, for the time being anyway. Attacking the Yugoslavs, Mussolini said, would be 'a humiliating fallback'.[45]

Mussolini's decision to go to war on Hitler's side had been long in the making. During the spring of 1940, as Germany scored one success after another, the caution so apparent in Rome over the previous eight months melted as quickly as the French divisions. Even Ciano's Germanophobia seems to have been pushed aside; not even the King and the armed services could stem the tide. Although the Italian chiefs of staff admitted their inability to conduct a war even on the limited scale, German victories in France, and his fear that the spoils would be all Hitler's, forced Mussolini's hand.[46]

The spoils of the summer of 1940 proved meagre for him. Extravagant Italian demands of France (Nice, Corsica, Tunisia and Savoy) were quickly toned down at Mussolini's meeting with Hitler and Ribbentrop in Munich on 18 June. Hitler wanted to offer terms which would make it easier for France to break with Britain and end her own resistance, while also sending a signal to London that a mutually acceptable and reasonable peace was still possible. Mussolini was left in no doubt who was calling the shots in the West. Frustrated, he turned his attention to the Balkans yet again. The South-East appeared the only area where he could enjoy some freedom of action, and where he could at least symbolically compensate for the success of his dominant, brutal friend.

In early July Mussolini ordered his General Staff to prepare plans for a simultaneous attack on both Yugoslavia and Greece. In the summer of 1940, however, Yugoslavia's neutrality still suited German interests. The Italians were left in no doubt of this fact by Hitler. He would formally agree with Italian designs in principle, but added that 'the time was not right' or that strategic conditions did not favour any such action in the Balkans. When Ciano expressed belligerent intentions towards Yugoslavia in a conversation with Hitler on 7 July, he received a firm rebuke.[47] Hitler was totally uninterested in any attack on Yugoslavia. He wanted peace on his southern border, and did not want to give the British an opportunity to create bases in Yugoslavia.

Ribbentrop spoke in the same vein to the Italian ambassador in Berlin, Alfieri, on 16 August, and spelt out the German absolute ban on any anti-Yugoslav adventure by the Italians.[48] Ribbentrop warned that not only the military, but also the political consequences of Italy's attack on Yugoslavia would be complex and problematic. But Hitler was still not reassured. By the end of the summer he sent Ribbentrop to Rome to calm Mussolini once again. The Germans in effect put a veto on Italian plans, and Mussolini had to accept it.[49].

Two weeks later Hitler and Mussolini met at the Brenner (4 October). Hitler talked of his plans concerning Spain, France and Britain.[50] However, he concealed from Mussolini that he had already issued orders for the entry of German troops into Romania - which happened only days later. Not for the first time, and certainly not for the last, Mussolini complained that 'Hitler always faces me with a fait accompli'.[51] He decided to take action unilaterally too, without giving Hitler an opportunity to frustrate him again. On 28 October 1940 Italian troops in Albania attacked Greece. Italy had brought the war to the Balkans.

The Italian attack on Greece made the geo-strategic and political position of Yugoslavia ever more precarious. Belgrade nervously waited to see whether the new conflict would remain localised. When this appeared probable after the first few days of fighting, the Yugoslavs issued a statement on 2 November 1940 - obviously aimed at Italy - affirming their policy of neutrality, and stressing the hope that this policy would be respected.[52] Yugoslav reliance on Germany in restraining Italian aggressive intentions during the summer of 1940 also gave rise to expectations in Belgrade that similar German benevolence would continue.[53] This was not to be.

German Pressure on Prince Pavle

Hitler was not pleased with Mussolini's action in Greece. Two factors subsequently had a decisive role in shaping German policy: British commitment to Athens - which started being implemented with the establishment of RAF bases in Crete - and Italian military defeats. Italian setbacks in Greece forced Germany not only to become more directly involved, but also to have a more explicit final word in this nominally Italian zone. Italy had no choice but to accept the further erosion of its role within the Axis. As usual, Italy's weakened position was the result of a self-inflicted wound.

From November 1940 Germany took the initiative in the Axis dealings with Yugoslavia. Increased German pressure on Belgrade could be felt even before Mussolini's Greek adventure. Initially this took the form of demands that the government of Yugoslavia make a 'candid adjustment of Yugoslav policy to the situation created by the German victory in the West'.[54] Prompted by Heeren, at the end of August, Prince Pavle felt compelled to indicate that Yugoslavia was forced by the circumstances to 'increase its reliance' on Germany.[55]

When Hitler talked to Ciano on 18 November 1940, he asked directly what Italy was prepared to offer to Yugoslavia in order to neutralise it, and immediately added that Salonika would be an appropriate inducement. The new German assertiveness in the matter was apparent in the way Hitler brushed aside Ciano's remark that this would be difficult for Mussolini to accept. Once its hand was forced by the Italian action in Greece, Germany proceeded with great determination to woo Yugoslavia to its side if possible, or to bully it into submission if necessary.

Prince Pavle's mood after May 1940 reflected a state of deep shock which the fall of France caused in Yugoslavia, especially among the traditionally Francophile Serb elite. To many, the final predominance of Germany in Europe seemed assured: the liberal democratic idea was nearing the end of its era, and a new order was emerging, with two totalitarian powers as its pillars. To offset their weight, Pavle was forced to establish relations with the third such power, Stalin's Russia, even though he detested Bolshevism and feared Soviet ambitions no less than the late King Aleksandar. Diplomatic relations between Moscow and Belgrade were re-established in June, and ministers exchanged in July

1940. The Germans disapproved, and the alleged increase in Soviet influence in Yugoslavia was added to their growing list of complaints against Pavle and his government.

Germany's impatience with Belgrade reflected a curious reversal of intra-Axis roles. For the best part of the previous two years Italy was adopting an aggressive posture towards its eastern neighbour, while Germany exercised a moderating influence. As 1940 drew to its close, German pressure on Belgrade became increasingly apparent, while Italy had given up any thought of an aggressive action against Yugoslavia. Bogged down in Greece, it welcomed the establishment of discreet contact between the two countries offered by a Belgrade lawyer and legal adviser of the Italian Legation there, Vladislav Stakić.[56]

That Prince Pavle and his ministers were now pinning their hopes on discreet diplomacy reflected their ever narrowing range of options. Stakić spoke to Ciano, who recorded on 11 November that Mussolini supported the idea of an Italo-Yugoslav entente. Ciano added a personal thought: 'I always considered an attack on Yugoslavia a difficult undertaking and not useful for the future equilibrium of Europe. Instead of bringing under our roof a mass of nervous and untrustworthy Croats, I believe it is better to create a solid basis of understanding with Yugoslavia'.[57]

While Stakić went to Rome, another secret emissary was sent to Berlin. This was Danilo Gregorić, a young Slovene who edited a right-wing Belgrade daily.[58] On his second visit to Germany Gregorić was told that Prince Pavle should come for talks with Hitler and Ribbentrop. The Prince sent Cincar-Marković instead, who was received by Hitler at the Berghof on 28 November 1940. Hitler suggested that Yugoslavia sign a non-aggression treaty with Germany and Italy.[59] He promised German backing for a consolidated Yugoslavia if it agreed to enter the new European order, and mentioned Salonika as an inducement. He hinted that the future relationship could go further, alluding to Yugoslavia joining the Tripartite Pact.

Prince Pavle assumed that Hitler would be satisfied with the Yugoslav acceptance of the 'non-aggression treaty' - especially since it was Hitler who had proposed it in the first place. The Yugoslav government replied on 7 December that it was prepared to sign such a treaty, 'based on the Italian-Yugoslav Treaty of March 1937'.[60]

To Pavle's chagrin, Hitler had changed his mind, and escalated his demands. After two weeks' silence he sent a reply to an increasingly nervous Belgrade, which stated that the non-aggression treaty 'would not satisfy' demands for closer links between Yugoslavia and the Axis, since it would still leave open the issue of its accession to the Tripartite Pact.[61]

Not surprisingly, the Prince was taken aback. Hitler's response may have been a calculated ploy designed to wear out the Yugoslavs psychologically; or he may have simply changed his mind - which he had in his power to do anyway. At the same time, Germany's combined diplomatic and military pincer movement had continued: one by one, Yugoslavia's neighbours to the north and east were joining the Pact and accepting German troops on their territory. Hungary joined the Tripartite Pact on 20 November 1940; Romania on 23 and Slovakia on 24 November. Bulgaria signed on 1 March 1941.

The primary objective of Germany was to prepare Operation Barbarossa; the secondary to reach Greece from the north-east, and attack it from Bulgaria. In the process, Yugoslavia found itself physically encircled. Most of Germany's new Balkan allies had some potential irredentist claim against Yugoslavia, which left the country vulnerable militarily and psychologically. In South-Eastern Europe in the winter of 1940-1941 it was not easy to enjoy the distinction of being the last 'Versailles state' to have its 1919 frontiers still intact.

It is ironic, and indicative of the desperate predicament of Prince Pavle and his government, that in trying to accommodate Hitler he sought a respite in closer relations with Rome. Encouraged by Stakić's talks there in November, he hoped to win Mussolini over to the idea of a bilateral or trilateral treaty based on the March 1937 model. Stakić went to Rome again in early 1941 and encountered Mussolini's encouraging response.[62] The Duce suggested that such treaty 'would suffice' as far as the demand for Yugoslavia's drawing closer to the Axis was concerned. Italy's weakness, however, meant that Mussolini's signals had little bearing on the final outcome. In effect, Yugoslavia's foreign policy was rapidly running out of time and options. Its makers were hoping against hope to find some constancy in Rome and Berlin by turns.

The Italians duly informed Berlin of their talks with Stakić. But Hitler would have none of this. He had serious business on his mind: getting Greece out of the way (Operation 'Marita', now firmly planned for early April) and a final settling of scores with Stalin. There was no room for ambiguities and *combinazioni* in the Balkans any more; to underscore the point, Gregorić was told yet again that 'total clarification' of relations with Belgrade was necessary.

Pressure From Britain and America

In early 1941 Prince Pavle was subjected to increasing pressure from what he had always considered a friendly quarter: Britain and America. As an inveterate and open Anglophile, until January 1941 he could take some comfort in the fact that there had been little discrepancy between the interests of Yugoslavia and those of Britain. As Regent he had discharged his duties in a manner consistent with his British education, friendships and outlook. His *soirees* with successive British ministers in Belgrade, his readiness to keep them well informed at all times, had been prompted not only by his desire for kindred companionship, but also by a deeper reverence for what he assumed were British 'standards' and values. 'In fact Pavle's trust of British representatives abroad was so profound that it was invariably taken for granted in official circles, and occasionally even taken advantage of by individuals.'[63]

The Foreign Office, in fact, took Prince Pavle for granted far too much. An example is provided by the way it simply ignored urgent appeals for economic aid, for expanded trade links, and for arms, which the Prince conveyed to London by various means, most notably through Lord Halifax in May 1939. In spite of vague verbal promises by Halifax, even that strong appeal was disregarded.

In June the British minister in Belgrade, Sir Ronald Campbell, sent a long report to the Foreign Office making 'a further plea for the offer by H.M.G. of more substantial assistance to (Yugoslavia). I never see the Prince Regent, the President of the Council, or the Minister of Finance that they do not, at some stage in our conversation, express surprise that we do practically nothing to help'. Again, no action was taken.

Aware of the pressing political need to secure new markets and new sources of supply, and rebuffed by the British, Prince Pavle sought to bolster his country's position by appealing to the United States. In the first half of 1939 the Yugoslav Minister in Washington, Konstantin Fotić, made repeated pleas for increased trade with the United States. He also asked the State Department to help secure Yugoslavia's lines of credit from the Export-Import Bank. For Pavle, disappointed in Britain's unresponsiveness, this was seen as an opportunity to reduce the country's near-total economic dependence on Germany.

Such pleas were totally ignored by Washington, too.[64] The War and Navy departments were not interested in acquiring a reserve stock of Yugoslav bauxite, which was one of the suggestions from Belgrade, and there had been no attempt by the State Department to encourage such purchase on political grounds. Furthermore, Export-Import Bank credits were denied to the Yugoslavs, following a letter to the Bank from Assistant Secretary of State Adolf Berle, who stated that 'the Department does not at the moment see any reason why such credit should be granted'. The need to reduce Nazi stranglehold on the Yugoslav economy evidently did not enter into the considerations of policy-makers in Washington.

In May 1939 Prince Pavle conveyed a confidential and personal request for American armaments to the U.S. Ambassador in France, William Bullitt. As the latter reported to Washington, the Regent 'knew' that all American telegrams to and from Belgrade were deciphered by the Germans, which was why he routed his request through Paris.[65] Nothing came of this initiative either, except for a somewhat indignant - and inaccurate - remark by an official in Washington that the code was safe from intrusion by German eavesdroppers.

Such apparent indifference in London and Washington prompted the Prince, shortly after Germany attacked Poland, to express his frustration with the 'slowness' of democracies to the American minister in Belgrade, Arthur Bliss Lane. Anticipating Roosevelt's words spoken a year later, he warned Lane that 'if Germany were to win the war, the American continent would then be threatened'.[66]

In the autumn of 1940 Lane asked Prince Pavle what would be the country's future posture in view of the changing strategic realities. There was a note of desperation in the Regent's reply: 'It is to be hoped that the United States Government will appreciate the position of the Yugoslav Government in endeavouring to keep out of the war at the same time as maintaining its self respect.'[67] The implication was clear: Yugoslavia probably would be forced to make some unpalatable choices before too long, and it would need understanding of its friends that its freedom of action was severely limited.

Such blunt enquiries coming from an American could be taken by Prince Pavle in his stride. He was understandably irritated, however, when the British - with whom he had always assumed the existence of a special relationship - started behaving in a clumsy and heavy-handed manner with him. The first such incident occurred in the spring of 1939, when the British minister, on instructions from Halifax, asked him 'what did Yugoslavia intend to do if Germany invaded Romania?' A furious Prince asked in return what Britain intended to do. To this Sir Ronald had no answer. Prince Pavle was concerned that Germany could only be irritated if Britain tried to force the Balkan countries to make formal declarations of this kind. None of them were capable of resisting Germany, neither on their own nor in any conceivable alliance, unless Britain was willing and able to offer massive help. No such help was promised, let alone delivered.

What Pavle got from London instead, in early 1941, was the news that not only Germany, but Britain, too, regarded Yugoslavia's continued neutrality as insufficient! On 12 January Campbell called on the Prince to inform him that Britain was going to send an expeditionary corps to Greece, and to propose the creation of a united Balkan front. Pavle was horrified. 'He considered the plan impetuous, irresponsible and doomed to failure...Britain would call for a Yugoslav act of suicide and in the end the whole of the Balkans would be overrun. It was the arrogance which infuriated him.'[68]

As if the increasing bullying by Germany and clumsy improvisations of Britain were not enough, Prince Pavle was faced with strong American pressure to resist German demands which was coordinated with London. Sudden American interest in Yugoslavia's predicament arose from President Roosevelt's desire to enhance the prospects of British resistance to German domination of Europe. Secretary of State Cordell Hull favoured a more cautious approach, but was overridden by the President, and generally pushed into the background as the war went on.

In January 1941, at Churchill's specific request, President Roosevelt sent his 'unofficial' representative, future director of the Office of Strategic Services, Colonel William (Bill) Donovan to the Balkans to encourage resistance to Germany and to promise American aid. Donovan arrived in Belgrade after visiting Athens and Sofia. In his conversations with Prince Pavle, prime minister Cvetković and Cincar-Marković, he argued for the rejection of German demands that Yugoslavia join the Tripartite Pact, adding melodramatic phrases about the preservation of national honour. Unsubtly, he followed this up with a thinly veiled threat that if Yugoslavia did not resist German demands, the United States would not act on her behalf at an eventual peace conference.[69]

Premier Cvetković's remarks in his memoirs could apply to many an American 'special envoy' of our own time: 'Colonel Donovan...proved to be one in a line of 'experts' who display total ignorance of the particular problems of the country they were visiting...Very superficially informed of Yugoslavia, which he was visiting for the first time - not knowing its language, its history, traditions, mentality, its political, economic and military situation - such a man could not form a proper idea of the problems of Yugoslavia in a few days...He did not know a thing about the Balkans'.[70]

It completely escaped Donovan's attention that Prince Pavle was turning into an almost broken man by that time, torn between his personal sympathy for Britain and the awareness that Germany had in her power to destroy Yugoslavia at will. As the dilemma deepened, abandoning the rules of diplomatic etiquette, he confessed to Lane some weeks later: 'I am out of my head; I wish I were dead!'[71] There was no bravado and no bellicose zeal in his demeanour. He would resist attack, but above all he would do all in his power to avoid it in the first place.

Donovan must have been comforted, however, by the meeting with two high-ranking Yugoslav officers, air force generals Dušan Simović and Bora Mirković. Resolutely anti-German, two months later they carried out a coup which toppled the government, and prompted German attack. While there is no reliable record of their conversation, some contemporaries believed that Donovan was aware of the generals' intent to act if the government signed the Pact.[72]

Britain continued to request American help in applying pressure on Yugoslavia.[73] On one occasion Lane went beyond his instructions to express a 'personal opinion' that 'countries which do not resist aggression are not worthy of independence'.[74] Some Yugoslav officials, quite appropriately, pointed out to Lane the fundamental contradiction in the American position. He summarised it for Hull: 'Officially we say that we do not intend to enter the war, yet unofficially we advise small countries to resist'.[75] Apparently caught off balance, Hull retorted rather weakly that 'if United States were threatened with invasion we would certainly resist and that we are not suggesting to Yugoslavia or any other country to take offensive action'.

A day later it was announced that Roosevelt's Lend-Lease Bill would apply to Yugoslavia and other countries 'that are now the victims of aggression or which might be threatened with aggression.'[76] Lane immediately asked to see Prince Pavle, with whom he had established a close relationship. The Prince thanked Lane for the President's expression of support, but stressed that Yugoslavia's military position would become quite untenable if the Germans entered Bulgaria.[77] The Prince was gloomy ('What do you expect me to do?'), pointing out - accurately, as it turned out - that even if the United States were to help his country, Yugoslavia would be finished before any such assistance arrived.

Lane's conversation with Pavle, which ended on a sombre note, prompted Roosevelt to send a new message to the Regent on 22 February. It contained the American argument in a nutshell:

> I fully appreciate the difficult and vital problems facing you and the Yugoslav Government, but I most earnestly wish to point out that the United States is looking not merely to the present but to the future. I wish to convey to you my feeling that the world in general regards with very real sympathy any nation which resists attack, both military or diplomatic, by the predatory powers.[78]

Roosevelt went on to cite the example of Abyssinia, China, Greece, and Norway: each of them had resisted against all odds, and stated further that those that succumbed would be restored after the war. For good measure, he repeated Donovan's threat that in the eventual peace settlement the treatment of a nation's claims would depend on its earlier attitude to the 'predators.' The President concluded, in effect, by appealing on the Yugoslavs to go the way of Ethiopia or Norway: resist gloriously, if necessary go down fighting, and trust in an eventual Allied victory.

The Pact

The Germans were not impressed by the British and American efforts. They knew that, while Churchill and Roosevelt relied on rhetoric and promises relating to the distant post-war future, the Reich had the more convincing set of arguments - in the form of motorised and Panzer divisions pouring into Hungary into Romania, and poised soon to cross the Danube into Bulgaria. In early February, as we have seen, they conveyed to Prince Pavle that time was running out and that Cvetković and Cincar-Marković should come to Berghof to clarify the issue of Yugoslavia's status.

They arrived there on 14 February 1941. Ribbentrop and Hitler duly cut short their initial suggestions of a 'neutral bloc' in the Balkans. For Yugoslavia it would be best to join the Tripartite Pact, Hitler said, and so ensure her position in the New Europe. His tone left no doubt in his visitors' minds that joining the Pact was, by that time, the only road open to their country. Cvetković and Cincar-Marković were also told that Prince Pavle himself needed to come for talks.

Aware that he was going to face a determined German assault, the Prince desperately tried the Italian card once again. This time the Germans intervened directly, asking the Italians not even to accept Yugoslav overtures, and to let Berlin know of all eventual Yugoslav proposals.[79] When Prince Pavle presented himself at the Berghof on 4 March 1941, he was alone in every sense.

What followed was a five-hour 'massage' by Hitler, in Prince Pavle's own words.[80] In the end the Regent still evaded a definitive answer, saying that he could not make a decision of such magnitude as joining the Pact without consultations. This was his way of saying he was unwilling, rather than unable, to do it alone.

The Prince returned to Belgrade on 5 March, undecided and deeply worried. For the following day he called a session of the Crown Council, which consisted of all three regents and several key government ministers. This was an *ad hoc* body, not provided for in the Constitution. He wanted to have a suitable forum endorse the seemingly inevitable acceptance of German demands. At the Council, after hearing bleak reports from Prince Pavle and Cincar-Marković on the foreign political situation, and from the war minister on the country's desperate military position, it was unanimously decided to sign the Pact, albeit with certain provisos.

A day later, on 7 March, Cincar-Marković informed the German minister, Heeren, of the Council's decision, and asked for written assurances from Germany and Italy on three points: that Yugoslavia's sovereignty and territorial integrity would be respected; that no military assistance from, or troop transfers through, Yugoslavia in time of war would be sought; and that Yugoslav interests in Salonika would be considered. Ribbentrop reluctantly accepted those demands, and even agreed that some of the provisions be made public, to placate Serb public opinion. The Yugoslav government were running out of excuses for further delays.

In the meantime, in the first week of March the Wehrmacht finally entered Bulgaria. At this late moment the British suggested military consultations between Yugoslav, Greek, and British staff officers, which took place in Athens on 8 and 9 March 1941. On that occasion the Yugoslavs definitively established that they could expect no meaningful assistance from the British, who were in need of help themselves, rather than able to offer any. Prince Pavle was driven to conclude that the British expected him to make a sacrifice, and could not promise anything in return. To his amazement his country was advised to 'attack first', to start a war against the Axis! By striking against the Italians in Albania - this remarkable argument went - they could grab the stocks of weapons there that could not be delivered from Britain, and hope for the best.

Following the totally unsatisfactory meeting in Athens both Prince Pavle and Prime Minister Cvetković changed the pitch in their answers to British and American enquiries about the Pact: they were now saying that Yugoslavia 'would not sign a pact with military clauses permitting occupation of the country'.[81]

After an agonising fortnight of final discussions, numerous messages exchanged between Belgrade and Berlin, and unprecedented German concessions to the Yugoslavs, the final decision to sign the Pact was made at the Crown Council on 20 March. It was confirmed at the Council of Ministers the following day. On 23 March Prince Pavle cut the knot, and sent Cvetković and Cincar-Marković to Vienna to sign the modified Pact. It was the best deal Yugoslavia could hope for. As van Creveld has observed:

> The Serbs had put on a brave show, but could not maintain their opposition for ever. The growing concentration of German troops in Romania spoke a stronger language than moral exhortations from England's friends...(Hitler's concessions) represented a great victory for the Serbs...By dragging their feet for so long, the Yugoslavs had shown quite unequalled courage in the face of a state so much stronger than themselves.[82]

The sustained pressure on Belgrade against the Pact had come from America, which was still out of the war, and from Britain, which was unable to offer any help and sought Yugoslavia's self-annihilation for no clear strategic reason. Furthermore, Britain and the United States did not - and could not - automatically take over the role of France in the perceptions and sympathies of Yugoslavia's ruling elites. Subsequently, both Lane, and his British colleague, Ronald Campbell, had a problem with credibility. They were visibly advising a course difficult to reconcile with a pragmatic assessment of Yugoslavia's national interests.

Under the circumstances, the only way to establish an alleged community of interest between Yugoslavia and the two democracies was by invoking moral principles, or making promises about the distant future. In either case the implicit - but perfectly clear - assumption was that Yugoslavia would be crushed and occupied by the vastly superior German forces, but that it should accept this fate, and even willingly invite it, for the sake of preserving its 'honour' and aiding Britain's war effort. Prince Pavle would have betrayed the trust placed in him in 1934 had he placed the interests of Britain before the preservation of his own country. He went out of his way to point out the absurdity of such 'advice' to those proffering, but to little avail.

Prince Pavle's policy of neutrality, pursued as long as possible, ostensibly ended at the Belvedere on 25 March 1941. The signing ceremony was described by one participant as reminiscent of a funeral. It was not an expression of the Prince's political will.

The Coup

The Prince and his ministers hoped that the watered-down version of the Pact - grudgingly accepted by Hitler - would calm the spirits at home. This failed because the government of Cvetković and Maček, and above all the Prince himself, did not enjoy the confidence of the Serb body politic. It was felt that the regime lacked the 'mandate' to sign. Had King Aleksandar been alive, he may have agreed to the Pact and kept the order internally. Prince Pavle could not do so, because he did not enjoy popular affection and the implicit confidence of his slain cousin.

In the early hours of 27 March 1941 a group of officers took power in an almost bloodless coup in Belgrade. This was a momentous event in Serb history. Even more than half a century later, this event arouses mixed emotions. There are still some who see it as an act which, for all its awful consequences, enabled Yugoslavia to avoid the otherwise allegedly inevitable slide into the Axis war camp.[83] This view was echoed in the streets of Belgrade and other Serbian cities in the demonstrators' slogan of *'Bolje grob nego rob'* ('Better grave than slave') and *'Bolje rat nego pakt'* ('Better war than pact'). It was an explicit rejection of 'realism' for transcendent goals.

With the benefit of hindsight the coup can be more accurately described as a criminal, or at least gravely mistaken attempt, partly inspired by covert British action, to alter Prince Pavle's course based on the pragmatic view of politics as the 'art of the possible.'[84] The officers' strike against Prince Pavle's government was not a responsible act based upon a coherent analysis of the situation. There was no long-term plan on what to do after the fall of the Regency. It was a mad adventure which inevitably ended in national disaster. Even the *post factum* claim that the coup decisively contributed to victory over Nazi Germany (allegedly by forcing Hitler to postpone his attack on Russia) has been proven to be false.[85]

It has been claimed that the coup was a British brainchild, and the belief that the Intelligence Service was closely involved persisted among both supporters and opponents of 'the 27th of March'. While there is no doubt that the British were active, both covertly and overtly, in trying to influence the course of Yugoslavia's policy, their input would not have been sufficient to induce the officers to act.[86] The mastermind of the Belgrade Putsch, General Mirković, had toyed with the idea of a coup way back in 1937, when the government of Milan Stojadinović embarked on a policy of improving relations with Italy.[87] He finally made up his mind, in March 1941, to act regardless of any vague promises of help and support from the British.

The conspirators of 27 March reflected a certain Serbian tradition which harked back to the *hajduks*, and which culminated in the ignominy of the regicide of 1903. This tradition had little to do with any notion of 'national interest', rationally defined and prudently pursued. Its proponents 'felt' what was to be done, and sought legitimacy in the alleged support of a mob. Their coup of 27 March 1941 was an incoherent scream of inarticulate *Angst*, all the more destructive for its heartfelt sincerity.

The coup was not 'imported' from without. Just as British and American pressure was not sufficient to dissuade Prince Pavle and the Cvetković government from signing the Pact, so British machinations, and American connivance, would not have been sufficient in pulling off the officers' revolt. The coup was a purely - and, one is tempted to add, typically - Serb affair.

Prince Pavle's political role ended on that day. His subsequent scandalously shabby treatment by the British, and his vilification by the victorious communists of Marshal Tito, cannot conceal the fact that he was a man of exceptional integrity, intellectual honesty, and highly developed sense of duty. Prince Pavle had done his best to avoid exactly the kind of catastrophe which befell his country after 27 March 1941, and which led, in an unbroken line, to the Calvary of the Serb nation in 1991-96. Prince Pavle died in Paris in 1976, at peace with his conscience. He could rest assured that any other outcome to the crisis of March 1941 would have been preferable to what has come to pass in the Balkans.

But that, as they say, is history. Yugoslavia was attacked within ten days of the coup. It was dismembered and plunged into Hobbesian chaos, into an orgy of terror and civil war, in which hundreds of thousands were to perish. Even if the country had been united in the will to resist and politically consolidated, the defence would have been hopeless. In April 1941 there were no military, economic, geographic, political or psychological foundations for a sustained defence of the Yugoslav state.

Unconsolidated Yugoslavia - or, rather, disoriented Serbia - did not 'find its soul,' as Churchill put it upon hearing of the coup in Belgrade. To some it may have looked that it opted for 'the Kingdom of Heaven' in the best mythical tradition of Prince Lazar, martyred at the Battle of Kosovo in 1389. Alas, it was pushed into a nightmare, on that euphoric spring day in 1941, and that nightmare is still continuing.

Notes

1 Lederer (1963), Chapters 1-2.

2 Balfour & Mackay (1980), p. 60.

3 Rusinow (1969), pp. 185-186.
4 Krizman (1975), p. 32.
5 Jarausch (1965).
6 Balfour & Mackay (1980), p. 85.
7 For a comprehensive study of Maček's policy see Boban (1974).
8 Krizman (1975), p. 84
9 Stojadinović (1970), pp. 368-369.
10 Hitler also urged the Italians to advise Hungary to arrive 'at a solid understanding with the Yugoslavs': Ciano (1948), p. 58.
11 Arhiv Jugoslavije (AJ), Fond M. M. Stojadinović, fasc. 14.
12 Krizman (1974), p. 97.
13 AJ, Fond M. M. Stojadinović, fasc. 14.
14 Wiskemann (1949), p. 29.
15 Ciano (1948), p. 100.
16 Documenti Diplomatici Italiani (DDI), ii, 5, No. 235.
17 Ciano (1948), pp. 98-105.
18 Ciano (1948), pp. 98-105.
19 Documents on German Foreign Policy (DGFP), C, Vol. 2, No. 381, Memorandum by the Director of Department II, 5 April, 1934.
20 Krizman (1975), p. 80 quotes a message to that effect that King Aleksandar sent to Berlin just before leaving for Marseilles.
21 DGFP, C, Vol. 2, Minutes of Hitler's meeting with Gombos.
22 Biber (1964), pp. 37-56.
23 Lowe & Marzari (1975), p. 291.
24 DGFP, D, Vol. 6, No. 94, Circular of the Foreign Minister, 25 March, 1939.
25 Stojadinović, p. 514.
26 Ciano (1948a), 19 January, 1939.
27 Ciano (1948a), 7 February, 1939.
28 The Cvetković Papers, Hoover Institution Archives.
29 Boban (1974), Vol. 2, pp. 49-50.
30 Balfour & Mackay (1980), pp. 168-169.
31 DGFP, D, Vol. 6, pp. 248-250, 252-253, 263, Memoranda on conversations between Goering and Mussolini, 15 April, 1939.
32 Ciano (1948a), 22-23 April, 1939.

33 DGFP, D, Vol. 6, No. 262, Record of conversation between Ribbentrop and Cincar-Marković, 25 April, 1939, and No. 271, Record of conversation between Hitler and Cincar-Marković, 26 April, 1939,
34 DGFP, D, Vol. 6, No. 341, Memorandum of talks between Ribbentrop and Ciano, 18 May, 1939.
35 Pavlović.
36 PA, Beuro Staatssekretaer, Italien, Bd. 1, Record of talks between Ribbentrop and Ciano, 23 May, 1939.
37 Krizman (1978), p. 322.
38 On Ciano's conversations with Ribbentrop and Hitler at Salzburg and Berchtesgaden see Ciano (1948a), 12 August, 1939, and DDI, viii, 12, Nos. 4, 21. For a German record see DGFP, D, Vol. 7, Nos. 43, 47, Records of conversations between Ciano and Hitler on 12-13 August, 1939.
39 Bonnet (1948), pp. 244-245.
40 DGFP, D, Vol. 6, No. 474, Ribbentrop's note on talks with Prince Pavle, 7 June, 1939.
41 PA, Beuro Staatssekretaer, Italien, Bd. 1, Foreign Minister's circular on the results of Prince Pavle's visit, 9 June, 1939.
42 See account Pavle's assessment by Alfonso of Spain quoted in Balfour & Mackay (1980), pp. 178.
43 See Shone to Halifax on Yugoslavia's foreign policy: PRO, FO 371, f-23885, R9975.
44 Ciano (1948a), 10 May, 1940.
45 Ciano (1948a), 13 May, 1940.
46 Lowe & Marzari (1975), p. 368.
47 DGFP, D, Vol. 10, No. 129, Minutes of talks between Ribbentrop and Mussolini, 19 September, 1940.
48 DGFP, D, Vol. 10, No. 353, and DDI, Vol. V, No. 431, Alfieri to Ciano, 17 August, 1940.
49 DDI, Vol. V, No. 617, Minutes of talks between Ribbentrop and Mussolini, 19 September, 1940.
50 DDI, Vol. V, No. 617, Minutes of talks between Ribbentrop and Mussolini, 19 September, 1940.
51 Ciano (1948a), 12 October, 1940.

52 DGFP, D, Vol. 11, No. 320, Minutes of Vauhnik's visit, 11 November, 1940.
53 DGFP, D, Vol. 10, Nos. 232, 395, Prince Pavle's and Cincar-Marković's expressions of concern to Heeren.
54 DGFP, D, Vol 9, No. 517, Heeren's report, 21 June, 1940.
55 DGFP, D, Vol. 10, No. 395, Heeren's report, 26 August, 1940.
56 See Stakić (1967), pp. 86-87, where Mussolini is reported to have said that Italy needed 'a strong and powerful Yugoslavia.'
57 Ciano (1948a), 11 November, 1940.
58 DGFP, D, Vol. 11, No. 324, Record of Gregorić's approaches, 12 November, 1940.
59 DGFP, D, Vol. 11, No. 417, Record of Hitler's talks with Cincar-Marković.
60 DGFP, D, Vol. 11, No. 467, Heeren's report, 7 December, 1940.
61 DGFP, D, Vol. 11, No. 549, Ribbentrop to Heeren, 21 December, 1940.
62 Stakić (1967), pp. 92-100.
63 Balfour & Mackay (1980), p. 169.
64 Foreign Relations of the United States (FRUS) 1939, Vol II, p. 893, Hull to Lane, 14 July, 1939.
65 FRUS 1939, Vol. II, p. 888, Bullitt to Hull, 24 May, 1939.
66 FRUS 1939, Vol. I, p. 447, Lane to Hull, 21 September, 1939.
67 FRUS 1939, Vol. I, p. 518, Lane to Hill, 22 September, 1939.
68 Balfour & Mackay (1980), p. 217.
69 van Creveld (1973), p. 139.
70 Cvetković (1965), Box 2.
71 FRUS 1941, Vol. II, p. 967, Lane to Hull, 24 March, 1941.
72 Cvetković (1965), Box 2.
73 FRUS 1941, Vol. II, p. 940, Halifax *aide memoire* to Department of State, 4 February, 1941.
74 FRUS 1941, Vol. II, p. 943, Lane to Hull, 11 February, 1941.
75 FRUS 1941, Vol. II, p. 944, Lane to Hull, 13 February, 1941.
76 FRUS 1941, Vol. II, p. 944, Hull to Lane, 14 February, 1941.
77 FRUS 1941, Vol. II, p. 946, Lane to Hull, 23 February, 1941.
78 FRUS 1941, Vol. II, p. 947, Hull to Lane, 22 February, 1941.
79 PA, Beuro Untersekretaer, Jugoslawien, Band 1, Nos. 129, 138. 28 February, 1941.

80 Krizman (1975), p. 145.
81 FRUS 1941, Vol. II, p. 955, Lane to Hull, 16 March, 1941.
82 van Creveld, pp. 127, 129.
83 Pavlowitch (1988), p. 9.
84 Cvetković (1965), Box 2.
85 van Creveld, pp. 69-183.
86 Stafford (1977).
87 Hoptner (1962), pp. 250-253.

References

Balfour, Neil & Mackay, Sally (1980), *Paul of Yugoslavia, Britain's Maligned Friend*, Hamish Hamilton, London.

Boban, Ljubo (1974), *Maček i politika Hrvatske seljačke stranke, 1928-1941*, 2 Vols, Liber, Zagreb.

Biber, Dušan (1964), 'Ustaše i Treći Reich: Prilog problematici jugoslovensko-nemačkih odnosa 1933-1939', *Jugoslovenski istorijski časopis*, No. 2, pp. 37-56.

Bonnet, Georges (1948), *Fin d'une Europe*, Geneva.

Ciano, Galaezzo (1948), *Ciano's Diplomatic Papers*, Oldham Press, London.

Ciano, Galaezzo (1948a), *Ciano' Diaries, 1939-1943*, Oldham Press, London.

Hoptner, Jacob B. (1962), *Yugoslavia in Crisis, 1934-1941*, Columbia University Press, New York.

Cvetković, Dragiša (1965), *Rat ili pakt: unutarna i spoljna politika namesništva*, Unpublished manuscript, Hoover Institution Archives, Cvetković Papers, Box 2, Stanford.

Jarausch, Konrad H. (1965), *The Four Power Pact 1933*, Madison.

Krizman, Bogdan (1975), *Vanjska politika jugoslavenske države 1918-1941*, Školska Knjiga, Zagreb.

Krizman, Bogdan (1978), *Ante Pavelić i ustaše*, Globus, Zagreb.

Lederer, Ivo (1963), *Yugoslavia at the Paris Peace Conference*, Yale University Press, New Haven & London.

Lowe, C.J. & Marzari, F. (1975), *Italian Foreign Policy, 1879-1940*, Routledge Keegan & Paul, London & Boston.

Pavlović, Kosta St. 'Jugoslovensko-britanski odnosi 1939-1945: Knez Pavle u poseti Rimu, Berlinu i Londonu prema britanskim dokumentima', *Glasnik Njegoš*, Vol. 9, No. 2.

Pavlowitch, Stevan K. (1988), *The Improbable Survivor, Yugoslavia and its Problems 1918-1988*, C. Hurst & Co, London.

Rusinow, Dennison (1969), *Italy's Austrain Heritage*, Clarendon Press, Oxford.

Stafford, David A.T. (1977), 'SOE and British Involvement in the Belgrade Coup d'etat of March, 1941', *The Slavic Review*, Vol. 36, No. 3, pp. 399-419.

Stakić, Vladislav (1967), *Moji razgovori sa Musolinijem*, Iskra, Munich.

Stojadinović, Milan (1970), *Ni rat ni pakt*, Otokar Keršovani, Rijeka.

van Creveld, Martin (1973), *Hitler's Strategy 1940-1941: The Balkan Clue*, Cambridge University Press, London & New York.

Wiskemann, Elizabeth (1949), *The Rome-Berlin Axis*, Oxford University Press, New York & London.

8 Dragoljub-Draža Mihailović

KOSTA NIKOLIĆ

Introduction

The collapse of the Yugoslav state and the defeat of its army in the brief April War of the 1941 was the most severely felt by Yugoslavia's Serbs. The Axis occupation meant that the Serbs lost their own state - a state in whose creation during World War I the Serbs had been the greatest contributors. Now they found themselves in a situation where their own biological existence was threatened. The occupiers wanted morally to humiliate the Serbs, to cripple their souls, to obliterate their historical consciousness and to forcefully deprive their nation of its name and identity. From the first moment of its military occupation, Germany introduced a system of total control in all aspects of life, with a conspicuous fear of any revival of a Serb State. The overall attitude of the occupying power towards the Serb population was that they were a lower race. Serbs were exposed to various measures of exploitation, political discrimination and destruction of their national pride and identity. All these measures were undertaken with the intention of suppressing any resistance. The enslaved people's desire to be liberated from their occupiers and oppressors could not, however, be so easily crushed.

In the tragic circumstances of overall disorganisation, a part of the Command of the Yugoslav Army, assisted by the efforts of civilian officials whose will to resist had not as yet been broken, did not wish to reconcile itself with the capitulation without any real resistance. In one of the most difficult periods of Serb history the fate of the national movement found itself in the hands of Colonel Dragoljub Mihailović. Who was Dragoljub Mihailović?

Military Career to the End of World War I

Dragoljub-Draža Mihailović was born on 14 April 1893[1] in the town of Ivanjica, the administrative centre of the Morava District, to father

Mihailo and mother Smiljana. Ill-fate followed this family. His father died when Dragoljub was only two-years-old, and when he was seven his mother passed away. Young Dragoljub and his two sisters, Milica and Jelica, were brought up by their uncle Vladimir who lived in Belgrade. In the autumn of 1904 Mihailović was enrolled in the 1st year of the Third Boys Gymnasium. He was a good student. In 1907 he transferred to the 2nd Belgrade High School which he attended until his enrolment in the Military Academy. Upon finishing the sixth grade, in 1910, the young Mihailović applied to enrol into the College of the Military Academy and was accepted as a cadet of the 43rd class.

Instead of the planned third year at the Academy, in September 1912 the 43rd class was sent to battle against the Turks in the First Balkan War. His first military duty was as adjutant to major Borivoje Tošić, commander of the 1st Battalion of the Fourth Infantry Regiment. The regiment was part of the Drina Division. The first military action occurred on 6 October, when the Turkish border watch-towers on the Javor were destroyed. Mihailović's 1st Battalion was involved in battles for the liberation of Sjenica on the 11 October on the 15 November a move was made towards Kosovo and Metohija. After the First Balkan War, on 18 July 1913 King Petar I of Serbia signed a decree promoting, to the rank of sub-lieutenant, each of the 28 sergeants of the 43rd class. Mihailović's name was in sixth place on the list.

Mihailović's return to the fourth year of the Academy was short-lived because of the so-called Albanian Rebellion. On 11 September 1913 Mihailović was assigned to the 4th Infantry regiment 'Stevan Nemanja'. As early as 17 September 1913 the regiment advanced toward Novi Pazar where it was incorporated into the Ibar Division. In that region sub-lieutenant Mihailović spent October and November, after which all the cadets of the 43rd class were again sent back to Belgrade to complete their education, which was again to be interrupted, this time by the whirlwinds of World War I.[2]

Sub-lieutenant Mihailović was mobilised in the 3rd infantry regiment of the Drina Division, a part of the 3rd Army at Valjevo. On 3 August 1914 the regiment encountered the Austro-Hungarian army at Sima's Hill south west of Cer. Over the next two days the enemy was driven out from that territory. Mihailović was the platoon commander of the 1st Battalion. As a result of heavy losses in the battles around

Kosjerić in September and October, Mihailović was appointed acting commander of the 2nd platoon of the 3rd battalion.

In official documents, Mihailović's soldiering in these battles was appraised as follows: 'Active infantry sub-lieutenant Dragoljub Mihailović, a young officer, distinguished himself with personal bravery and skilful platoon command of inexperienced conscripts from the new areas for which he should be awarded a gold medal for bravery.'[3] After the defeat of the Austro-Hungarian army in the battle of Kolubara, his regiment saw no action until 25 September 1915 when it engaged German army units north of Požarevac. Due to the massive enemy attack, retreat to the south began. From 7 November the Golgotha of the 3rd regiment and the whole Serbian Army began. Of Mihailović's entire regiment only two battalions remained. The number of soldiers diminished daily. On 1 December 1915 they bivouacked at Podgorica, on the way to Skadar and on 31 December they were ordered to move to Drač-Valona.

Mihailović, with the remnants of his regiment, arrived at the camp at Valona in Albania on 26 January 1916 and two days later the survivors were boarded on the ship 'Kraljica Jelena' bound for Corfu. After his recovery at Corfu, on 22 April 1916 Mihailović joined the newly formed 23rd infantry regiment of the Vardar Division and was sent to the Salonika Front. In early August in the battles against the Bulgarians near the lake of Ostrovo, lieutenant Mihailović commanded the machine-gun platoon. On 11 September Mihailović was wounded for the first time; the second time was on 25 April 1917. For his bravery Mihailović was awarded the British Military Cross and on the 14 January 1918 the Serb White Eagle with Swords of the Fourth Order. Some time later the whole of his second machine-gun platoon received a gold medal for bravery. At the end of August 1918, the Entente force attacked the Central Powers' defences at the Salonika Front, and on the 1 September, on the day of the artillery's preparation for the final assault, Mihailović was promoted to the rank of full lieutenant. Mihailović's regiment saw its last action in World War I on 18 September 1918 at Štip.

From there the Yugoslav Division, of which Mihailović's regiment was a part, began to move toward Metohija to suppress an Albanian uprising. Mihailović spent the whole of 1919 in various garrisons across the unsettled Metohija. Finally, in mid-year, Mihailović's regiment was relocated to Skopje to 'Kralj Petar I' barracks, where it was renamed the 28th infantry regiment. As the best officer in the regiment, he was recommended for transfer to the King's Guard in Belgrade in September 1919.[4]

The Interwar Years

Lieutenant Mihailović, however, remained in Belgrade for just over than four months. He was charged with spreading Bolshevik propaganda. According to Mihailović own account of this matter he 'spent New Years Eve (1919) in the restaurant 'Sloboda' in the company of lieutenant Stefan Bohunjić who, when making a toast, touched on the Bolshevik revolution citing that our freedom should come from the East. My comrade continued his toast addressing it to me when from the adjacent table came a threat from the citizen Svetozar Pribićević. I pulled out my gun, placed it on the table and said: 'Let me see who is a better Serb than I!' I loaded my gun and held it in front of me.'[5] Disciplinary action against Mihailović consisted of 15 days of imprisonment after which, on 25 January 1920, he was ordered back to his 28th regiment in Skopje as an adjutant to the regiment's commander. Lieutenant Mihailović was not out of favour for long. On 11 April he was awarded the gold medal for bravery and on 26 August 1920 he was given permission to marry Jelica, the daughter of the late lieutenant Jevrem Branković. On 14 October 1920 he was promoted to the rank of captain, second class. Next year his first son, Branko was born; another, Vojislav, was born in 1924 and a daughter Gordana was born in 1926.

In September 1921 he was admitted to Upper School of the Military Academy where, two years later, he completed his course as sixth in his class. Upon completion of the course with such success, he was appointed a trainee general-staff officer in the General Staff Headquarters where he spent another year and a half in the intelligence section. In December 1925, having passed the appropriate examinations, he was promoted to the rank of major. In the following year Mihailović was appointed as the acting adjutant to the Chief-of-Staff of the Danube District Division. In January 1927, in recognition of his loyalty and professionalism, he was transferred to the Headquarters of the King's Guard. Mihailović retained this position in the King's Guard until 1935. As a lieutenant-colonel in the Guard, in 1932 he was sent on a study tour of France and the French army and, in March 1932, was appointed commander of the Guards' 3rd battalion of the infantry regiment.

A new chapter in Mihailović's career commenced in 1935 when, on 28 May, he was appointed military attache in Bulgaria and, on 6 September, promoted to the rank of colonel. Mihailović monitored Bulgarian units positioned near Yugoslavia, Bulgarian arms supplies and the activities of the Internal Macedonian Revolutionary Organisation. He established contacts with opposition circles and with the Bulgarian Captains' League which was leaning towards a Bulgarian-Yugoslav rapprochement. From this post he was removed following an official Bulgarian request. The appointment of colonel Mihailović as a military attache in Czechoslovakia followed on 22 May 1936. From this post he was first transferred in April 1937 to the Headquarters of the Drava Division in Ljubljana and then, in April 1938, to the post of the commander of the 39th infantry regiment at Celj, so that he could fulfil one of the conditions for promotion to the rank of brigadier-general. In this period Germany annexed Austria, and Celj, having a large German minority, presented a complex political problem, as was the case with the whole area of responsibilities of Mihailović's 39th regiment. A year later he was made chief-of-staff of the fortification of Ljubljana.

Apart from his military duties Mihailović performed political duties in Slovenia. As he did not show sufficient tact in his relations toward Germans and also made contacts with Slovene Yugoslav Nationalists, on the request of the Slovene governor of the Drava *Banovina* (province), he was relieved of his duties and left the region. On the eve of World War II, on 30 August 1939, Mihailović was appointed a permanent lecturer at the Military Academy in Belgrade. At that time he was punished by the Minister of the Army, general Milan Nedić with 30 days of house arrest because he wrote an essay in which he was very critical of the state of Yugoslavia's military preparedness. He demanded an urgent reorganisation and a separation of the Yugoslav Royal Military according to national origin - Serbs would defend their lands and Croats their lands and so on. Mihailović himself said: 'I stressed that an army as it was organised at the time, was marching toward ruin and chaos. I asked for the dismissal of (former) Austrian officers.'[6] Because of the punishment, he took only took up his appointment at the Academy on 17 December 1939. In the Military Academy Mihailović was a lecturer of strategy. After only a semester, on 29 January 1940, he was transferred to the position of the head of the general section of the General Inspectorate of the army.

Early in October 1940 at a reception in the English consulate he gave a lecture in which he supported Yugoslavia's joining the war against Germany. He fiercely attacked Hitler and German politics. Following a protest from the German envoy Viktor von Heeren, Minister Nedić punished Mihailović with 30 days' house arrest. In addition, as further punishment, Mihailović was transferred to the duty of assistant chief-of-staff of the Primorska Military District with headquarters in Mostar. He arrived there on the 30 October 1940 and served his punishment in Mostar until the 3 November 1940. There he participated in the preparations for the trial mobilisation ordered on the 18 February 1941. He was in Mostar at the time of fateful events of March 1941 - the Yugoslav government's signing of the Tripartite Pact and the military coup toppling the signatories of the pact which led to the April War with Germany.

During his peacetime service, Dragoljub Mihailović was officially appraised as a diligent worker and an excellent officer. His warrior schooling in World War I contributed to the formation of his character and to his sense of military duty, and ethical and political responsibility. He developed a loyalty towards the Western allies which he continued to uphold during World War II, even when these very same allies turned their backs on him and effectively handed over his movement to his communist opponents. He was a quiet and loyal officer, but was able to express his own opinion which, among other things, caused him to be sentenced to house arrest three times. He also demonstrated independence and initiative in his work which brought him into conflict with a rigid military bureaucracy. His anti-German orientation was one of the consistent traits of his character and attitude.[7]

The April War, 1941

The April War in 1941 found Colonel Mihailović acting as the Chief-of-Staff of the Operative section of the 2nd Army which was deployed to defend Yugoslavia's border with Hungary. The headquarters were stationed in the Djakovo bishopric and it was there the Mihailović witnessed the disintegration of the Royal Yugoslav Army and the treason of some of its Croat officers and soldiers. After the proclamation of the Independent State of Croatia on 10 April 1941 the High Command ordered withdrawal of the 2nd Army south of the river Sava aiming to stabilise the front. Mihailović crossed Sava at Šamac and on the Bosnian side arrived at Brčko on the 11 April. The next day there were the first clashes with Croat Ustaša forces on the Vinkovci-Brčko road, and the bridge on the Sava was blown up. At the same time contact with the High Command was lost and from then on Mihailović acted independently. From the 41st and 72nd infantry regiments he formed an 'express squad' on 14 April and suppressed the Ustaša revolt in Derventa. On the way to Bosanski Brod, at the station of Sevarlia, on 15 April, his unit clashed with German forces. The same day Mihailović and his group arrived at Doboj where his participation in the April war ended. Upon learning that on 17 April the Yugoslav High Command had formally capitulated to the Axis forces, Mihailović decided to switch to a guerilla type of warfare. He separated from the body of the 2nd Army and set out towards the Drina river. He did not wish to capitulate and rejected the order to negotiate with the Germans. His idea was to push through to the Drina river, convinced he would find a front there. At the time of the Army's disintegration in Bosnia and Croatia, he thought that the situation in Serbia was much better and that it was possible to continue with resistance to the occupation in Serbia. Mihailović soon realised that this was not the situation. On 15 April Mihailović started to pursue independent military action which, upon his arrival in Serbia, he turned into the first resistance movement in the Nazi-occupied Europe.[8]

The Četnik Resistance and Civil War

Mihailović's group of around 80 men started from Doboj and reached the river Drina on 27 April 1941. Upon crossing it the Germans were immediately informed by the local gendarmerie. Lieutenant Brabenter with an artillery section and a unit of the German military police, was sent in pursuit on 3 May. A short battle was fought at a distance of 400-500 metres after which Mihailović's group slipped away. The Germans continued to search the area on 4 May but the group managed to evade them. The march was continued to the Suvobor mountain and eventually to Ravna Gora (610m above sea-level, on the western slopes of Suvobor, and half way between Valjevo and Čačak) where the group arrived on 11 May 1941. With Mihailović there were seven officers - major Miodrag Palošević, captains Milojko Uzelac and Milenko Reljić, lieutenants Ilija

Pazina and Borivoje Ilić, sub-lieutenants Pavle Mešković and Vladimir Lenac - and about 20 non-commissioned officers and soldiers.

On arrival at Ravna Gora, Mihailović and his men confronted a dilemma. Did they belatedly give themselves up to the occupational authorities and thus be severely punished, or did they remain as the nucleus of the resistance? The second option was chosen. The first headquarters were established at Ravna Gora and it became the seat of activities and a symbol of the whole movement to which gave it its name - the Ravna Gora Movement. Mihailović set up the command of the 'Četnik Detachments of the Yugoslav Military - Mountain Headquarters No. 1.' Later, during the summer, the name was changed to 'Četnik Military Detachments'. Even though the name 'Četnik' was borrowed, the organisation was not based on a prewar Četnik association nor on the association of old Četnici, nor did it arise from the Četnik command of the old Yugoslav Army, formed in April 1940. The name 'Četnik' symbolised the old tradition of Serb guerilla fighting.

From mid-May until August 1941 Mihailović's focused on the gathering of new personnel, enlisting volunteers and the preparation of mobilisation lists. His units collected arms and set up ammunition caches, organised communication equipment and planned strategic defences. In the early days of his organisation's formation, Mihailović stressed the need for secrecy in organising and the promotion of civilian disobedience. The aim was to continuously disrupt the occupier and create a feeling of insecurity among German troops. In addition, secret units in all towns and villages as well as small Četnik companies in the mountains were to be formed with a view to obtaining a good intelligence network. As he organised resistance in the country, Mihailović stressed that in April 1941 only the first battle had been lost. His organisation's main aims were as follows: organising the people for the struggle for freedom which would come with a mass rebellion at the moment when its success would be certain; the toppling of the occupying power's regime; maintaining law and order in the country; preventing organised pillage by the occupier; obstructing regular traffic and use of communications; and the punishment of all traitors and criminals. As for the Serbian collaborating authorities, he held that their propaganda was to be countered. However, he did not want to undo any beneficial effects upon the population which the collaborating authorities conferred. Rather he sought to prevent the occupier from gaining any advantage from such collaboration. On the other hand, he did seek to eliminate obvious traitors.

In his orders Mihailović warned that Yugoslavia was still at war with her enemies - Germany and her allies. For Mihailović his oath to his King and country meant it was his duty to, at any cost, liberate his homeland. He believed that the honour and pride of his people and the glorious tradition of his ancestors demanded the struggle for freedom to expel the long-standing enemy of his homeland. Mihailović expected his officers, soldiers and all patriots to answer 'the call of the Fatherland' and help the struggle by any means. For Mihailović the price to be paid and sacrifices to be made would be great and bloody, but success would be of historical importance in the times to come. Freedom, the greatness of the nation, and the well-being of all South Slavs, united in a 'Great Yugoslavia' were all at stake. He drew the attention of all military conscripts to the fact that they were still under oath and every failure to answer calls to mobilise would be treated as treason All officers and non-commissioned officers had an immediate duty to assume command functions for the newly-formed units.

The first Četnik units were usually given the name of a mountain or a river in their district. Those units which formed spontaneously were to be incorporated into his organisation once Mihailović's officers arrived and took over command. Units consisted of 150 to 300 men and had a certain independence in their actions, which was, in the beginning unavoidable due to difficulties in communications with Mihailović's headquarters, and by demands of specific local circumstances. Soldiers were mainly of peasant origin, deeply steeped in Serb traditions and the philosophy of the village. Units enlisted even men without weapons and trained them when the demands of village life permitted.

The first military actions in Serbia started during July and August 1941 and were mainly of a diversionary character. However, on 31 August Četnik units under the command of Veselin Misita liberated the city of Loznica. Ninety-three German soldiers were captured but Misita was killed. This was the first city in Europe liberated from German occupation. In September the two anti-fascist movements - the People's Liberation Movement, popularly known as Partisans, under the leadership of the Communist Party of Yugoslavia (CPY), and Mihailović's Četnici - carried out their first coordinated actions and the rebellion thus became a mass national uprising. As a result of the combined operation, on 28

September, of the Takovo Četnik unit and Takovo People's Liberation Movement unit, under the over-all command of Mihailović's officer, lieutenant Zvonimir Vučković, the first German garrison in World War II surrendered - the garrison at the town of Gornji Milanovac. As a result of further German surrenders, such as that of 40 German soldiers on 4 October 1941 at the village of Majdan near Takovo, the Četnici established a prisoner-of-war camp for German soldiers at the village of Planinica - the first such camp in the history of the resistance in Nazi-occupied Europe.

The first steps towards cooperation and a united war effort of Četnici and Partisans were at the same time dogged by disputes of a military and political nature. The matters over which disputes arose were numerous: the questions of rank and command, of tactical approach to battles and to military operations, the attitude to 'kulaks' and the 'fifth columnists', as well as issues concerning the division of authority in liberated areas, the distribution of weapons, methods of mobilisation, and the future political system of the country. Relations between the two movements worsened daily. Mihailović and his men, as opposed to the communist Partisans, were more realistic in their appraisal of the superiority of German military strength. Četnik military doctrine was guerilla warfare and the Četnik command structure was also mindful of the need to avoid civilian casualties. Mihailović pointed out that actions without a chance of inflicting serious harm to the occupying forces should be avoided. The German reprisal policy of killing 100 hostages for every German soldier killed made such military actions counter-productive. Mihailović was against acting too hastily. The civilian population had to be shielded from further losses. In contrast, Josip Broz Tito, the general secretary of the CPY and leader of the Partisans, wanted to change the structure of political authority in Yugoslavia by force. As an internationalist, he viewed the situation in Yugoslavia in the light of the politics of the Soviet Union, accepting instructions from Moscow, which did not take into account of the fate of the Serb people.

The first open confrontation between Partisan and a Četnik forces took place on 30 September 1941 at Petrovac. The Požarevac Partisan unit attacked the Homolj Četnik unit led by Velimir Piletić. The Partisans took 61 Četnici prisoners and captured a large amount of weapons and ammunition. Constant German reprisals against the civilian population also contributed to making an already tense situation in liberated territory unbearable. In an attempt to prevent an escalation of the conflict into all-out civil war, on 22 October 1941 Mihailović wrote to the Partisan General Headquarters pointing out the importance and dire need of resolving the many misunderstandings between the two movements. He stressed that the military situation was too serious to allow any incidents of this type to lead to mutual distrust and thus become obstacles to agreement between the Četnici and Partisans. In particular, in Mačva the uprising was under threat and there was a danger of losing Užice unless urgent combined measures were undertaken. In this situation Mihailović believed that both sides should do everything possible to overcome any differences, and to prevent, at all costs, any further confrontations between Četnici and Partisans.

Civil war, however, could not be avoided. The CPY insisted on the second phase of the struggle - the social revolution. By way of contrast the Četnici claimed to be the legal bearer of the continuity of Yugoslavia and the defender of monarchism. Such diametrically opposed national political platforms made co-existence and co-operation between these two anti-fascist movements impossible. The Partisan-Četnik battles in Serbia in autumn 1941 resulted in a lasting conflict between Partisans and Četnici, leading to new frontlines across all of the Serb-populated territory of Yugoslavia. They became the principal opponents of each other, singling out each other as their main internal enemies. For the Partisans, Četnici became 'domestic traitors, servants of the occupier, and Great-Serb reactionaries'. For the Četnici, Partisans were 'traitors of the Serb nation, Ustaša criminals and Communist madmen'.

At the height of the civil war, the military arm of the Četnik movement was reorganised when the Yugoslav government-in-exile and the government of Great Britain, on 15 November 1941, recognised Mihailović as the 'commander of all patriotic forces in Yugoslavia'. On the 7 December he was promoted to the rank of brigadier general and on 11 January 1942 he was appointed the minister of war in the new Yugoslav government-in-exile led by Slobodan Jovanović. Further, on the 19 January he was promoted to the rank of the division general and renamed his forces the 'Yugoslav Army in the Fatherland', the official name which was to remain until the end of war, as a symbol of continuity of the Kingdom of Yugoslavia.

On 3 December 1941, as part of its operations against the uprising in Serbia, the German command ordered its 342nd infantry division to annihilate Mihailović's Četnici. The German offensive began on 6 December 1941 by an attack against Struganik where majors Aleksandar Mišić and Ivan Fregl were taken prisoner, and later executed at Valjevo. The German advance was then directed towards Ravna Gora but Mihailović managed to escape the German pursuit. As a part of the German operation, a reward of 200,000 German marks was offered for the capture of Mihailović. He thus became the first resistance leader in Europe on whose head the German occupying authorities had put a price.

The German command believed that, after the defeat of the uprising in Serbia, Mihailović escaped to Bosnia. However, the Četnik commander, after ordering his units to split into smaller groups, spent the winter of 1941-42 in the forests around Valjevo and Čačak, hiding in mountain huts, staying in safe-houses, often changing his place of residence. To ensure complete secrecy, Mihailović ordered a complete termination of personal, courier and radio communications. The Germans, along with the communist leaders, believed that he had left Serbia and had found refuge with major Jezdimir Dangić in eastern Bosnia. Mihailović operated mainly in the region of around Rudnik mountain. He celebrated Christmas 1942,[9] with a few followers, at the Vračevšnica monastery and then visited several villages in the Takovo region explaining the tactics and strategy of the struggle ahead. In early March 1942 he moved to the mountain Golija. On 13 April 1942 German units of the 717th Division carried out 'Operation 'Fortstrat', whose aim was to search for and capture Mihailović. The operation was unsuccessful and was terminated on 17 April. Mihailović managed to slip through the German-Italian demarcation lines and retreated into Montenegro.

His decision to move the High Command of the Yugoslav Army in the Fatherland to Montenegro and then again in 1943 to Bosnia-Hercegovina, was made in anticipation of receiving Allied aid as well an eventual invasion of Yugoslavia from the Adriatic Sea. Mihailović's main strategic target was coastal security and sabotage of the most important German and Italian communications facilities. Prior to its departure for Montenegro the High Command assembled at the village of Preljina, near Čačak. From Preljina, across the Western Morava river and the mountain Jelica, the High Command arrived at the mountain Čemerno in south-western Serbia on the left bank of the river Ibar. Having evaded the German offensive, Mihailović moved toward the mountain Zlatar, and from there he made his way to Lipovo, a village near Kolašin, where on the 1 June 1942, he established his headquarters and re-established radio communication with the Allied command in Cairo and his commanders throughout Yugoslavia.

The Struggle Against the Germans

In mid-1942 the Yugoslav Army in the Fatherland was re-organised, and, by the order of king Petar II of the 10 June, Mihailović was named Chief-of-Staff of the High Command and on 17 June promoted to the rank of army-general. Mihailović regarded his movement as purely military and, therefore, above all political parties. His view was that the war excluded political differences, party frictions, and the division of people on a political basis. Such occurrences could have dire consequences under the conditions of occupation. To further develop his organisation Mihailović formed separate commands for Serbia, South Serbia, Vojvodina, Eastern Bosnia, Montenegro and Boka, Stari Ras, Croatia, Slavonia, Dalmatia and Lika, and Slovenia. The military organisation of his unit was based his 'Instruction No 5' which set the 'četa' (company) as the basic unit, with a battalion made of 2-3 companies, a brigade consisting of 3-5 battalions, and a corps of 2-5 brigades. Companies were further differentiated by their degrees of mobility, duties and composition. This organisation was based on territorial principles, so to avoid reprisals, save on provisions, and retain as many men as possible for agricultural work in their villages but in readiness for the final military operations at the appropriate time. In the course of 1942 and 1943, 68 corps with 90,000 armed men were organised across Yugoslavia. After Mihailović left Serbia, his forces continued to operate from several centres from which Četnici disarmed units under the command of the collaborators Kosta Pećanac and Milan Nedić, sabotaged railways and attacked smaller German units. The most important centres were situated in south-western Serbia, on the mountains of Homolje and in the region of Kopaonik-Goc-Jastrebac.

In the second half of 1942, following the failure of Rommel's offensive in Africa and the fall of Tobruk to Britain, Mihailović intensified the activities of his forces. According to reports of 21 November made by the German Commander of the South-East to field marshal Willhelm Keitel, the Chief-of-Staff of Wehrmacht land forces, Mihailović initiated a policy of civil disobedience towards the occupier, the replacement of municipal mayors with his own men, the intensification of sabotage, the collection of intelligence and the monitoring of the south-bound movements of German troops. The newly formed 7th SS division 'Prinz Eugen' started its first military operation code-named 'Kopaonik' against the Rasin Četnik unit commanded by major Dragutin Keserović. The operation was unsuccessful as Keserović managed to escape the encirclement. Further actions against Mihailović's Četnici were carried out during 1942. According to 'The War Journal of the High Command of Wehrmacht' in Serbia, in the period between 13 November and 28 December 1942, 482 Četnici were killed in reprisal actions or in direct confrontations with the Germans. During a military conference, attended by Hitler, on 12 December 1942, General Alfred Jodl, the Chief-of-Staff of the Operative Section of High Command of the Wehrmacht, advised that arrests were continuously being made in Belgrade and that every day, on an average between 15 and 30 of Mihailović's followers were being executed.

The German attitude toward Mihailović is well illustrated by a report dated 9 February, 1943 written by the chief of German intelligence in Eastern Europe, General Gelen, which stated that the followers of Mihailović come from all levels of society and he enjoyed the support of over 80 per cent of the Serb population. Gelen noted that Mihailović's organisation was founded on the fanatical will of its supporters and, as such, could acquire, as a revolutionary movement, a notable political and military significance in the Balkan at any critical moment.

During 1943 Mihailović and his movement found themselves under German attack within the framework of two large German operations - 'Weiss' and 'Schwartz'. The Germans expected an Anglo-American invasion from the Adriatic coastline and in this context they wanted to clear Yugoslavia of enemy formations by manipulating the rival Yugoslav resistance forces. The German High Command believed that it was essential, within the framework of 'Operation Weiss', to disarm all Četnik formations. Hitler saw dangers in Mihailović's long-term plans to either destroy or disarm Italian units in Hercegovina and Montenegro. Consequently he ordered the elimination of all Mihailović's forces in regions occupied by German troops. The German attitude was firm in its insistence that it could not tolerate even temporary accommodations between Italian forces and the Četnici and that the latter had to be destroyed wherever possible. After the planned destruction of Tito's

Partisan forces, a concentrated attack on the main centre home Četnik strength would begin. Hitler specifically insisted that upon the obliteration of 'Tito's state', the Četnik movement was also to be annihilated so as to eliminate any possible attacks on Germans from the rear in the event of an Allied landing from the Adriatic. Mihailović's Četnici thus came under attack as the result of the German policy of systematically eliminating all its adversaries.

In his order of 14 May 1943 to general Walter Shetner, the commander of the 1st Mountain Division, general Lohr stated: 'In cooperation with Italian occupying troops, all armed units found in the area of Berane-Andrijević-Kolašin are to be disarmed and imprisoned. Execution of this order relates to Četnici who were until now in league with Italians. They must be disarmed by force. Most importantly, the headquarters of D. Mihailović is to be captured and, together with his helpers and officers for communication, obliterated.' Shetner's division inflicted heavy losses on the Četnici in Montenegro. On 14 May 1943 German units entered Kolašin and captured major Pavle Djurišić with about 2,000 men. In this situation Mihailović was forced to retreat from Montenegro. In early June 1943 Mihailović succeeded in moving to Serbia. But on 19 June the Germans began preparations for operations against Četnik units at Suvobor, Maljen and Medvednik. However, after seven days of pursuit, which resulted in the death of 11, and the capture of 453, Četnici, the action ended unsuccessfully. German forces were, yet again, unable to capture Mihailović. The German command in Serbia again offered a reward for the capture of Mihailović, this time in the amount of 100,000 German marks in gold. This German effort also proved fruitless. Just how intensive Četnik operations were at this time is reflected in the fact that in Serbia, during 1942-1943, 1048 Četnici were executed by Germans.

The Beginning of the End

In the last phase of war in Serbia in 1944, Mihailović's movement suffered a complete collapse. After heavy fighting with Communist-led units in August 1944, defeat could not be avoided, especially when it became clear that the Soviet Red Army would assist the Partisans. Defeat, however, was apparent much earlier. That Mihailović's movement was going to be discarded by its most important ally, Great Britain, was clear by the latter part of 1943. In late 1942 the British Foreign Office was dissatisfied with Mihailović and was preparing to establish contact with the communists in Yugoslavia. In September 1943, with the arrival of brigadier Fitzroy Maclean as the head of the British mission to the Partisans, Great Britain recognised the Yugoslav Partisans. This political change was supported by the Special Operations Executive (SOE) branch in Cairo. On 19 November the SOE officially presented arguments in support of the discontinuation of the British aid to the Četnici and for the recall of British liaison officers at Mihailović's headquarters. On the 25 November this was also recommended by the Allied combined intelligence committee. British commander-in-chief for the Near East, general Henry Wilson felt that Mihailović should be left 'alone to waste away and fall off like rotten fruit'. In November 1943 all deliveries of war material to Mihailović and his movement were stopped. Furthermore, at the Teheran Conference, in November 1943, the Allies formally recognised the Partisans as allies, and all military, political and diplomatic support was transferred to them.

Why did Great Britain abandon general Mihailović? That question is difficult to answer, even today, fifty years after the end of the war. The Cairo headquarters of SOE employed a number of staff of leftist or communist political orientation. The main role in discarding Mihailović was played by Basil Davidson, the officer responsible for Yugoslavia. Davidson controlled Mihailović's communication channels and controlled all messages from and to him. He also controlled the British mission at Mihailović's headquarters and all missions with his units. For example, he sent an instruction to Mihailović supposedly from the Foreign Office which it neither issued nor approved. In Cairo, Davidson's superior, major James Klugmann altered reports from the head of the British mission to Mihailović, brigadier Charles Armstrong, and censored news from Yugoslavia. These two officers sought the fall of Mihailović and worked at the creation of the Partisan legend and on the myth of its leader, Tito. Did they cause a change in the British policy towards the Yugoslav resistance or was their anti-Mihailović orientation only a consequence of such a change? This question cannot be answered until secret British Foreign Office and SOE records become accessible. Nevertheless, James Klugmann belonged to the same group of Soviet agents as did Guy Burgess, Donald Maclean and Kim Philby, all of them students of the University of Cambridge, who became agents of the Soviet Union at the start of the 1930s.[10] In any case, communists in the SOE in Cairo sabotaged the programme for provision of war material to Četnici from Cairo, and provided incomplete or one-sided information to official circles in London about the resistance in Yugoslavia. For example, in their reports to London they accused Mihailović of being passive in autumn 1943 at the very time he was the more active in his attacks on the Germans than at any time since November 1941.[11] In addition, the head of the British mission to the Partisans and great admirer of Tito, brigadier Maclean consistently accused Mihailović of being chauvinistic and promoting reprisals against Croat population in revenge for the Ustaša terror over the Serbs in Croatia and Bosnia-Hercegovina. Thus it became clear that Mihailović, whatever his policies and beliefs, did not suit British plans for the postwar reconstruction and internal organisation of Yugoslavia. This suggests that the decision to cast Mihailović aside was of a purely of political nature.[12]

The British Foreign Office, in February 1944, finally decided to remove Mihailović from the leadership of the Yugoslav resistance. The British officials at the time even considered mounting a coup which would replace Mihailović with an officer more suited to the British. This plan did not propose Mihailović's liquidation. Instead of the coup, the British decided to resort to official channels through King Petar II. In February 1944 all remaining British officers were recalled from Mihailović's headquarters, and in May the British pressured the king to dismiss Božidar Purić's Yugoslav government-in-exile. King Petar II dismissed this government in June 1944 and named Dr Ivan Subašić as the new prime minister. The dismissal of Purić's cabinet automatically removed Mihailović from his post of the minister for war in the government-in-exile.

The Ravna Gora Movement and its Policies

The Ravna Gora Movement announced its programme for the political and social structure of a postwar Yugoslavia at its People's Congress, held at the village Ba from 25 to 28 January 1944. The Ba Congress was attended by more than 300 representatives from all of Yugoslavia and all political parties except for the CPY. The Yugoslav Democratic Union was formed, the legitimacy of the Karađorđević dynasty was recognised and the renewal of a trialistic federation consisting of Serbia, Croatia and

Slovenia was proclaimed. The Serb unit would, according to democratic principles, gather all Serb people within its territory as would the Croat and Slovene units. The old boundaries between Serbs and Croats, which were, before and during the war, established without legitimate Serb representatives, were not recognised. The Ba Congress annulled both the formation of the Croatian *Banovina* (which resulted from the *Sporazum* (Agreement) of August, 1939, negotiated by Dragiša Cvetković, the then Yugoslav prime minister, and Dr Vladko Maček, the leader of the Croat Peasant Party), and the occupier's division of Yugoslavia including the formation of the so-called Independent State of Croatia, and rejected the communist project of forming six federal units in postwar Yugoslavia. At the Ba Congress the borders between the future Serb and Croat federal units were not determined, but a fundamental principle was defined as follows: 'In tomorrow's Yugoslavia, which we are adopting as our state and existential framework, the union of all Serb lands must be realised. Serb lands are all those where Serb blood was spilled and where Serb heads fell, because by their very sacrifice they irrefutably marked the boundaries of Serbdom.'

The Ravna Gora Movement insisted that the Serbs could only enter the new Yugoslavia under the condition that their ethnic and historical territories be determined. It was pointed out that the 'Croat question' had plagued Yugoslavia for more than twenty years and that it would not be wise to battle for the next twenty years over the 'Serb question'. In its proclamation, the movement stressed that being aware of not only the common, but also their own, interests, Serbs should not be apprehensive about the new Yugoslavia: 'Our salvation in the present and our progress in the future depends on Serb unification and the political, spiritual and moral unity of the Serbs, based on freedom and justice'.[13]

The Ravna Gora Movement often emphasised the missionary role of Serbia as the Piedmont of the South Slavs, proclaiming that Serbia should be constituted with all her rights, and spiritual and moral values, so that as a land of real democratic freedoms, she could join a better union, the federation of Yugoslavia. Major reforms were planned for the economic, social and cultural sectors so that in a future Yugoslavia political liberties, economic equality and social justice would be ensured. Federal units would have the widest self-government. Common national issues, foreign relations, military and financial affairs would be conducted by the central government. In all other matters federal units would have their own ministers. Separate national representative bodies would elect representatives for the federal *Skupština* (Assembly). The Ravna Gora Movement was a faithful supporter of a Yugoslav state, but on the condition that in such a state Serbs would have a leading role and that their service to this state be publicly recognised.

The Ravna Gora Movement's general stance towards the Croats was Yugoslavist, in keeping with the fundamental concept of Yugoslavia's renewal. However, it was qualified by the movement's stance towards the genocide of Serb people in the Ustaša Independent State of Croatia and the widespread treason of Croat officers and soldiers in the April War of 1941. General Mihailović, in instructions to his officers stressed that Yugoslavia would still exist and that Croats would still live in it. But, what borders Croatia would have and what rights Croats would have would be dependent exclusively on their contribution in the struggle for the new Yugoslavia and their abandonment of the Ustaša regime. Mihailović often called for the Croat conscripts of the Ustaša-led *Domobrani* (Home Guard) to abandon the Ustaša regime and to join his units. In his addresses to the Croat people Mihailović denied that Četnici were preparing revenge for murdered Serbs. But, he warned, Croats must know that Yugoslavia needs peace and order, and that all those who betrayed their Fatherland and spilled their brothers' blood would be put on trial.

The Ravna Gora Movement's attitude towards the Croats was often subject to contradictory interpretations within the movement itself, and the policies towards the Croats often depended on international relationships at the time, and on the problem over the future structure of Yugoslavia. Nevertheless, it was always stressed that the Croats as a people were not the same as the Ustaša, for whom there would be no mercy. To the radical branch of the movement, given that the Serbs in Croatia were threatened with extermination, this was tantamount to giving in to the Croats for the sake of future co-existence. Meanwhile the communist movement's propaganda portrayed the Ravna Gora Movement as anti-Croat and this view was eventually accepted by the Allies.

Mihailović made special efforts to win over the Muslims for the Ravna Gora Movement. He accordingly ordered punishment for only those Muslims who fought alongside the Ustaša. In his New Year's message to Muslims in 1944 general Mihailović called on all Muslims to unite with Serbs in battle, pointing out the examples of Mustafa Pašić and Ismet

Popovac in Hercegovina, Fehim Musakadić in Sarajevo and Hamdija Čengić in East Bosnia. The general policy of the Ravna Gora Movement was directed towards a 'most honourable rapprochement of Serbs and Muslims' so that 'the wounds of the past could be healed, and foundations for a harmonious and happy life in the new Federation of Yugoslavia could be created.' Mihailović's project concerning the status of Muslims provided for full religious freedom without the imposition of the Serb national identity, total Islamic autonomy (with the widest legislative competencies) and a guaranteed right to co-operate with other Islamic nations. In political matters Muslims were to have full equality within the Serb federal unit. In addition a Muslim national committee, with its seat in Sarajevo and regional centres in Banja Luka, Mostar, Tuzla, Belgrade, Novi Pazar, and Kosovska Mitrovica, would be formed. In military matters Mihailović planned the organisation of separate Muslim units within the framework of his Yugoslav Army in the Fatherland, so that by united fighting the country could be liberated and the spread of communism curtailed. The military organisation of Muslims was entrusted to major Šefket Hasandedić.

The Last Days of Mihailović's Movement

The decisive battle for Serbia began on 28 July 1944, with the penetration of the three Partisan divisions into Serbia. On 4 August they succeeded in crossing to the river Ibar's right bank with the aim of penetrating into the area of Jablanica and Toplica, and in co-operation with Serbian Partisan units, capturing control over the areas of Župa and Rasina. Mihailović's general plan in the last phase of the war was to establish a unified front in the battle for the final liberation of the country. He sought Allied support to end the civil war, but with no success. The Allied decision to support the Partisans as the only resistance movement was interpreted as incitement of the civil war, a preference for one side in the confrontation, and as prejudicing the future social and political order in Yugoslavia. The Allies were asked to form two operative zones for separate actions by each resistance movement, so that the country could be freed, leaving all political arguments to be resolved after the war. However, nothing came of all this. In the summer and autumn of 1944, in Serbia, instead of a war of liberation, a bloody war between Partisan and Četnik forces was fought. The Partisan divisions directed their attack towards the Četnik units of the 4th Mobile Corps under the command of major Dragoslav Račić, who commanded all operations in Serbia, and the Rasinski-Toplički corps under the command of Dragutin Keserović. On 1 September 1944 Mihailović, proclaimed a 'general mobilisation' so that Yugoslavia could be liberated both from external and internal enemies. However, the mobilisation was poorly enforced and had no effect. A general disintegration of the Yugoslav Army in the Fatherland ensued.

Early in September 1944 the Red Army was at Turn Severin, on the Romanian side of the Danube. Mihailović considered it essential that his units be the first to come into contact with the Soviet troops. He ordered that the Russians could not be attacked but should be welcomed as allies and friends. He believed that the Red Army would treat his forces as an ally and would not actively side up with Partisans. This turned out to be his first major miscalculation. On the 26 August colonel Robert McDowell, the last chief of the American military mission still with his High Command, convinced Mihailović that the advance of the Red Army into Yugoslavia would cause a conflict with the Western allies. He also tried to get the German forces in the Balkans to surrender to Mihailović but the Germans refused. The attempt at co-operation with the Red Army was also a failure. After initial friendly contacts with the Krajina corps under colonel Velimir Piletić, and the Red Army-Četnik joint actions to liberate Kruševac and the Western Morava Valley in October 1944, Red Army units turned against Mihailović's units.

The hardest blows to Mihailović came from where he least expected it - from his sovereign. First, on 24 August 1944 King Petar II signed an act of abolishing the High Command of the Yugoslav Army, so that Mihailović could not be its chief-of-staff. Then in his speech of 12 September he called on all of Mihailović's fighters, as well as all Serbs to come under the command of Marshal Tito. For the Četnik movement this act was equal to treason. To Mihailović, he and his men had been abandoned by the king for whom they sang songs and in whose name they died in battle.

Confronted with a defeat in Serbia, but bolstered by his unwavering optimism that the tides of war would change in his favour, Mihailović decided to transfer his remaining units to Bosnia in the expectation of a conflict between the West and the Soviet Union. Following a session of his Central Committee, on 8 and 9 September 1944, in the village of Milićevci (near Čačak), the High Command, under threat from Partisan forces, retreated over the mountain Suvobor. By 24 September Mihailović and the High Command were crossing into Bosnia. The entry of the Red Army into Serbia posed an insoluble dilemma for the Četnici. In his diary, the commander of the 2nd Šumadija corps, major Aleksandar Milošević, wrote: 'Fighting them (the Red Army) would be beyond any logic. There is nothing left but a retreat to the west, before them. We have no other way out.' A key decision was made at the conference of all corps and group corps commanders on 21 October 1944 in Ivanjica, and called by major Dragoslav Račić, at which it was decided to move toward Bosnia so Serbian units could join the High Command and Mihailović. The rationale behind this decision was a vain hope that the western allies would land on the Adriatic coast and then together with Četnik units advance into Serbia to liberate her from communism. This was the second major miscalculation which would lead the Četnik movement to its final collapse. The decimated units of the Yugoslav Army in the Fatherland, some 25,000 men, moved towards its last battleground in Bosnia. The main idea was, in accordance with Mihailović's instructions, to prepare to continue the war and await the opportune moment to strike against the enemy, regardless of the external situation. Existing forces had to be saved and, if possible, maximally strengthened. Winter had already arrived and Bosnia, burnt and ravaged, was ready to provide the backdrop for the last act of the war. There was little food from anywhere, even less arms and ammunition. Mihailović kept saying that the struggle would continue until the final liberation of Serbia. He also expected his army to still maintain their loyalty towards all its former allies. In all his optimism, Mihailović appraised the situation in autumn 1944 in confidential orders as 'one of confusion which bordered on panic and chaos'. Moving through harsh conditions and an epidemic of typhus, already disorganised units became more demoralised. There were many desertions. The most important event in 1945 was the battle against the Ustaša for the liberation of Modrič from 6 to 12 January. On liberating the town, an opportunity arose for the Četnici to rest and make further plans. Mihailović was still convinced of ultimate victory. From his soldiers and his officers he demanded discipline, decisive command and a maximum commitment to all assignments. He endeavoured to gather around him Croats and Muslims, 'in the struggle against the Partisan tyranny'. He demanded of his soldiers correct behaviour towards that population, forbidding pillage and abusive conduct.

During February 1945 Mihailović moved westward, along the river Bosna. His aim was to get to western Bosnia, to Banja Luka where his forces could be rallied for further fighting. He continued to believe in Allied help. He also believed that the people in Serbia would rebel against communist rule, which was his third major miscalculation. In March, Mihailović's closest supporters abandoned him: lieutenant-colonel Pavle Djurišić and colonels Zaharije Ostojić and Petar Bačović. All the regional differences in the Serb nation surfaced - between Montenegrins and Hercegovinians on one side and Serbs from Serbia on the other. Furthermore, major Blagoje Brajević, commander of the South Morava group, left Mihailović and joined Djurišić. The commander of the Rudnik corps, captain Dragomir Topalović followed suit as he did not want to be under the command of Neško Nedić. The last reorganisation of what was left of the Yugoslav Army in the Fatherland was carried out on 10 March 1945 in Modrič. Unit numbers were reduced to critical levels. These forces remained on the mountain Vučjak until mid-April. Here Mihailović changed his earlier plan and instead of Banja Luka, decided to advance towards Serbia. As his units moved from Vučjak, they were engaged in exhaustive battles with more numerous and rested Partisan forces. In these battles Mihailović's son Vojislav was killed. The personal tragedy was further heightened by the fact that his son Branko and daughter Gordana had both joined the Partisans.

The decisive battle was fought on 13 May 1945 on Zelengora. In the encounter with the 38th Partisan division, Četnik units suffered their last defeat. There were over 4,000 dead, wounded and captured. The battle was faithfully described by Major Milošević: 'Our persistence to carry out our orders and the communist persistence to inflict the last blow upon us turned into a fearful clash. The confusion of the firing of all kinds of weapons overtook the universe. It seemed that the earth shook and collapsed pursuant to the titanic power of its inner forces. Just as before a volcanic eruption, the earth gathered all its might. And then, disappearing somewhere in the distance, it would tear itself apart into screams of terror, like something that tears the muscle, breaks bones and summons human wailing in the grievous tortures of death's throes.' The Yugoslav Army in the Fatherland ceased to exist as an organised formation.

Mihailović's Capture and Execution

Mihailović went into hiding as the new authorities started to search for him. It must be stressed that under no circumstances did he want to leave his country, refusing several offers to that effect from the United States. He often pointed out that he would, until the last moment, share his destiny with his people. Optimism never left him, even in the critical moments. On 15 June 1945 he wrote: 'We must endure as after the breakdown of Nazism and Fascism in Europe, because we have came under the occupation of the Red Terror'. He asked his few remaining followers to fight a guerrilla war against communist rule which he considered to be temporary.

In September 1945 Mihailović and his small staff were located in eastern Bosnia. His remaining forces were distributed into four corps, but there were no serious battles any more. In October 1945 the new government undertook wide-ranging actions to apprehend Mihailović. The Yugoslav communist police followed Mihailović's movements via radio stations and codes belonging to captain Raković (who later committed suicide), and capitalising on the betrayal of Mihailović by Major Trifun Kostić, and Lieutenant Nikola Milovanović, the commander for communications in Serbia. Mihailović's Lieutenant-Colonel Nikola Kalabić, the commander of the Mountain Guard also agreed to collaborate with the communist Department for the Protection of the People. It was due to his collaboration that General Dragoljub Mihailović was apprehended during the night between 12 and 13 March 1946, and on 13 March brought to Belgrade.

Mihailović's trial on charges of treason began on the 10 June 1945. Twenty three persons were tried with him. Among them there were close Mihailović's supporters - Stevan Moljević, Mladen Žujović, Živko Topalović, Đuro Vilović - as well as prominent politicians and soldiers from the royal government-in-exile - Slobodan Jovanović, Božidar Purić, Momčilo Ninčić, Petar Živković, Radoje and Živan Knežević, Milan Gavrilović and Konstantin Fotić. They were all tried *in absentia*.

The Mihailović verdict was delivered on 15 July 1996. It was 'guilty' and the punishment was death. An appeal for a pardon was rejected by the Presidium of the People's Assembly, and on 17 July 1946 Mihailović was executed.

(Translated from the original Serbian by Lana Panić)

Notes

1 The date is according to the 'Old' Calendar and corresponds to 26 April, 1893 according to the 'New' or Gregorian Calendar.

2 On Mihailović's career during the Balkan Wars see Dimitrijević (1996), pp. 32-42.

3 Quoted in Dimitrijević (1996), p. 71.

4 On Mihailović's career during World War I see Dimitrijević (1996), pp. 43-70.

5 Quoted in Dimitrijević (1996), p. 78.

6 Quoted in Dimitrijević (1996), p. 135.

7 On Mihailović's interwar career see Dimitrijević (1996), pp. 73-166.

8 On Mihailović's service in the April War see Dimitrijević (1996), pp. 71-232.

9 Christmas in the Serbian Orthodox Church is celebrated, according to the Gregorian calendar, on 7 January.

10 The thesis that Allied abandonment of Mihailović was instigated by communist influence in SOE Cairo is detailed in Lees (1990) and Martin (1990), and has been accepted by Lamb (1991), pp. 250-275, and Weinberg (1994), p. 524. The thesis has been rejected by McLynn (1992), pp. 247-260 and Davidson (1996), although the latter does note, at p. 20, that the Allied switch from Mihailvić was 'one valuable project in partnership with Moscow, more precisely with the Comintern, (that) was mounted and carried through.'

11 A detailed chronological list of anti-Axis actions undertaken by Mihailović's forces from August to December, 1943 can be found in Martin (1990), pp. 129-148.

12 Various interpretations of Allied policy towards Mihailović and the resistance movements in Yugoslavia can be found in Roberts (1973),

Deroc (1988), Wheeler (1980), Đuretić (1985), and Petranović (1992), pp. 569-632.

13 The Resolution of the Ba Congress is reprinted in Petranović & Zečević (1987), Vol. I, pp. 816-821.

References

Deroc, M. (1988), *British Special Operations Explored, Yugoslavia in Turmoil 1941-1943 and the British Response*, East European Monographs, New York.

Dimitrijević, Bojan (1996), *Đeneral Mihailović, Biografija, I Deo (do maja 1941. godine),* A.L.X., Belgrade

Đorđević, Dimitrije (1994-1995), *Ožiljici i opomene*, I & II, Bigz, Belgrade.

Đuretić, Veselin (1985), *Saveznici i Jugoslovenska ratna drama*, Narodna Knjiga & Balkanološki Institut SANU, Belgrade.

Kesar, Jovan & Lukić, Dragoje (1990), *Ne osećam se krivim, Draža Mihailović pred sudom, Stenografske beleške sa suđenja vođi četničkog pokreta*, Akvarius, Belgrade.

Lamb, Richard (1992), *Churchill as War Leader, Right or Wrong?*, Bloomsbury, London.

Lees, Michael (1990), *The Rape of Serbia, The British Role in Tito's Grab for Power 1943-1944*, Harcourt Brace Jovanovich, San Diego, New York & London.

Martin, David (1990), *The Web of Disinformation, Churchill's Yugoslav Blunder*, Harcourt Brace Jovanovich, San Diego, London & New York.

Matić, Milan B, (1995), *Ravnogorska ideja u štampi i propagandi četničkog pokreta u Srbiji 1941-1944*, Institut za savremenu istoriju, Belgrade.

McLynn, Frank (1992), *Fitzroy Maclean*, John Murray, London.

Nikolić, Kosta & Vesović, Milan (1996), *Ujedinjene srpske zemlje: Ravnogorski nacionalni program*, Vreme Knjige, Belgrade.

Petranović, Branko (1992), *Srbija u Drugom svetskom ratu*, Vojnoizdavački i Novinski Centar, Belgrade.

Petranović, Branko & Zečević, Momčilo (1987), *Jugoslovenski federalizam, Ideje i stvarnost, Tematska zbirka dokumenata*, I & II, Prosveta, Belgrade.

Ristović, Milan (1991), *Nemački novi poredak i jugoistočna Evropa 1940/41-1944/45*, Vojnoizdavački i Novinski Centar, Belgrade.

Roberts, Walter R. (1973), *Tito, Mihailović and the Allies, 1941-1945*, Rutgers University Press, New Brunswick.

Weinberg, Gerhard L. (1994), *A World at Arms, A Global History of World War II*, Cambridge University Press, Cambridge.

Wheeler, Mark C. (1980), *Britain and the War for Yugoslavia 1941-1943*, East European Monographs, New York,

9 Slobodan Milošević

LENARD J. COHEN

> Why did the Serbian people desire this illusion named Slobodan Milošević? I emphasise the Serbian people wanted the illusion. And it has been living quite long under this illusion, as you can see, despite all that has happened to them, and is happening.
>
> Ivan Stambolić (1995)

Introduction

Slobodan Milošević's manipulation of Serbian nationalism as a political tool during the late 1980s and early 1990s had a significant influence on the collapse of the 'Second Yugoslavia', and also on the horrendous warfare that followed in its wake. In the context of the emotional political controversy surrounding the assignment of responsibility for the savage fighting in the Balkans, Milošević has frequently been described as an ultranationalist adherent of 'Greater Serbianism', or even less generously pilloried as a 'demagogue', 'fascist', 'war criminal', 'butcher', or 'bully'. Considering the heated political climate and tendency to over-simplification prompted by the recent Balkan conflict, it is important to carefully reconsider and evaluate how and why Slobodan Milošević first achieved power during the twilight of the communist regime. This analysis will revisit the fascinating story of Milošević's emergence as a major figure in Serbian political life during the waning years of the Titoist regime, and also some important features of Serbian political culture that assisted his consolidation of political power.

Prelude to Power: The Ambitious Young Titoist

Slobodan Milošević was politically spawned and shaped by the very Yugoslav communist regime that he would eventually help destroy. Indeed, the features of Milošević's early political socialisation, and his profound political metamorphosis during the second half of the 1980s, illustrate the internal dynamics, serious defects, and tortuous disintegration of the now defunct Yugoslav socialist experiment. The collapse of the communist regime, and the emergence of Milošević as the leader of the rump Yugoslav state, are two separate, but closely related stories.

Raised in a communist family - both his mother, a school teacher, and his father a Serbian Orthodox priest, were party members[1] - Milošević's formal commitment to the values and organisational structure of the Yugoslav socialist regime had been nurtured well before his teenage years. indeed, Milošević was literally a 'child of the revolution'. He was born on 29 August, 1941 in the provincial city of Požarevac (about 100 kilometres southeast of Belgrade), only four months after Yugoslavia's dismemberment by Nazi Germany and its allies, and two months after Tito and the Yugoslav Communist Party began a guerrilla struggle against the fascist occupation and various anti-communist nationalist groups. During the period of Milošević's secondary education (1953-1958), Tito's maverick model of communism evolved into a political amalgam comprised of a one-party oligarchy, a conservative police apparatus, a spurious federal system, and a novel structure of promising, but politically powerless, workers' councils. Young people during those years were expected to imbibe the values of 'Yugoslav socialist patriotism', a belief system premised on the expectation that ideological bonds among 'producers' would gradually transcend traditional ethno-regional forms of identity.

In 1959, at the age of 18, Milošević joined the League of Communists (until 1952 the Communist Party of Yugoslavia). A year later he entered the faculty of law at Belgrade University; the faculty that excelled in preparing educated officials for service in Serbia's communist establishment. While studying law in Belgrade during the first part of the 1960s, Milošević served as a secretary for ideological political work in the League of Communists' Belgrade University Committee, and subsequently became president of that committee's Ideological Commission. It was at law school that Milošević forged a close friendship with another young communist, Ivan Stambolić. Stambolić, five years older than Milošević, was the nephew of Petar Stambolić, one of Serbia's and Yugoslavia's leading communist officials. By the time he had met the well-connected Stambolić, Milošević was married to his high school sweetheart, Mirjana (Mira) Marković, whose father and uncle were prominent communist officials. The post-secondary education of the young Milošević couple, and their early working life, coincided with a decade of steady Titoist reform. It was also a phase when the regime officially recognised that the 'national question' had re-emerged as a major problem in Yugoslavia, and that social conflicts constituted a normal facet of a socialist society.

Milošević's friends from his law school days generally point out that the young Slobodan's commitment to marxism was rather superficial, and that he tended to view adherence to communist orthodoxy primarily as a vehicle for career advancement.[2] In this regard, Milošević was not atypical of political activists from his particular generation and milieu. Indeed, he exhibited an exceptionally high aptitude for exploiting one of the most characteristic features of Titoist Yugoslavia (and other one-party states), namely, the use of patron-client networks for early career advancement. Milošević's major patron was Ivan Stambolić. Thus, during the two decades after Milošević's graduation from law school in 1964, Stambolić generously helped the younger Slobodan assume a succession of jobs which had already been pre-tested and successfully occupied by Stambolić himself. As Stambolić advanced up the economic and political ladder in Yugoslavia, the ambitious Milošević eagerly took advantage of posts offered to him by his successful comrade and friend. For example, after holding some minor posts in the Belgrade city administration, Milošević served (1970-1973) as Assistant General Director under Stambolić at the enterprise, 'Tehnogas', which manufactured industrial gases. He then followed Stambolić to become the firm's General Director (1973-1978). In 1978, Stambolić, who had become the president of the Belgrade City Chamber of Commerce, also helped Milošević to get appointed president of UBB (*Udružena beogradska banka*), one of Belgrade's leading banks.

Entering the Political Fray: Serbian Politics and the Stambolić Line

In 1982, after spending over a decade as a political manager in the economic sector, Milošević followed Stambolić into the sharply factionalised and hardball world of Serbian politics. Stambolić, already a member of the communist establishment owing to his family ties, had actively joined the Serbian political elite near the end of Tito's life. Serving as Prime Minister of Serbia in the late 1970s and early 1980s, Stambolić had responsibility for managing a large and important republic. Mastering the game of musical chairs among political professionals, referred to by Yugoslav communist officials as the 'rotation of cadre', Stambolić made sure that his close friend, Slobodan, was not left standing idle. In 1982, while still a bank president, Milošević became a member of the Presidency of the Serbian League of Communists. That post, although a non-professional political position, served as an important vantage point from which to observe and become involved in the dynamics of his republic's power structure. He was also the president (another avocational position) of the Communal Committee in Belgrade's biggest commune, Stari Grad, a post that provided an important power base for his future political career. In the spring of 1984, Milošević assumed his first solo role as a leading Serbian political functionary when he became President of the City Committee of the League of Communists in Belgrade (a post that had been held by Stambolić from 1982 to 1984). Bound closely by ties of friendship and common perspectives, Stambolić and his friend Slobodan formed a unified team in Serbian political life. The younger and less visible Milošević was, however, clearly the team's junior partner.

During the early 1980s the Serbian communist leadership was preoccupied with three closely related negative legacies of the Tito era: (1) an economic crisis growing out of structural problems in the economy and economic mismanagement; (2) an inter-nationality crisis traceable to the persistence of deep inter-ethnic conflicts, and; (3) a political crisis arising from the general delegitimation of the long-ruling League of Communists. The political and economic crises were interdependent, and both crises stimulated, and in turn were exacerbated by the problem of ethno-nationalism in the perennially fragile country. During the mid-1980s, the Serbian political scene was still dominated by the same clique of passive, obedient, and uninspired political leaders whom Tito had foisted on the republic a decade earlier. Tito's move had been connected with a purge of the republic's liberal leaders that began with the removal of independent-minded Croatian communists in late 1971, and had subsequently spread to other republics. Thus, the political delegitimation of the Serbian communist leadership was well underway in 1981, when, only a year after Tito's death, the republic was hit by growing economic difficulties and a serious escalation of tensions between Albanians and Serbs in the province of Kosovo.

Lacking a strategy to deal with its multiple crises, the republic's communist establishment turned to its seasoned tactics of repression and drift in order to maintain power. Indeed, throughout the last decade of

Tito's life, Serbian leaders had avoided taking any innovative steps with regard to the issue of politicised ethnicity. Thus, all non-socialist forms of ethnic participation were officially prohibited, while extreme or vocal expressions of nationalism on the part of any ethnic group were strongly condemned and often harshly punished. The regime's policy for dealing with resurgent nationalism was rarely consistent, or able to remedy the serious problems that motivated ethnic conflict. Although a violent outburst of nationalism by Albanian nationalists and their sympathisers in Kosovo during 1968 was quashed, Tito, together with the weak Serbian communist leadership, permitted Albanian communist leaders in Kosovo to consolidate their hold on the province's political machine.

For Serbs, Tito's policy in Kosovo amounted to a process of officially sanctioned 'Albanianisation' which, they believed, threatened the influence and survival of the local Serbian community in the province. When the prominent Serbian writer and longtime communist, Dobrica Ćosić, warned in 1968 of dangers connected with Albanian nationalism, he was promptly expelled from the League. Outside public view, however, intellectual concern regarding Serbian rights in Kosovo intensified during the 1970s, along with popular dissatisfaction with the regime's policy toward Serbian interests generally. The republican leadership's political position was further weakened by crudely managed repression of neo-marxist dissidents and other political non-conformist Serbs in the mid and late 1970s, and also by the Belgrade regime's failure to adequately address the republic's looming economic problems. Thus, in the first years following Tito's death in mid-1980, the Serbian leadership faced a groundswell of dissatisfaction within both the general population and the ranks of the Serbian intelligentsia.

Ivan Stambolić tended to regard creative constitutional engineering as the best strategy for deflecting anti-communist and anti-regime criticism in Serbia. Like Stambolić, many Serbs felt that the republic's major economic and ethnic difficulties were fundamentally related to flaws in the 1974 federal Constitution which had essentially fragmented Serbia by granting the republic's two autonomous provinces, Kosovo and Vojvodina, near republican-level status. The devolutionary and divisive trends stimulated by the 1974 Constitution were viewed by many Serbs as having encouraged Albanian nationalism in Kosovo, and stimulated a growing drive for political autonomy by leaders in Vojvodina. In order to rectify matters, and also to reverse the regime's debilitated image, many Serbian leaders argued for a full-scale revision of the 1974 Constitution.

The outbreak of the 1981 round of Albanian nationalist demonstrations in Kosovo once again brought the issue of provincial powers and ethnic relations within Serbia to the top of the political agenda. Thus, during the first part of the 1980s, Ivan Stambolić would have to spend much of his time trying to assuage an upsurge of Serbian dissatisfaction by dangling the promise of constitutional and economic reforms that would, he maintained, reassert Serbian paramountcy vis-a-vis its two provincial units, as well as improve the republic's alleged weakness within Yugoslavia. While such claims identified problems and raised expectations, promises of eventual constitutional change did not resolve immediate ethnic and economic discontent. Thus, political resentment against the constitution and regime grew, while gratification continued to be postponed.

Throughout this period, Stambolić attempted to calm the atmosphere in Serbia and reassure communist leaders in the other Yugoslav republics. Thus, while downplaying the dangerous political potential of assimilationist policies favoured by extreme Serbian ultranationalists, he was not reluctant to speak out against the growing chorus of strident Serbian nationalism that had appeared both within and outside communist ranks. For example, in May 1985 at a meeting of the Serbian Central Committee dealing with ideology, Stambolić warned against any 'reconciliation' between Partisan perspectives on nationalism and the officially discredited view of the anti-communist Četnici. 'Nationalist views and action', Stambolić insisted, 'must be beaten everywhere and at all times. We have realistically grasped this danger and have tried to examine its roots and causes'. Stambolić also cautioned that Serbian communists must take a 'permanent militant attitude to nationalistic poisoning of the young'.[3]

During the entire period from roughly 1981 through early 1987, Slobodan Milošević appeared to adhere very closely to the Stambolić line. Indeed, statements by Milošević regarding political matters amounted to little more than ritualistic incantations of accepted Titoist orthodoxy, and uninspired variations of the latest views espoused by Stambolić. For example, at the May 1985 Serbian Central Committee Meeting on Ideology, Milošević, who was the first speaker on the roster, attacked efforts by the 'old dogmatic opportunists' and new anti-communists to 'question the fundamental values' of Yugoslav society, including the 'reality of the concept of brotherhood and unity'. Milošević's ostensible orthodoxy and loyalty to his sponsor were rewarded in early 1986 when Stambolić advanced Milošević's name as the sole candidate for the important post of President of the Central Committee of the Serbian League of Communists.

Stambolić hoped that Milošević could assist him in obtaining a moderate resolution of Serbia's internal problems, and also improving relations with the other republics. In April 1986, just one month before securing Milošević's promotion as leader of Serbia's communists, Stambolić had visited two communities in Kosovo Polje, the heart of Kosovo's Serbian ethnic community. During his visit, Stambolić had urged that 'paranoia and ghosts' be placated, and he pleaded for 'disinformation which introduces confusion to be prevented'. Stambolić also commented on the serious threats to the security of Serbs in Kosovo, on the unfortunate emigration of Serbs and Montenegrins out of the province, and on the need to challenge 'irredentists' and 'separatists'. But the Serbian leader also warned his listeners that they should not seek to resolve their local difficulties by a broader mobilisation of Serbian nationalist solidarity, especially through rallies and demonstrations. 'This is a great evil and is playing with fire', he warned.[4] One year later, the citizens of Kosovo Polje would receive another guest from the Belgrade communist leadership. However, the second visitor's response to Serbian concerns in Kosovo would depart significantly from the Stambolić line.

Milošević's Metamorphosis: 'Power Above Ideas'

In late September 1986, the Belgrade newspaper, *Večernje Novosti*, published sections of a draft 'Memorandum' which had been under preparation by members of the Serbian Academy of Arts and Sciences (SANU) since May 1985. Serbia's top political leaders were aware that the SANU document was being written, but had no idea of the controversial details which would soon engender a firestorm of critical comment throughout Yugoslavia. Among other things, the Memorandum asserted that since before World War II, when the Comintern directed the underground Communist Party of Yugoslavia, Yugoslav communist leaders had adopted policies contrary to Serbian interests; a longtime anti-Serb coalition had existed between Croatian and Slovenian communists which was responsible for Serbia's growing difficulties; the anti-Serb coalition had deliberately weakened Serbia by strengthening the power of the republic's two provinces, and; except for the period of the Independent State of Croatia during World War II, the position of the Serbian minority communities in Croatia and Bosnia-Hercegovina had never been worse.[5]

The events set out in the Memorandum were also alleged to have contributed to the communist regime's repression of the Serbian cultural intelligentsia in Yugoslavia, as well as the dire situation reputedly faced by the Serbs of Kosovo. In essence, the Memorandum characterised the entire Titoist approach to the 'national question' as an elaborate deceit and failure that had seriously harmed Serbia, and also had stimulated inter-ethnic and inter-regional conflict throughout the country. Although the solutions recommended by the Memorandum's authors indicated their loyalty to marxist political ideals, and to the potential reformability of Socialist Yugoslavia, their attack sharply undercut the political and constitutional legitimacy of the Titoist regime.[6] As for Serbia itself, the Memorandum urged that after 'four decades of Serbian passivity', it was time for the republic 'to define and declare its own national interests'. Only through 'Social Democracy', and the assertion of Serbian equality in Yugoslavia, the Memorandum suggested, could Serbs overcome the legacy of an 'historically-worn out ideology'.[7]

The publication of the Memorandum naturally added grist to the mill of those political forces in Yugoslavia, and also in Serbia, who believed that the Serbian communist leadership was committed to the goal of restoring Serbian hegemony in Yugoslavia on both the federal (vis-a-vis the other republics) and republican (vis-a-vis Serbia's two provinces) levels. Thus, Stambolić and his leadership group were immediately forced to respond to the controversial contents of the Memorandum, and also to adopt an attitude toward the Serbian Academy and Serbian intellectuals who had prepared the document. Interestingly, Milošević, who for years had passionately voiced his devotion to Titoist precepts regarding inter-nationality relations, adopted an unusually cautious and ambiguous approach to the Memorandum. For example, his remarks about the Memorandum at a February 1987 meeting of the Belgrade City Committee of the League of Communists amounted to a lukewarm and rather hesitant condemnation of the SANU members who, he suggested, must change their views and exercise 'responsibility toward their communist consciences'.[8] Although Milošević took a somewhat harsher view of the

Memorandum behind closed doors, he left public condemnation of the document's contents to Stambolić and other Serbian party leaders.

Polemics concerning the Memorandum continued to preoccupy Serbian politicians throughout the late fall of 1986. In early 1987, however, attention once again shifted to Kosovo as relations worsened between the province's Serbs and Albanians.[9] Near the end of April, Milošević was invited to make an official visit to Kosovo Polje - a journey Ivan Stambolić encouraged him to accept - where the Serbian community was politically mobilised and in a state of considerable agitation. On 24 April at 8:30 in the evening, Milošević and local Albanian communist leaders arrived at the hall of Kosovo Polje's cultural center (*Dom kulture*), where an unexpectedly large crowd of approximately 15,000 Serbs and Montenegrins had gathered to meet the visiting communist officials. The crowd surged forward chanting slogans, and trying to break through the police cordon in order to speak directly to Milošević. When Milošević and his delegation finally entered the hall the crowd outside began shouting insults and throwing stones at the building and windows. Members of the crowd again tried to break through police lines and into the building, but they were brutally clubbed and beaten back by the police (composed mainly of Albanian officers). Informed of what was taking place outside, Milošević exited the building and approached the still highly volatile crowd. According to reports at the time, the Serbian leader was visibly upset and physically shaken. When a dialogue ensued between the demonstrators and Milošević, they complained to him about the rough police tactics. Milošević quickly responded with his soon-to-be legendary remarks: 'No one will be allowed to beat you! No one will be allowed to beat you!'

Acting on a journalist's suggestion that he re-enter the hall and speak to the crowd though a window, Milošević invited the demonstrators to send in a delegation to discuss their grievances. That meeting was to last twelve hours and would become a major benchmark in contemporary Serbian history. As the crowd outside dissipated, Milošević listened to a litany of complaints by local Serbs and Montenegrins. It was one of those rare occasions in Eastern Europe when a high communist official was forced to come face to face with the views of the working class, in this case, the aggrieved members of the shrinking Serbian and Montenegrin ethnic group in Kosovo. Before leaving Kosovo Polje, Milošević reassured the members of his audience that they were entitled to reside safely in

Kosovo, and to struggle for their rights. 'We must not let the misfortunes of people to be exploited by nationalists', Milošević told those who remained. 'We must preserve brotherhood and unity as the apple of our eye'. But, he added:

> We cannot and we do not want to divide people into Serbs andAlbanians *but we must draw the line that divides the honest and pwgressive people...from the counter-revolutionaries and nationalists* on the other side. This is your country. Your homes, your fields, your gardens, your memories are here. Surely you will not leave your land because it is difficult to live there and you are oppressed...You should stay here because of your ancestors and because of your descendants. Otherwise you should disgrace your ancestors, and disappoint your descendants. (Author's emphasis.)[10]

At the conclusion of his remarks, Milošević reassured the Serbs and Montenegrins that 'Yugoslavia does not exist without Kosovo. Yugoslavia disintegrates without Kosovo, Yugoslavia and Serbia will not give Kosovo away.'[11] It was a remarkable exchange between members of an angst-ridden ethnic community and a communist official who was still by no means the advocate of their ethnic interests. And it was a remarkable performance by a communist functionary whose previous speeches and style were hardly dramatic or exceptional among his peers.

The intensity of the views advanced by the demonstrators at Kosovo Polje in their dialogue with Milošević undoubtedly had a major impact on both his perception of the seriousness and depth of nationalist feeling in the province, and also his subsequent decision to derive political capital from politicised nationalism. Milošević certainly recognised, well before his arrival in Kosovo, the political benefits that might accrue from a skilful use of Serbian nationalist grievances. However, the particular dynamic of the episode at Kosovo Polje, and the results of his intuitive response to the demonstrators, constituted the elements for a major turning point in Milošević's, and ultimately Serbia's, political development.[12] Serbian analysts who have researched the events of April in Kosovo Polje claim that the episode had a profound affect on Milošević's behaviour as a politician. When he arrived at Kosovo, he had been a cautious and reserved Titoist apparatchik offering the population words from a lexicon of well-honed and officially condoned platitudes. Leaving Kosovo,

Milošević had acquired a far more intimate appreciation of nationalist sentiments in Serbia - feelings which the local Serbs regarded as legitimate defensive or reactive nationalism - and also the limitations of existing Serbian communist methods and policies to address those concerns. After Kosovo Polje, one observer noted that Milošević was 'a different man'.[13] He had still not determined, however, just how to exploit his revelation and opportunity.

As word of Milošević's Kosovo meeting spread among Serbs within and outside Serbia, his popularity rapidly grew. The Serbian leader's instinctive decision to protect the demonstrators against the police was interpreted as a sign of bravery and Serbian patriotism. The nature and setting of his encounter in Kosovo Polje - a nighttime meeting in an unimpressive hall located in a remote European province - hardly seemed the stuff of momentous historical change. But for the nationally downtrodden Serbian psyche, and for many members of the Serbian intelligentsia searching for an event to excite national consciousness in the general population, Milošević's visit to Kosovo Polje began to take on certain idealised and romantic overtones.

Prior to April 1987, Milošević had rarely commented officially on the situation in Kosovo. During the mid-1980s, like other Serbian leaders, Milošević had supported the idea of amending the 1974 Constitution in order to reassert Serbian control over its provinces. In one meeting of the Serbian Central Committee held in November 1984, he had also made some interesting remarks about the need of Serbian communists to liberate themselves from a sense of guilt about the historic nationalism of the Serbian bourgeoisie. On the contrary, he observed that Serbian communists were untainted by 'unitarism', had no reason to cover their heads in shame, and should say what they think.[14] At the time, such remarks were not unusual or at odds with dominant Serbian communist thinking and the Stambolić line. After his April 1987 encounter in Kosovo Polje, however, the issue of Serbian-Albanian relations and Kosovo became frequently recurring themes in Milošević's speeches. The Kosovo experience had undoubtedly changed Milošević's outlook in many respects, but he still had not decided how or when to openly break with his fellow leaders regarding the matter of nationalism, and particularly its growing attraction to the Serbian intelligentsia. Milošević was on the verge of playing his own 'national' card, but only after he had completely prepared the political ground. Meanwhile, he took the occasion of a closed meeting with communists from the Federal Secretariat of Internal Affairs on 4 June, 1987 - just ten weeks after the episode in Kosovo Polje - to make an uncharacteristically impassioned attack on the infamous Memorandum.[15] Considering his remarks in light of the policies he would later espouse, and the impact of those policies on the disintegration and aftermath of the Second Yugoslavia, Milošević appears to have been a master of political guile who was willing to both attack and forecast his own course of action. Only a short time after making this speech, Milošević would begin appropriating and encouraging viewpoints which he had earlier condemned as examples of the 'darkest nationalism', and within a year would also coopt many of the Memorandum's authors and supporters as an intellectual brain trust.

During mid-1987, Ivan Stambolić's position within the Serbian elite and federal political leadership was significantly weakened by various factional struggles and intrigues within both the higher ranks of the League of Communists and the military establishment. It was at this juncture that Milošević decided to step completely out the shadow cast by his former mentor and friend. The pretext for Milošević's move was a controversial news conference held on 11 September, 1987 by Dragiša Pavlović, the President of the City Committee for the Belgrade League of Communists (who had held the job since 1986 when he had replaced Milošević).[16] Most of Pavlović's comments - made to a political group composed of chief editors from the media and local party secretaries - offered a relatively moderate and sensible assessment of how the League could best manage growing nationalism in Serbia, and particularly the grievances of Kosovo Serbs regarding Albanian nationalism. Pavlović warned that a dangerous atmosphere had arisen in Serbia, and that any sober words uttered against ascendant Serbian nationalism were wrongly being construed as yielding to Albanian nationalism. In preserving their rights, Pavlović cautioned, the Serbian people 'must not be led astray through wrongly chosen methods of struggle...Inflammatory words result in nothing, but a conflagration'.[17] Pavlović was clearly encouraging Serbian public leaders to exercise responsibility when dealing with the highly incendiary 'national question'. But his remarks were also undoubtedly a thinly veiled indictment of Milošević's intemperate response to the demonstrators at Kosovo Polje the previous spring, not to mention the media's sensational celebration of that incident during the following months. Still riding the wave of his experience in Kosovo, where he had established a special plebiscitarian-type bond with the province's aggrieved Serbs, Milošević was in no mood to accept such criticism from one of his junior colleagues in the Belgrade political establishment.

On 18 and 19 September, 1987, at the Eighth Session of the Central Committee of the Serbian League of Communists, Milošević, together with a coalition of prominent Serbian political and military figures which he had been assembling over the past several months, launched a sharp assault on Dragiša Pavlović and his policies. Their major target was the leading moderate and anti-nationalist in the Serbian political leadership, Ivan Stambolić. At Kosovo Polje in April, Milošević had cannily identified the instrument necessary for his political advancement; now, less than six months later, he began to openly wield that political tool. Milošević had also undoubtedly determined that the substance and style of his future approach to Serbian-Albanian relations, and more broadly toward the assertion of Serbian interests within Yugoslavia, could be modelled on the emotional and populist dynamics of Kosovo Polje. Having committed himself to this new course of action, Milošević had also made the cold-blooded decision to completely end his past alliance and mentor/follower relationship with Ivan Stambolić.

The Eighth Session turned into an intense and lengthy debate between Serbian party moderates and Milošević's adherents. Many members of the latter group had only recently migrated over to Milošević's side. Such repositioning derived from a variety of motives, including the issue of Serbian nationalism. Faced with a torrent of criticism and a proposal for his dismissal, Pavlović attempted to explain his earlier remarks, claiming that he may have 'exaggerated something', and that at his news conference he did not have Milošević or the Serbian party leadership in mind. Stambolić proved more pugnacious in standing up to the new Milošević line. Pavlović was being thrown out, Stambolić observed, because 'in one of his (Pavlović's) sentences Slobodan Milošević or some others saw an allusion to themselves'.[18] Stambolić chastised Milošević for always speaking about party 'unity', but taking measures which actually encouraged dissent in the ranks of the League. He also urged his formerly junior colleague to 'manifest a greater degree of ability' and to avoid conflict. After all, Stambolić lectured Milošević, 'nobody is right about everything and nobody is wrong about everything'.[19]

When Stambolić had completed his remarks Milošević took the floor, and denounced Stambolić's efforts to personally link him with the assault on Pavlović, claiming that such remarks were 'insulting' to the Central Committee Presidium. As the Session came to an end, Milošević remained unapologetic about his orientation to the issues under debate, and was especially enigmatic in his commentary about Serbian nationalism. Removing Pavlović was not a 'purge' or 'squaring of accounts', Milošević claimed. He further observed that it was 'politically unacceptable for the leaders of the Serbian League of Communists to be threatened with accusations of Serbian nationalism'.

> Serbian nationalism today is not only intolerance and hatred of another nation or nations, but is itself a serpent deep in the bosom of the Serbian people...Serbian nationalists would do the greatest harm to the Serbian people today by what they offer as being allegedly the best thing, namely isolating the Serbian people...No one can label us Serbian nationalists because we want to, and really will, resolve the problem of Kosovo.[20]

The events at the Eighth Session publicly signalled that Slobodan Milošević had assumed full political control of Serbia. At the same time, by defending Dragiša Pavlović and personally attacking Milošević, Ivan Stambolić had signed his political death warrant. At the conclusion of the Eighth Session, Pavlović was removed from his position on the Serbian Party Presidium (he had already resigned from the Belgrade Committee). Stambolić was replaced as President of Serbia's collective presidency in mid-December 1987. Not long afterward he left political life and resumed a career in Serbian banking.[21]

For some observers, such as several Serbian opposition journalists from the Belgrade weekly, *Vreme*, the SANU Memorandum has been viewed as being the intellectual impetus and framework for the Eighth Session. Thus, it has been argued, the authors and supporters of the Memorandum constituted a kind of 'nationalistic pseudo-opposition' ready 'at the signal' to endorse Milošević.[22] According to this perspective, members of the intelligentsia who, only a few months earlier, Milošević had accused of endorsing 'the darkest nationalism', actually engaged in a tacit or secret alliance with the Serbian leader in order to ensure his political victory. What seems more likely, however, is that Milošević, buoyed by his new-found popularity and seeking to expand his power through the immoderate style of leader-mass interaction which he had experienced at Kosovo Polje, had decided to push aside Stambolić and other moderate Serbian communist leaders. While it is still not known exactly what contacts occurred between Milošević and the authors of the Memorandum during the summer of 1987, it does not appear that by the time of the Eighth Session in September, Milošević had fully consolidated his ties with the leading nationalist intellectuals; although he was undoubtedly counting on their tacit support, and was preparing to unabashedly appropriate various components of their nationalist platform. The Memorandum, as Stambolić would later observe, represented the 'great divide' between two factions in the Serbian League of Communists: 'the dogmatists (potentially nationalistic) and the reform currents'.[23] Sensing the mood in Serbia, after his long night at Kosovo Polje, the ambitious Milošević deftly took advantage of the split in party ranks and enlisted the dogmatists and disgruntled nationalists in order to topple the principal reform figure who stood in his way.

Explaining Milošević's Appeal: Patriotism and Political Culture

Answering the question of why Milošević chose to play the nationalist card is easier than explaining the reasons why his ethnic constituency found his appeal so attractive, and also how he managed to retain popular support during the recent and extremely difficult stage of Serbian national development. As Gale Stokes has aptly pointed out, political leaders typically adopt nationalist programs in order to acquire and maintain power. What is more difficult to understand is why the message of such leaders so often proves successful.[24] Thus in one sense, Milošević's rise to power can be viewed as a classic case of unbridled political ambition and brilliant political opportunism. In that regard, Aleksa Djilas has correctly described Milošević's exploitation of nationalism as an inspired 'act of political cannibalism' by a communist seeking to develop a new legitimating formula for his politically bankrupt, but still power-hungry party machine. Thus, Djilas observes: 'The opponent (of the communists), Serbian nationalism, was devoured and its spirit permeated the eater. Milošević reinvigorated the party by forcing it to embrace nationalism'.[25]

But beyond the all too familiar drives and cynical methods of power-seeking politicians, Milošević also intuitively understood and could effectively express the nationalist yearning of large numbers of Serbs on both the elite and popular levels. Indeed, Milošević's presumptuous decision to become the 'voice' of the Serbian people, his shifting political tactics toward apparent friends, close associates, and former opponents, and also the strident tone of his statements on behalf of Serbian interests, all represented the kind of pragmatic and plebiscitarian political style that has had a deep resonance in the Serbian and Balkan body politic.

Jettisoning the political constraints and exhausted platitudes of the Titoist apparatus, Milošević's political techniques and methods clearly exhibited many aspects of the 'heroic', patriarchal, and aggressively patriotic characteristics associated with Serbian political culture. While many 'national-anthropological' features of Serbian political tradition are often deprecated by educated and urban Serbs, those attitudes remain deeply engrained facets of Serbian political life. Milošević not only clearly perceived what was troubling the majority of his ethnic brethren, he also very shrewdly anticipated how they would respond to his rhetoric and problematic remedies. Thus, the hundreds of thousands of Serbs who attended rallies organised by the Milošević-controlled Serbian communist party machine during 1988 and 1989 did not feel they were exponents of radical, expansionist, or potentially violent nationalism, but rather supporters of a genuine and long-overdue outpouring of democratic patriotism.

While aspects of political repression, electoral chicanery, and media manipulation would later emerge as prominent components of Milošević's management style, his political ascendancy and initial consolidation of power depended as much on factors having to do with the cultural underpinnings of the Serbian polity, as on its structural features. Granted, during his early ascent to power, Milošević patiently consolidated his hold on the machinery of Serbia's League of Communists, both in Belgrade and in the republic's smaller towns, and also on winning the votes of party officials for his move against Stambolić. But, he also shrewdly appreciated the way in which the cultural components of Serbian society could work in his favour. Thus during the second part of the 1980s, Milošević appealed to patriotic sentiments, which were deeply rooted in Serbian political culture, as a means to enhance his popularity within the Serbian working class, agricultural population, employees of the state apparatus, and segments of the intelligentsia. Milošević discerned that many urban and highly educated Serbs with liberal-democratic leanings might view his reliance on mass rallies and 'street democracy' as expressions of authoritarian manipulation. However, he recognised that most Serbs would regard such populist tactics as an appropriate method with which to forge the traditional linkage between strong Serbian leaders and the Serbian people; a legitimating bond that had the added value of circumventing the established intermediacy of discredited communist bureaucrats and the largely powerless edifice of 'self-managing' institutions.

In his early career as an enterprise manager and a bank president, Milošević exhibited signs of non-ideological pragmatism, a situation leading some observers to believe that he was a committed liberal technocrat and a moderniser. However, at the time, few appreciated his talent and appetite for power, and also his very unusual chameleonic character. Moreover, in view of the fact that he was politically socialised in the oppositionless and bureaucratic environment of the Tito regime's restricted pluralism, and that in the early 1980s he became deeply enmeshed in the network of patron-client communist recruitment, it is hardly surprising that the ambitious Milošević ultimately utilised political techniques drawing upon the illiberal facets of Serbian political culture. An inventory of such historically shaped facets of that political culture would include: support for traditionally centralised modes of political control; a popular penchant for 'heroic leaders' who can maintain political order and preserve the 'unity' of the nation; a disinclination to accept rules-of-the-game which would allow the fragmentation of the Serbian nation among different Balkan political units (or any kind of minority status for Serbs within a multi-national state dominated by other ethnic groups); and an exaggerated emphasis on sanguinity - 'Serbian blood and origins' - territorial control, and national religious myths as defining features of collective identity.[26] Such features might be regarded as the dominant components of the traditional Serbian elite and mass political mindset, although - particularly in the modern history of urban Serbia - such perspectives are certainly not all-pervasive, nor unchallenged by important strands of liberal thought and outlook.

While it is analytically difficult, and even dangerous, to extrapolate from the presence of such dimensions in the historically conditioned Serbian political mindset directly to contemporary and current political dynamics, the importance of cultural factors in understanding Serbian politics should not be ignored. Indeed, many analysts of Balkan historical development have pointed to the important role of patriarchal patterns stemming from tribal society, and especially the *zadruga* form of landholding and family organisation, as major elements shaping contemporary Serbian political culture.[27] Thus although important elements of 'democratic' participation - for example, the right of members of the community to openly express their individual ambitions and views - can be identified as dimensions of tribal society and the *zadruga* system, the overall collectivist nature of the patriarchal legacy gives the Balkan notion of 'democracy' a 'somewhat different meaning than in the Western world'.[28]

Under the strong influence of the patriarchal tradition, it has been argued, the meaning of democracy in Serbian and other Balkan contexts came to include strong imperatives for politicians and policies to reach unanimity, to overcome minority non-conformism, and to assert the 'sole truth'. The influence of patriarchal and aggressively patriotic components in Serbian political culture appear to be particularly strong among Serbs living in, or originating from, the Dinaric areas of the Balkan region, which include most of Bosnia-Hercegovina, southwestern Serbia (Kosovo), southeastern Croatia, and Montenegro.[29] Dinaric Serbs are characterised as extremely patriotic, and having a highly developed 'consciousness of nationality'. For example, according to the ethnographer, Jovan Cvijić, who provided a rich and detailed, if rather idealised, portrait of Dinaric Serbian characteristics: 'Dinaric people feel themselves just as closely connected with their national heroes as with blood relatives.'[30] According to Cvijić, Dinaric Serbs have a consuming and often violently expressed commitment to the 'national mission' Moreover, he asserts: 'They will stop at absolutely nothing. It does not matter in the least if they 'drown in blood' so long as they preserve the heroic traditions, their great name and their 'sacred freedom'.[31]

Cultural explanations of Serbian politics cannot, of course, neglect the influence of Western liberal values in Serbian society and intellectual circles, especially during the nineteenth and twentieth centuries. However, it is the illiberal facets in the Serbian political legacy reinforced by the long period of Ottoman rule, and subsequently by one-party communism,[32] that appear to be predominant and most enduring. Thus, while enthusiasm for 'instinctive democracy', 'self-determination', and 'democratic' participation are often noted as major components of the Serbian 'national character', it has been frequently noted that Serbian political culture places even more emphasis on the value of strong leaders who can achieve their community's national mission and constrain tendencies toward 'democratic chaos'[33] and 'excessive individualism'.[34]

If deeply engrained facets of Serbian political culture provided especially fertile soil for Milošević's patriotic populism and anti-establishment rhetoric, survey research during the late 1970s and early 1980s has also revealed that popular Serbian attitudes congruent with such cultural expectations and values remained highly salient dimensions of the prevailing political mood. Surveys conducted by the Belgrade Institute of Social Sciences, for example, pointed to an increasing disenchantment with, and abandonment of, regime-sponsored values connected with self-management socialism, and also a growing preference for a 'traditional syndrome' of beliefs. Thus, survey results demonstrated an emerging or re-emerging mentality in Serbian society which reflected a deep strain of authoritarianism. Such attitudes were highly supportive of social conformism, egalitarianism, and an immoderate devotion to preferred political leaders that bordered on 'idolatry'.[35] Aspects of what are characterised as an 'authoritarian syndrome' were particularly apparent among the agricultural population in the rural and underdeveloped regions of Serbia, as well as among unskilled, semi-skilled, and highly skilled industrial workers.

'Patriarchal Patriotism' in the Intelligentsia

Milošević's alliance with sections of the Serbian cultural intelligentsia during the second part of the 1980s also represented a fascinating case where re-emergent 'patriotic' political values converged with mutual political interests. For the savvy Milošević, the creative intelligentsia and particularly the SANU intellectuals, represented an established opposition bloc that needed, from his perspective, to be coopted and contained. They were also a group, Milošević calculated, that could provide an intellectual underpinning for his national-patriotic programme. Meanwhile, many of the intellectuals who had broken with the communist regime, and who now espoused an eclectic blend of nationalist and communist views, saw Milošević as a unique opportunity to advance their own agenda. For many intellectuals, Milošević represented the first Serbian politician since Aleksandar Ranković (removed by Tito in 1966) who was willing to remain ideologically committed to socialism, but still take a strong stand on behalf of Serbian national interests. Thus, by the summer of 1988,

Milošević was closely collaborating with the authors of the Memorandum, or the same intellectuals he had conveniently criticised during 1986 and 1987.

Badly disappointed by the failures and repression of the communist regime, many of the SANU intellectuals, and their peers, reverted to a framework of beliefs that has usefully been characterised as 'patriarchal patriotism'. Among other things, such views prescribe a 'morality of simple but inflexible duties towards one's nation'.[36] Thus, many of the intellectuals embracing such patriotic attitudes found it profitable to idealise Milošević as the personification of the best Serbian political principles and traditional values. For example, Antonije Isaković, the President of the SANU commission that prepared the Memorandum, claimed that Milošević's mode of behaviour and policies combined the positive features of the nineteenth century Serbian politicians, Karađorđe (Đorđe Petrović, known as Kara or Black Đorđe) and Miloš Obrenović; the first political figure allegedly exhibiting the principles of a well-meaning revolutionary nationalist, and the second leader typifying aspects of an 'evolutionary' but essentially pragmatic, conspiratorial, and sometimes ruthless (Obrenović eventually murdered Karađorđe) administrator and politician. While most Serbs, including his supporters, often characterise Milošević's aloofness and reclusiveness as rather 'strange' behaviour, Isaković's sycophantic and rather defensive description of the same traits illustrates how such idiosyncrasies may be perceived and recast as qualities that serve the interests of the nation.[37]

Viewing Milošević's alliance with the SANU intellectuals in retrospect, some Balkan and foreign analysts have incorrectly assumed that the Serbian leader sympathetically observed the preparation of the Memorandum during 1985 and 1986, and plotted from the very outset to exploit its general principles as part of his own pursuit of power.[38] It would also be wrong to assume that the blueprint for the entire course of events connected with the disintegration of Yugoslavia, the subsequent wars in Croatia and Bosnia, and various policies such as 'ethnic cleansing', were all part of some master plan or conspiracy hatched by Milošević and a coterie of Serbian intellectuals during the 1987-1988 period.

What can be concluded, however, is that after an initial political career (1982-1987) in which he exhibited no traces of an aggressively nationalist orientation, Milošević decided - once having seen that Ivan

Stambolić had turned his back on the politically rich opportunities deriving from Serbian ethnic grievances, and after having experienced the potential force of those grievances at Kosovo Polje - to utilise nationalism as a political weapon. Only after removing Stambolić, did Milošević establish a calculated alliance with the SANU academicians in order to give his views a patina of intellectual respectability and coherence. He thereby also obtained an important vehicle for disseminating and defending his policies in the Serbian media and Serbian cultural circles. In his drive to maintain and enlarge his power after 1987, Milošević selectively appropriated the views and energies of leading Serbian national ideologues. But it was Milošević's interests, instincts, and imperatives, not the Memorandum or its authors, that guided Serbian policy in the late 1980s and 1990s, and ultimately provoked the violent disintegration of the Yugoslav communist federation. Thus as the political situation evolved in the decade after 1987, Milošević would frequently demonstrate his willingness to callously, and even ruthlessly sacrifice those Serbian nationalists who previously appeared to be his close friends and allies. Unlike most Balkan politicians in the 1990s for whom power was a means to achieve their nationalist goals, for Milošević nationalism was simply the paramount instrument to achieve and solidify political power. Astutely understanding his cultural milieu, he knew precisely how to package and convey such nationalist appeals, and also when to adopt a new style of political discourse.

Milošević's political pragmatism and non-ideological style also contributed to his appeal among segments of the intelligentsia that had previously remained more or less committed to the communist regime. For example, Milošević was able to coopt a small sub-group of neo-marxist dissidents who had conducted a protracted struggle with the political establishment throughout the 1970s and early 1980s. Thus, well-known and vocal Belgrade University professors such as Mihajlo Marković and Svetozar Stojanović - whose espousal of participatory forms of socialist democracy and ideological distance from the Tito regime had made them the darlings of the neo-marxist community around the world - decided (like the SANU intellectuals who had broken completely with the League of Communists in the 1960s and 1970s) that Milošević's creatively mixed cocktail of skin-deep socialism and Serbian patriotism justified their return to the mainstream of what was still a one-party regime. Meanwhile, most members of the communist cultural intelligentsia in Serbia, who had worked loyally for the regime, simply continued their allegiance to Milošević as the new head of the political establishment.[39]

Milošević's appeal to the communist and neo-marxist intelligentsia was clearly enhanced by the political role of his wife. Mirjana Marković's well-known communist family background,[40] and her orthodox Yugoslav communist views, provided a natural bridge to sections of the intelligentsia who had remained suspicious of Slobodan Milošević's break with Titoist policy on the national question, and uncomfortable with his unconventional populist tactics. Thus in 1988, Mirjana Marković would help coordinate a 'hard Marxist-Leninist core' at Belgrade University where she worked as a sociology professor. In October 1989, she also became more directly involved in the Belgrade City League of Communists. Following the advent of multi-party politics in 1990, she emerged as a top leader and chief ideologist of the 'League of Communists - Movement for Yugoslavia' which served as an adjunct to Milošević's newly formed Socialist Party of Serbia (a reconfigured combination of the Serbian League of Communists and the Serbian Socialist Alliance) in maintaining links to conservative communist politicians, military officers, and pro-regime intellectuals. Like her husband, who brazenly and often reiterated his opposition to nationalism (despite the connection of his policies at various times with the most aggressive and egregious aspects of Serbian patriotism), Mirjana Marković has frequently maintained that she is repelled by the explosion of nationalist views in the 1980s and 1990s, not to mention extreme policies which contributed to 'Serbian apartheid'.[41] As with many other communist and neo-marxist intellectuals, Milošević's wife - who has been his closest political confidante - undoubtedly has felt, or has needed to convey, that she has been participating in a patriotic (as opposed to a nationalistic) regime devoted to socialist principles.

Although Milošević was successful at coopting the bulk of the patriotic dissidents at SANU, as well as most neo-marxist and communist intellectuals, a sizeable portion of the intelligentsia, and especially the anti-communist nationalists and the small group of liberal-democrats, remained steadfastly opposed to his regime. Personal and political divisions within the ranks of the anti-Milošević intelligentsia, however, made it difficult for them to mount a viable opposition during the late 1980s, or even after the advent of pluralist politics in the early 1990s. Moreover, once Milošević was ensconced at the summit of the socialist regime, and could claim to be the official representative of Serbian national interests, it became very difficult for his intellectual opponents to attract popular support on the basis of their own patriotic programmes. Indeed, often unwilling to completely transcend or forego the emotional and illiberal components of their own appeals to Serbian nationalism, the self-styled 'liberal opposition' often found it difficult to either steal Milošević's thunder, or claim they were offering citizens a genuine democratic alternative.[42] Meanwhile, in the climate of the 1980s and early 1990s,[43] those few Serbian intellectuals who did advance a truly non-nationalist and liberal democratic programme were largely marginalised and ostracised.

Looking back at Milošević's political career during the last phase of the communist regime, one is most impressed by his proficiency in utilising specifically Serbian notions of patriotism and democracy as a means of sustaining a diverse coalition of seemingly incompatible constituencies. As incisive journalists from the Belgrade magazine, *Vreme*, have observed: 'He succeeded in tricking both the communists and the nationalists; the communists believed he was only pretending to be a nationalist, and the nationalists that he was only pretending to be communist'.[44] Caught up in their yearnings to overcome the perceived political subordination of the Serbs in Yugoslavia, few of Milošević's supporters during the second half of the 1980s fully considered where his still evolving and ostensibly patriotic programme would eventually lead. Those that did speak out regarding the dangers of runaway Serbian nationalism, either within or outside the League of Communists, proved powerless to resist the culturally-based infatuation with Milošević on the part of so many of his ethnic brethren. Thus, having successfully consolidated his hold on the communist regime from 1987 to 1989 using both the machinery of the League of Communists and a wily admixture of culturally appealing socialist and nationalist rhetoric, Milošević would go on to successfully utilise the same factors - complemented by the perks and full technology of modern state power (he was elected the last communist President of Serbia in May 1989) - to win several competitive, albeit not fully democratic, elections in the 1990s.

It was only after 1992, when the citizens of Serbia began to experience for themselves the full consequences of the Second Yugoslavia's disintegration, and especially the negative effects of war-related difficulties and international sanctions, that Milošević could no longer depend upon Serbian nationalism as a tool for power-maintenance and political mobilisation. Perhaps it was the politically ill-fated Ivan Stambolić who has offered the best insight into the changing tactics of Slobodan Milošević:

> He came to power by advocating my policy, he broke with me and with his wife's policy when he adopted the policy of the Serbian nationalists, he thereby disintegrated Yugoslavia and ushered in a war. By accepting the policy of the international community he now (1995) wants peace! And if he does have a policy of his own, it's a policy of retaining power.[45]

Notes

1 Milošević's mother and father, who were both of Montenegrin origin, separated after the war. His father left for Montenegro where he worked as a language teacher at a religious high school, while Slobodan and his brother (who regards himself as a Montenegrin) stayed with their mother. Both of his parents later committed suicide; his father in 1962, when Slobodan was on a student excursion in Russia, and his mother in 1973.

2 Stephen Engelberg, 'Carving Out of Greater Serbia', *New York Times Magazine*, 1 September, 1991, p. 23.

3 BBC Summary of World Broadcasts, EE/7939/B/1, 1 May, 1985.

4 BBC Summary of World Broadcasts, EE/8229/B/6, 10 April, 1986.

5 Srpska Narodna Odbrana (1987).

6 Aleksandar Pavković (1994).

7 Srpska Narodna Odbrana (1987) pp. 41-42.

8 Đukić (1992), p. 189.

9 The following two paragraphs draw heavily on Đukić (1992), p. 122-130.

10 Foreign Broadcast Information Service, Daily Bulletin Eastern Europe (FBIS), 27 April, 1987.

11 FBIS, 27 April, 1987, p. 18.

12 In September 1995, Milošević's wife told the BBC that, prior to his going to Kosovo Polje, she and her husband had discussed 'how he should speak and what he should say. I felt that he should speak constructively, offering the Serbs the support that belongs to them'. 'Vreme' News Digest Agency (VND), 13 November, 1995, No. 215. Ivan Stambolić claims that prior to the trip to Kosovo, he had warned Milošević 'not to yield to emotions', but that Milošević 'succumbed to the atmosphere. He even fuelled the fire'. Stambolić (1995) p. 167.

13 Đukić (1992), p. 127.

14 Milošević (1989), p. 34.

15 Internal Bulletin of the League of Communists in the Federal Secretariat of Internal Affairs, 'Naše aktuelnosti', June 1987, cited in VND, 16 August, 1993, No. 99, p. 15.

16 Milošević had been unenthusiastic when Pavlović was brought into the political elite by Ivan Stambolić. Two years younger than Milošević, Pavlović had completed the faculties of both machine engineering and economics, and had a doctorate in political science. Đukić (1992), pp. 108-109.

17 FBIS, 8 October, 1987, pp. 49-51.

18 FBIS, 16 October, 1987, p. 62.

19 FBIS, 16 October, 1987, p. 62. Stambolić would later admit that he had been 'set up' by Milošević. Stambolić also claims that he had reservations about Milošević when he advanced him for high office, and had received strong warnings about Milošević's character from others. Stambolić recounts that he ignored such warnings, believing that he could control Milošević's 'vices', or that they would 'disappear'. Stambolić (1995), pp. 135-136, 138-139, 141.

20 Nedeljne informativne novine (NIN), No. 1918, 4 October, 1987, pp. 12-13.

21 His successor was retired General Petar Gračanin. Pavlović's views on the Eighth Session can be found in Pavlović (1988).

22 Milos Vasić, Roksanda Ninčić, and Tanja Topić, 'A Tired Serbia', VND, No. 52, 21 September, 1992.

23 Stambolić (1995), p. 131.

24 Stokes (1993).

25 Djilas (1993), p. 87.

26 For the impact of Serbian historical patterns on political culture see Melčić (1993), and Hehn (1986).

27 For important studies of this aspect of Serbian political culture as it relates to democracy and the mobilisation of nationalist sentiments see Cvijić (1965), pp. 79-135; Dvorniković (1939), pp. 193-250, Jovanović (1990), Erlich (1966), pp. 373-393, Tomasevich (1955), pp. 192-197, 247-249; Burić, (1976), and Lucev (1974).

28 Erlich (1966), p. 393.

29 Milošević's Montenegrin family background and also his origins in Šumadija place his roots squarely in the 'Dinaric Zone'.

30 Cvijić (1930-31), p. 381.

31 Cvijić (1930-31), p. 383. It is important to note that aspects of the syndrome of Dinaric characteristics described by Cvijić and other analysts are also exhibited by members of several Balkan ethnic groups, and particularly by Croats and Moslems living in the 'Dinaric zone'.

32 Zagorka Golubović argues that the mentality and operation of Yugoslavia's communist state bureaucracy - including its monopoly over the agencies of political socialisation - reinforced traditional habits and attitudes despite the self-management system. Golubović (1988), pp. 285-391.

33 Cvijić (1930-31), p. 383.

34 Nearly a half century ago, for example, such dual and seemingly contradictory features of Serbian political culture were noted by Cvijić in his incisive inventory of Serbian folkways. 'The whole national tradition is democratic in trend. It is true that we have a long succession of famous emperors, heroes, and martyrs: but the Serbs regard this in a way of their own...one does find individual persons or families who seem to have a natural instinct towards leadership: and for this reason people consider that we have undemocratic tendencies. These are individual cases however, and do not occur often'. Cvijić (1930-31a), pp. 676-678.

35 The discussion of survey results that follows is based on several studies by Dragomir Pantić: Pantić (1981), Pantić (1988) and (Pantić (1990).

36 Pavković (1993). Pavković argues that the Serbian cultural intelligentsia is strongly attached to patriotic values expressed in traditional Serbian folk epics, nineteenth century Serbian literature, and historiography. In his opinion, both patriotically oriented intellectuals, and those who were more attracted by the European liberal tradition, rejected communist rule.

37 NIN, No. 2158, 8 May, 1993, pp. 18-21. As an example of the Miloš Obrenović style of behaviour, Isaković gave the example of Milošević's willingness to support the interests of the Krajina Serbs in Croatia - in the name of 'all Serbs living in one state' - and then (in 1992, after the cease-fire in Croatia and the arrival of United Nations peacekeeping troops) to pragmatically inform Krajina leaders that such a position was no longer tenable. The Belgrade journalist, Slavoljub Đukić, has described Milošević's distinctive patron-client relationship with intellectual subordinates in a rather less favourable light than Isaković: 'Tito never had as much control and influence over his supporters as Milošević does...There is a tremendous division between the first man (of Serbia) and all others. While alongside Tito there arose many personalities of considerable capability, Milošević has gone in an entirely opposite direction...Among (his) Socialists there doesn't exist a second and third personality as you found Kardelj, Ranković and Djilas next to Tito...Between Milošević and his party comrades there exists an unbridgeable gap...Between Milošević and his allies and enemies there is no hate, nor love or disappointment, and least of all any ideological burden. Only raw interest exists. People are (politically) secure, only if they are indebted. In general one does not deal with biographies'. NIN, No. 2285, 14 October, 1994, p. 29.

38 It is true that since the late fall of 1984, Milošević had become associated with the view that Serbs should not feel guilty about expressing their patriotic feelings, or have a 'complex' about the misdeeds of Serbs in the past. Moreover, there is also evidence that while Milošević played the role of a loyal member of the Stambolić

team, his wife, Mirjana Marković, was ambitiously laying the groundwork in Belgrade's intellectual and political circles for her husband's political advancement. For example, she has observed that it was in November 1984 that her Belgrade circle of left-wing university intellectuals (and presumably her husband who spoke out in the same vein at the time) began their 'just and fine struggle for the national affirmation of all the interests of the Serbian people in Yugoslavia'. She also claims, however, that by 1989 various 'primitive' nationalists perverted such legitimate cultural and national sentiments into 'aggressive nationalism'. Marković (1993), p. 209, and Marković (1994) pp. 163-164. I am indebted to Chip Gagnon for directing my attention to Marković's views on this issue. Milošević's wife also had played a key role behind the scenes at the important Eighth Session of the Central Committee of the Serbian League of Communists (drafting his speeches, communicating with allies, etc.) However, Milošević appears not to have established a close working political relationship with the Memorandum authors until mid-1988, that is, a year after his visit to Kosovo Polje, and months after he played the nationalist card against Pavlović and Stambolić in the latter part of 1987.

39 Milošević could also count on the loyalty of conservative political and managerial elites on the local level throughout Serbia, who - particularly in the less developed and rural areas - were more interested in job security than democratic reform or economic change. See Bolčić (1991).

40 Milošević met his future wife, Mirjana Marković, at the beginning of secondary school. Her mother, Vera Miletić, was shot during the war when she was head of the Belgrade Communist Party organisation. Mirjana's father was Moma Marković, an influential communist political leader for several decades, and her aunt was Davorjanka Paunović, who was Tito's secretary and mistress during the war.

41 Washington Post, 17 June, 1993, p. 5.

42 For interesting discussions of problems faced by the democratic opposition see Srdja Trifković (1992), Gligorov (1991), Popović, (1993).

43 For the views of one of Serbia's leading non-nationalist intellectuals see Pešić, (1993).

44 Milos Vasić, Roksanda Ninčić, and Tanja Topić, 'A Tired Serbia', VND, No. 52, 21 September, 1992, p. 6.

45 Stambolić (1995), p. 151.

References

Bolčić, Silvano (1991), Nejednakosti i protivre!nosti u preobražavanju nedovoljno razvijenih područja u Srbiji' in Mihailo V. Popović et al. (1991), *Srbija krajem osamdesetih*, Institut za sociološka istraživanja, Belgrade.

Burić, Olivera (1976), 'The Zadruga and the Contemporary Family in Yugoslavia' in Robert F. Byrnes (ed), *Communal Families in the Balkans: The Zadruga*, University of Notre Dame Press, Notre Dame, 117-138.

Cvijić, Jovan (1930-31), 'Studies in Jugoslav Psychology (I)', *The Slavonic Review*, Vol. 9, No. 26.

Cvijić, Jovan (1930-31a), 'Studies in Jugoslav Psychology (II)', *The Slavonic Review*, Vol. 9, No. 27.

Cvijić, Jovan (1965), *Iz društvenih nauka*, Vuk Karadžić, Belgrade.

Djilas, Aleksa (1993), 'A Profile of Slobodan Milošević', *Foreign Affairs*, Vol. 73, No. 2, pp. 81-96.

Dvorniković, Vladimir (1939), *Karakterologija Jugoslovena*, Kosmos, Belgrade.

Đukić, Slavoljub (1992), *Kako se dogodio vođa: borba za vlast u Srbiji posle Josipa Broza*, Filip Višnjić, Belgrade.

Erlich, Vera St. (1966), *Family in Transition: A Study of Three Hundred Yugoslav Villages*, Princeton University Press, Princeton.

Gligorov, Vladimir (1991), 'The Discovery of Liberalism in Yugoslavia', *East European Politics & Societies*, Vol. 5, No. 1, 5-21.

Golubović, Zagorka (1988), *Kriza identiteta savremenog Jugoslovenskog društva*, Filip Višnjić, Belgrade.

Hehn, Paul (1986), 'Man and the State in Serbia, From the Fourteenth to the Mid-Nineteenth Century: A Study in Centralist and Anti-Centralist Conflict', *Balkan Studies*, Vol. 27, No. 1, pp. 3-27.

Jovanović, Slobodan (1990), 'Jedan prilog za proučavanje Srpskog nacionalnog karaktera', in Radovan Samardžić & Živorad Stojković (eds), *Sabrana dela Slobodana Jovanovića*, Vol. 12, Bigz, Belgrade, pp. 543-582.

Lucev, Ivan (1974), 'Socialni karakera i politička kultura', *Sociologija*, No. 1, pp. 23-41.

Marković, Mirjana (1993), *Odgovor*, BMG, Belgrade.

Marković, Mirjana, (1994), *Noć i dan*, BMG, Belgrade.

Melčić, Dunja (1993),'Communication and National Identity: Croatian and Serbian Patterns', *Praxis International*, Vol. 13, No. 4, pp. 360-363.

Milošević, Slobodan (1989), *Godine raspleta*, Bigz, Belgrade.

Pantić, Dragomir (1981), *Vrednosne orijentacije mladih u Srbiji*, SSO Srbije, Belgrade.

Pantić, Dragomir (1988), *Klasična i svetovna religioznost*, Institut društvenih nauka, Belgrade.

Pantić, Dragomir (1990), *Promene vrednosnih orientacija u Srbiji*, Institut društvenih nauka, Belgrade.

Pavlović, Dragiša (1988), *Olako obećana brzina*, Globus, Zagreb.

Pavković, Aleksandar (1993), 'Intellectuals and Politicians: Serbia 1990-1992', *Meanjin*, Vol. 52, No. 1, pp. 107-116.

Pavković, Aleksandar (1994), 'The Serb National Idea: A Revival, 1986-1992', *Slavonic & East European Review*, Vol. 72, No. 3, pp. 440-455.

Pešić, Vesna (1993), 'The Cruel Face of Nationalism', *Journal of Democracy*, Vol. 4, No. 4. pp. 100-103.

Popović, Srdja (1993), 'Political Opposition in Serbia', *New Politics*, Vol. 4, No. 4, pp. 91-97.

Srpska Narodna Odbrana, (1987), *Nacrt memoranduma Srpske Akademije Nauka u Beogradu*, Srpska Narodna Odbrana, Toronto.

Stambolić, Ivan (1995), *Put u bespuće*, Radio B-92, Belgrade.

Stokes, Gale (1993), 'Cognition, Consciousness, and Nationalism', *Ethnic Studies*, Vol. 10, pp. 27-42.

Tomasevich, Jozo (1955), *Peasants, Politics and Economic Change in Yugoslavia*, Stanford University Press, Stanford.

Trifković, Srdja (1992), 'Illiberal Legacy in Former Yugoslavia as an Impediment to Market Reforms', *Serbian Studies*, Vol. 6, No. 4, pp. 5-20.